Cultivating Interest and Competencies in Computing

AUTHENTIC EXPERIENCES AND DESIGN FACTORS

Barbara M. Means and Amy Stephens, *Editors*

Committee on the Role of Authentic STEM Learning Experiences in Developing Interest and Competencies for Computing

Board on Science Education

Division of Behavioral and Social Sciences and Education

Computer Science and Telecommunications Board

Division on Engineering and Physical Sciences

A Consensus Study Report of

The National Academies of
SCIENCES · ENGINEERING · MEDICINE

THE NATIONAL ACADEMIES PRESS
Washington, DC
www.nap.edu

THE NATIONAL ACADEMIES PRESS   500 Fifth Street, NW   Washington, DC 20001

This activity was supported by contracts between the National Academy of Sciences and Google (Award # 552112 and Award # 638539) and Grable Foundation (Award # 193D18). Any opinions, findings, conclusions, or recommendations expressed in this publication do not necessarily reflect the views of any organization or agency that provided support for the project.

International Standard Book Number-13: 978-0-309-68215-2
International Standard Book Number-10: 0-309-68215-0
Digital Object Identifier: https://doi.org/10.17226/25912
Library of Congress Control Number: 2021933324

Additional copies of this publication are available from the National Academies Press, 500 Fifth Street, NW, Keck 360, Washington, DC 20001; (800) 624-6242 or (202) 334-3313; http://www.nap.edu.

Suggested citation: National Academies of Sciences, Engineering, and Medicine. (2021). *Cultivating Interest and Competencies in Computing: Authentic Experiences and Design Factors*. Washington, DC: The National Academies Press. https://doi.org/10.17226/25912.

The National Academies of
SCIENCES · ENGINEERING · MEDICINE

The **National Academy of Sciences** was established in 1863 by an Act of Congress, signed by President Lincoln, as a private, nongovernmental institution to advise the nation on issues related to science and technology. Members are elected by their peers for outstanding contributions to research. Dr. Marcia McNutt is president.

The **National Academy of Engineering** was established in 1964 under the charter of the National Academy of Sciences to bring the practices of engineering to advising the nation. Members are elected by their peers for extraordinary contributions to engineering. Dr. John L. Anderson is president.

The **National Academy of Medicine** (formerly the Institute of Medicine) was established in 1970 under the charter of the National Academy of Sciences to advise the nation on medical and health issues. Members are elected by their peers for distinguished contributions to medicine and health. Dr. Victor J. Dzau is president.

The three Academies work together as the **National Academies of Sciences, Engineering, and Medicine** to provide independent, objective analysis and advice to the nation and conduct other activities to solve complex problems and inform public policy decisions. The National Academies also encourage education and research, recognize outstanding contributions to knowledge, and increase public understanding in matters of science, engineering, and medicine.

Learn more about the National Academies of Sciences, Engineering, and Medicine at **www.nationalacademies.org**.

The National Academies of
SCIENCES · ENGINEERING · MEDICINE

Consensus Study Reports published by the National Academies of Sciences, Engineering, and Medicine document the evidence-based consensus on the study's statement of task by an authoring committee of experts. Reports typically include findings, conclusions, and recommendations based on information gathered by the committee and the committee's deliberations. Each report has been subjected to a rigorous and independent peer-review process and it represents the position of the National Academies on the statement of task.

Proceedings published by the National Academies of Sciences, Engineering, and Medicine chronicle the presentations and discussions at a workshop, symposium, or other event convened by the National Academies. The statements and opinions contained in proceedings are those of the participants and are not endorsed by other participants, the planning committee, or the National Academies.

For information about other products and activities of the National Academies, please visit www.nationalacademies.org/about/whatwedo.

v

Preface

In a world increasingly shaped by digital technologies, the size and composition of the workforce in computer science and computing-intensive fields is of great importance on grounds of both economic competitiveness and social justice. Computing fields are projected to grow in terms of number of job openings and are among the best-paid occupations. Failing to provide opportunities for all young people to discover these fields and to develop expertise in them if they so choose means limiting the size of our computing workforce and missing out on the creative contributions of individuals with diverse experiences and perspectives. It also reinforces existing income inequalities and stereotypes. And beyond concern with the computing workforce, there is the realization that full and effective participation in social, civic, learning, and financial aspects of life today requires everyone to have a basic understanding of computing. If this imperative was not obvious before the COVID-19 pandemic, the months when students could participate in schooling only through the Internet have provided ample proof.

The question addressed by this consensus study is whether authentic science, technology, engineering, and mathematics (STEM) learning activities can provide an entree to the development of interest and competencies in computing. Broadening participation of groups historically underrepresented in computing fields—students of color, women, and those from low-income backgrounds—was emphasized in the charge to the committee and in the committee's deliberations over a period of 15 months.

This consensus report calls on readers to critically examine the concept of authentic STEM learning experiences. While some have used the phrase to denote certain pedagogies involving inquiry or project- or problem-based learning, the committee asked the question "Authentic to whom?" In dealing with authenticity both from the perspective of authenticity to the profession as it is practiced today and from the perspective of authenticity to the learner, the committee brought together empirical findings from different research traditions and weighed the evidence on the importance of both kinds of authenticity. The committee found that programs and learning experiences stressing professional authenticity may be uninteresting and unwelcoming in the eyes of learners from groups underrepresented in STEM. Programs and learning experiences designed to reflect the interests and cultures of particular underrepresented groups, on the other hand, may engage these learners but impart few of the skills and competencies used in computing-intensive professions. The committee concluded that personal and professional authenticity do not need to be in opposition to each other, and that learning experiences can and should be designed to embody both forms of authenticity.

This report was written with multiple audiences in mind. Researchers studying computational thinking, the acquisition of computer science knowledge and skills, or participation in computer science and related fields will find a conceptual framing of the development of computing expertise and engagement as well as a summary of the available evidence for the effectiveness of different kinds of programs.

Policy makers and funders will find recommendations as to the kinds of efforts that are intense enough and of sufficient duration to plausibly influence the course of a young person's life.

Those designing programs and learning activities to foster interest and competencies in computing will find descriptions of a wide array of existing programs, a summary of available evidence on their impacts, and a set of design principles they can use in designing and implementing new programs and activities.

This consensus study would not have been possible without the sponsorship of Google and the Grable Foundation. These organizations worked with the Board on Science Education of the National Academies of Sciences, Engineering, and Medicine, in collaboration with the Computer Science and Telecommunication Board to develop the charge to the study committee, but were not involved in shaping the way in which the committee went about its work or in influencing committee findings and recommendations.

Soon after the committee's fourth meeting in February 2020, the world changed with the spread of COVID-19. Two virtual meetings replaced the committee's planned fifth in-person meeting, and both committee members and National Academies staff performed the necessary integration of the different themes in this report while working from home.

Members of the National Academies staff played significant roles in production and refinement of this report. Throughout the process, I was grateful for the tireless work of Amy Stephens, the National Academies study director, who integrated and aligned the written contributions of committee members as well as keeping the committee's work organized and on schedule. Heidi Schweingruber, director of the Board on Science Education, and Kerry Brenner, senior program officer, participated in committee meetings, sharing their insights and making the committee aware of other, related work going on within the Academies.

Most importantly, I want to express my gratitude for the wisdom, open-mindedness, and hard work of the committee members themselves. Having served on a number of National Academies committees in the past, I can say with confidence that these members were outstanding in their commitment to making a significant contribution with their report and in their willingness to seek out information sources that were new to them, challenge each other's assumptions, and write and rewrite as the committee's thinking evolved over time.

In the end, the committee found support that personally and professionally authentic STEM learning experiences, when well implemented, can increase participants' knowledge, skills, and participation in STEM. Evidence regarding the impacts of specific programs or practices specifically for computing knowledge, skills, and participation was sparse, however, and judged to be suggestive rather than definitive. Nevertheless, the committee's examination of the range of in-school and out-of-school contexts in which children and young people encounter computing and computational thinking enabled it to identify conditions and practices associated with greater professional and personal authenticity.

I know I speak for the entire committee in expressing my excitement about the potential for multiple formal and informal education institutions to work together to broaden access and incorporate the authentic assets that underrepresented youth can bring to computing. By leveraging the contrasting strengths of different organizations within a coordinated, developmental and ecological approach to designing and implementing authentic learning experiences in computing, communities can make a difference in the opportunities available to their young people.

> Barbara M. Means, *Chair*
> Committee on the Role of Authentic STEM
> Learning Experiences in Developing Interest
> and Competencies for Computing

Acknowledgments

This report would not have been possible without the many individuals who provided their expertise, including those who served on the committee as well as those who participated in discussions with the committee. We recognize their invaluable contributions to our work. The first thanks are to the committee members, for their passion, deep knowledge, and contributions to the study.

This report was made possible by the important contributions of Google and the Grable Foundation; in particular Jen Phillips (Head of Program Management, Open Source Programs Office) and Calvin Johnson (Program Manager, Open Source) at Google and Gregg Behr (Executive Director) at The Grable Foundation.

Members of the committee benefited from discussion and presentation by many individuals who participated in our fact-finding meetings.

- At the first meeting, we had the opportunity to talk with our contacts at Google, Jen Philips and Calvin Johnson, to get further clarity on the statement of task. We also heard from Kamau Bobb (Georgia Institute of Technology), Carrie Tzou (University of Washington Bothell), and Sepehr Vakil (Northwestern University) who spoke to considerations around equitable access to authentic STEM learning opportunities.
- At the second meeting, the following topics were explored:
  - **Robotics Competitions and Engineering Programs: Reaching Diverse Populations.** Presenters included Alan Melchoir (Brandeis University) and AnnMarie Thomas (University of St. Thomas).

- o **Hobbies, STEM Outcomes, and Implications for Computing and Technology.** Presenters included Gail Jones (North Carolina State University) and Flávio Azevedo (University of Texas at Austin).
- The third meeting included a workshop featuring three panels followed by open discussion:
  - o Panel 1 discussed **Authentic STEM Activities for Computing and Technology—Defining "Authentic,"** including Tamara Clegg (University of Maryland), Ron Eglash (University of Michigan), Emmanuel Schanzer (Bootstrap), and Shirin Vossoughi (Northwestern University).
  - o Panel 2 described **Authentic STEM Outcomes for Computing and Technology.** Panelists included Jill Denner (ETR), Sonia Koshy (Kapor Center), Keliann LaConte (Space Science Institute), Jean Ryoo (University of California, Los Angeles), and David Weintrop (University of Maryland).
  - o Panel 3 focused on **Designing and Implementing Hands-on STEM Learning Experiences—Implications for Computing and Technology,** including Lisa Brahms (Monshire Museum of Science), Loretta Cheeks (Strong TIES), Amon Millner (Olin College), and Kylie Peppler (University of California, Irvine).

The committee is very grateful for additional discussions with experts to include Kate Aubin (Teen Educator) and Karisa Tashjian (Director of Education) at the Providence Public Library, Juan Rubio (Digital Media and Learning Program Manager) at the Seattle Public Library, and Claudia Haines (Youth Services Librarian) at the Homer Public Library in Alaska. We would also like to thank the students who spoke to members of the committee to share their experiences with computing to inform the cases used in this report.

This Consensus Study Report has been reviewed in draft form by individuals chosen for their diverse perspectives and technical expertise. The purpose of this independent review is to provide candid and critical comments that will assist the institution in making its published report as sound as possible and to ensure that the report meets institutional standards for objectivity, evidence, and responsiveness to the study charge. The review comments and draft manuscript remain confidential to protect the integrity of the deliberative process. We thank the following individuals for their review of this report: Jan Cuny, Khoury College of Computer Sciences, Northeastern University; Colleen Lewis, Department of Computer Science, Harvey Mudd College; Amon Millner, Computing and Innovation, Olin College of Engineering; Kylie Peppler, Informatics and Education, University of California, Irvine; Nichole Pinkard, Learning Sciences, Northwestern

University; Emmanuel Schanzer, Office of the Co-Director, Boostrap; Steve A. Schneider, Science, Technology, Engineering, and Mathematics, WestEd; and Brett Wortzman, Paul G. Allen School of Computer Science and Engineering, University of Washington.

Although the reviewers listed above provided many constructive comments and suggestions, they were not asked to endorse the content of the report nor did they see the final draft of the report before its release. The review of this report was overseen by Marcia C. Linn, Graduate School of Education, University of California, Berkeley, and Edward D. Lazowska, Paul G. Allen School of Computer Science and Engineering, University of Washington. They were responsible for making certain that an independent examination of this report was carried out in accordance with institutional procedures and that all review comments were carefully considered. Responsibility for the final content of this report rests entirely with the authoring committee and the institution.

Thanks are also due to the project staff. Amy Stephens, senior program officer for the Board on Science Education directed the study and played a key role in the report drafting and review process. Kerry Brenner (senior program officer for the Board on Science Education) and Judith Koenig (senior program officer for the Committee on National Statistics) provided critical assistance in project direction, organizing the report, and revising the writing. Emily Grumbling (program officer for the Computer Science and Telecommunications Board) helped early on in the study process, in particular with thinking through setting up the committee. We also thank Clair Geary (Christine Mirzayan science and technology policy fellow) who assisted with information gathering during the report writing process. Leticia Garcilazo Green, research associate with the Board on Science Education, managed the study's logistical and administrative needs. Jon Eisenberg (director of the Computer Science and Telecommunications Board) and Heidi Schweingruber (director of the Board on Science Education) provided thoughtful advice and many helpful suggestions throughout the entire study.

Staff of the Division of Behavioral and Social Sciences and Education also provided help: Laura Elisabeth Yoder substantially improved the readability of the report; Kirsten Sampson Snyder expertly guided the report through the report review process; and Yvonne Wise masterfully guided the report through production. The committee also wishes to express its sincere appreciation to Rebecca Morgan in the National Academies Research Center for her assistance with helping to identify potential committee members and conducting literature searches.

Contents

Summary

The influence of computing on society is pervasive and profound. Computing in some form touches nearly every aspect of day to day life and is reflected in the ubiquitous use of cell phones, the expansion of automation into many industries, and the vast amounts of data that are routinely gathered about people's health, education, and buying habits. Computing is now a part of nearly every occupation, not only those in the technology industry. Given the ubiquity of computing in both personal and professional life, there are increasing calls for *all* learners to participate in learning experiences related to computing including more formal experiences offered in schools, opportunities in youth development programs and after-school clubs, or self-initiated hands-on experiences at home. At the same time, the lack of diversity in the computing workforce and in programs that engage learners in computing is well-documented.

Given the pressure to expand access to, and engagement in, learning experiences related to computing, it is important to consider how to increase access and design experiences for a wide range of learners. Authentic experiences in science, technology, engineering, and mathematics (STEM)—that is, experiences that reflect professional practice and also connect learners to real-world problems that they care about—are one possible approach for reaching a broader range of learners. These experiences can be designed for learners of all ages and implemented in a wide range of settings. However, the role they play in developing youths' interests, capacities, and productive learning identities for computing is unclear.

In response to the need to better understand the role of authentic STEM experiences in supporting the development of interests, competencies, and skills related to computing, the Board on Science Education (BOSE) of the National Academies of Sciences, Engineering, and Medicine, in collaboration with the Computer Science and Telecommunication Board (CSTB) convened an expert committee to examine the relevant evidence. In particular, the committee was asked to focus on the evidence on learning and teaching using authentic, open-ended pedagogical approaches and learning experiences for children and youth in grades K–12 in both formal and informal settings. The committee was asked to give particular attention to approaches and experiences that promote the success of children and youth from groups that are typically underrepresented in computing fields.[1]

The committee recognizes that computing is more than just coding or computer science. Rather, computing refers to a broad range of fields, including the disciplinary field of computer science, that utilize computational methods. This broad framing means that the outcomes of interest go beyond a narrow focus on coding to include a larger set of foundational knowledge and competencies.

Authentic learning experiences for computing may include recreational pursuits such as playing video games or engaging with online creative communities as well as more structured activities in out-of-school learning institutions (e.g., community-based programs, museums, and public libraries) and in classroom settings. Long-term interest, skills, and participation in computing are influenced by a wide range of experiences at home, school, online, and in the local community as well as by individual factors. The social interactions that take place and the relationships that develop in the context of these activities can be an important driver for engagement and continued participation for learners.

Authentic learning experiences in computing that are designed to closely mirror professional practice—professional authenticity—may engage some learners. However, historical inequities in computing, biases, and stereotypes may also make these kinds of experiences unattractive to learners from communities that have typically been excluded from computing. Learning experiences in computing that are designed with attention to learners' interests, identities, and background—personal authenticity— may attract and retain more learners from underrepresented groups in computing because of their gender, race, ethnicity, or perceived ability than learning experiences that focus solely on professional practice. These aspects of authenticity do not need to be in opposition and a given experience can be designed with attention to both.

Authentic learning experiences in computing can occur in a wide range of settings, including classrooms, community organizations, and homes as well as online. Each setting brings constraints as well as affordances with

---

[1]The full statement of task appears in Box 1-1 in Chapter 1.

respect to the potential to provide experiences that combine both personal and professional authenticity. Many learners will need multiple experiences with computing to develop enduring interest in and competencies for computing. These experiences will likely need to include both in-school and out-of-school opportunities.

While the evidence based on experiences for computing is still emerging, the committee was also able to leverage the larger body of research on authentic experiences in other STEM fields. Taken together, this body of research points to the importance of careful design of authentic experiences so that they are appropriate for the context in which they are implemented, are targeted at a defined set of outcomes, and account for learners' prior interests and experiences in their homes and communities.

The report takes up issues of design and institutional/organizational infrastructure to highlight the particular contexts that may best support the development of learners' interest and competencies for computing. It provides guidance for educators and facilitators, program designers, and other key stakeholders on how to support learners as they engage in authentic learning experiences.

RECOMMENDATIONS

The committee's recommendations are outlined below. The committee also developed a research agenda for the field.

RECOMMENDATION 1: Program designers should be intentional in the design and implementation of programs offering *authentic* learning experiences that build interest and competencies for computing. This includes:

- having clear and explicit programmatic goals and continuous refinement of the program to ensure alignment to those goals;
- designing for personal authenticity that builds on learners' interests, identities, and backgrounds while also designing for professional authenticity;
- ensuring that the participants include people who are underrepresented in computing because of their gender, race, ethnicity, or perceived ability;
- considering inclusion of families and community members as well as learners in opportunities to co-create activities;
- ensuring educators and facilitators have adequate preparation and access to necessary materials and resources; and
- reflecting on whether the communication, outreach, and operation of the program are inviting for learners who are underrepresented

in computing because of their gender, race, ethnicity, or perceived ability.

RECOMMENDATION 2: Practicing teachers in schools and facilitators in out-of-school time settings should seek opportunities and materials on how to incorporate effective practices for creating authentic learning experiences in computing within an existing program that includes utilizing problem-/project-based learning strategies, allowing learner choice among activities, and considering learners' contexts outside of school time.

RECOMMENDATION 3: Preservice and in-service teacher educators and trainers of out-of-school time facilitators should ensure that educators and facilitators are equipped to engage learners in personally authentic learning experiences in computing. This includes providing ongoing opportunities for educators to learn and practice using inclusive pedagogical approaches, as well as having access to materials and resources that build on learners' interests, identities, and backgrounds.

RECOMMENDATION 4: School leaders should consider a variety of ways to provide access to authentic learning experiences for computing. These include (1) addressing challenges (e.g., lack of instructional time and teacher expertise) associated with integrating authentic computing experiences into instruction in a variety of subjects, (2) increasing access to stand-alone computing courses, and (3) ensuring schools have adequate resources such as equipment, reliable broadband Internet, and time.

RECOMMENDATION 5: Program providers in out-of-school settings should increase efforts to expand access to authentic learning experiences for computing through growth of opportunities and active program promotion within underserved communities and in rural areas. This includes considering ways to reduce barriers to participation such as time, cost, and transportation. It also includes offering programs multiple times or during the evening and weekends, reducing program costs or offering financial assistance, and subsidizing transportation.

RECOMMENDATION 6: Program evaluators should develop and apply robust models of evaluation that take into account the distinctive features of authentic learning experiences in computing. More specifically, this includes attending to personal and professional authenticity, considering connections across settings, and to the extent possible, disaggregating findings and examining differences between and within

groups (e.g., gender, race, ethnicity, socio-economic status) for computing outcomes as a central part of model building and evaluation.

RECOMMENDATION 7: There should be a broad-based effort to
cultivate a network of opportunities, as well as supports for learners
to navigate between them both in and out-of-school to increase access
and opportunities for sustained engagement with computing. To
achieve this:

- funders should support initiatives that make connections across
  settings—both formal and out-of-school settings including home
  and online—and between industry and educational efforts for
  authentic learning experiences in computing;
- designers and educators across formal and out-of-school settings
  should consider tailoring to the community context, learners' backgrounds and experiences, and attending to cultural relevance;
- local STEM institutions, schools, and out-of-school providers
  should develop partnerships that allow them to develop complementary programs that fill in gaps and connect learners to other
  opportunities within the network; and
- stakeholders in the network should be sure that they are providing
  opportunities in communities of underrepresented learners.

1

Introduction

The impact of computing can be seen all around us. This impact is perhaps most visible to people in moments when they engage directly and intentionally with computing, such as using a computer to access information, using GPS to navigate while driving, and using a smartphone to connect and engage through social media. Overall, the pervasive use of computing has dramatically transformed our personal, professional, and public lives.

Today's learners will enter as adults into a world that is different from the world as it is today. Progress in computing has led to significant advances (e.g., artificial intelligence and automation), and these technologies will continue to evolve. It is even possible that programming may become less essential. A recent report by the National Academies of Sciences, Engineering, and Medicine ([NASEM], 2018a) defined computing as a "term used broadly to refer to all areas of computer science, all interdisciplinary areas computer scientists work in, and all fields using computer science or computational methods and principles to advance the field. This includes both academic and occupational fields, such a bioinformatics, medical informatics, library sciences, digital archives, computational sciences, and more" (p. 17).[1] Because nearly all jobs involve computing, it is important to consider the ways computing will likely continue to shape the future workforce and how learners today are educated. Realizing the

---

[1] This report also defined computer science as "[T]he study of computers and algorithmic processes, including the principles, their hardware and software designs, their applications, and their impact on society" (NASEM, 2018a, p. 17).

profound impact of computing on the *future* workforce has led to debates centering on the importance of learners engaging with computing in the present. These debates have largely been positioned in two ways: workforce development and computing literacy for civic participation.

When considering workforce development, it is important to envision the *potential* workforce needs, given advancements in technology and computing (Guzdial, 2015). A number of federal strategy documents produced over the past couple of years acknowledge the trends and needs for growing sectors of the workforce (e.g., artificial intelligence, computer science, data science). For example, the development of the computing workforce is called out in the 2019 report *National Artificial Intelligence R&D Strategic Plan: 2019 Update*[2] and the 2018 report *National Strategic Overview for Quantum Information Science*.[3] Throughout these reports, and others (see the 2019 report *National Strategic Computing Initiative Update 2019*[4]), there is an emphasis on developing a more diverse workforce, stemming from recognition that the science, technology, engineering, and mathematics (STEM) workforce, including computing, has lacked representation among women and individuals of color.

In addition to workforce development, debates about learner engagement in computing have also focused on the development of computing literacy for civic participation. The 2018 report *Charting a Course for Success: America's Strategy for STEM Education* produced by the National Science & Technology Council[5] stresses that computing is a necessary critical skill for understanding our changing technological and social landscape (Lee and Soep, 2016; Vee, 2013). Computing literacy goes beyond simply knowing how to use a computer or engaging with technology, it also includes being able to use computing to make and create new products (Ito et al., 2019; Kafai, Fields, and Searle, 2019; Rushkoff, 2010). As learners continue to have computing opportunities that leverage "making with," they are able to learn and understand the complex issues and approaches that are necessary for true digital literacy (Buckingham, 2007, 2013; Guzdial et al., 2012; Marty et al., 2013).

These shifts in computing have also emphasized the need to develop skills that are essential to life in the 21st century, calling attention to the need to emphasize teaching computational thinking (Blikstein, 2018;

---

[2] The full report is available at https://www.whitehouse.gov/wp-content/uploads/2019/06/National-AI-Research-and-Development-Strategic-Plan-2019-Update-June-2019.pdf.

[3] The full report is available at https://www.whitehouse.gov/wp-content/uploads/2018/09/National-Strategic-Overview-for-Quantum-Information-Science.pdf.

[4] The full report is available at https://www.whitehouse.gov/wp-content/uploads/2019/11/National-Strategic-Computing-Initiative-Update-2019.pdf.

[5] The full report is available at https://www.whitehouse.gov/wp-content/uploads/2018/12/STEM-Education-Strategic-Plan-2018.pdf.

Buitrago Flórez et al., 2017; Shein, 2014; Vogel, Santo, and Ching, 2017; Wing, 2006). Wing (2006) described computational thinking as: (1) conceptualizing, not programming, (2) fundamental, not rote skill, (3) a way that humans, not computers, think, (4) complements and combines mathematical and engineering thinking, (5) ideas, not artifacts, and (6) for everyone, everywhere. Conversations continue to focus on how to define these important skills, whether as a set of practices emerging from computer science (Wing, 2006), a set of dispositions (Computer Science Teachers Association [CSTA] and International Society for Technology in Education [ISTE], 2011), or a way of thinking (National Research Council [NRC], 2011a). Although its boundaries and definitions are often contested (Tedre and Denning, 2016), there is some consensus that computational thinking is a valuable skill for learners to engage in an increasingly technological and computational world (Grover and Pea, 2013; NRC, 2011a).

Computational thinking can also be valuable as a method for developing disciplinary understanding (diSessa, 2000; Papert, 1980). Computational thinking includes engaging in logical thinking and problem-solving and is observed in national standards for mathematics (i.e., Common Core State Mathematics Standards)[6] and science (i.e., Next Generation Science Standards [NGSS]; NRC, 2013).[7] As such, there is a close resemblance between aspects of scientific inquiry and aspects of computational thinking, such as data collection and analysis. In engineering, for example, the computational thinking practices of defining problems through abstraction and approaching solutions systematically parallel typical applications of working with robots and testing solutions iteratively.

In the past decade, computer science (CS) education has been, and continues to be, supported broadly through public policy and a growing number of public K–12 institutions. For example, the increased interest and emphasis in computing and CS education is observed nationally through broader educational initiatives such as the CSforALL movement as well as through private-sector support (see Box 1-1).[8] It is also observed in the creation of a framework for K–12 CS education and subsequent national standards.[9] These national endeavors have called for the development of interdisciplinary approaches to the integration of computing within STEM teaching and learning; building capacity within the educational system to support CS education; and examining ways to broaden access and partici-

---

[6] For specific information regarding the mathematics standards, see http://www.corestandards.org/Math.

[7] For specific information regarding the science standards, see https://www.nextgenscience.org.

[8] For more information, see https://www.csforall.org.

[9] For more information on the framework, see https://k12cs.org/ and for more information on the standards, see https://www.csteachers.org/page/about-csta-s-k-12-nbsp-standards.

BOX 1-1
The Role of the Private Sector

The current movement for computing and learning has been catalyzed and supported by unique public, non-profit, and private partnerships. Many in-school initiatives for K–12 STEM+C have been funded and implemented by corporations (e.g., AT&T Aspire, Tata TCS goIT, Google Code Next, Cisco Networking Academy, and Microsoft TEALS). Code.org has developed a number of activities to expand access to computing opportunities in school (e.g., providing computer science curriculum, teacher professional development, and the Hour of Code campaign).

The private sector has been a key driver of tools and programs that support STEM experiences and help develop computing interests and competencies. This involvement includes (1) corporate funding and support for computer science and maker-oriented educational programs and institutions, (2) computing learning programs and tools developed by the educational technology industry, (3) technology learning experiences fostered through recreational engagement commercial games and technology platforms, (4) corporate-developed training and curriculum, and (5) corporate support for employee volunteer opportunities.

The private sector has also been a longstanding supporter of out-of-school STEM learning and making programs. Intel was a key sponsor of the Computer Clubhouse Network. Other companies have also sponsored technology centers and makerspaces such as the Best Buy Teen Tech Centers. The maker movement and the Maker Faire were, until recently, championed by the for-profit company Maker Media, which also helped launch non-profit educational efforts such as Maker Ed.[a] Many of the early maker education efforts were seeded, and continue to be sponsored, by corporations such as Cognizant, Google, Infosys, and Chevron, among many others. Family and community foundations, as well as federal agencies, have also played critical roles, but corporate funds supported the momentum of these initiatives, developed in in-school and out-of-school-time spaces alike. Smaller local businesses are often also critical to a maker program's fundraising and community building.

While large corporations have supported public-sector and non-profit computing programs such as Code.org, other companies have developed businesses centered on afterschool and summer programs for STEM learning. Summer camp providers such as ID Tech, Galileo, and Rolling Robots offer programs that can cost more than $1,000 a week to learn robotics, coding, and digital creation. A number of for-profit afterschool centers offer programming and computing experiences for youth, although their membership dues are often prohibitive for large portions of the youth population. A smaller number of startups have sought to establish online STEM learning programs and platforms, such as DIY.org and Apex Learning.

---

[a] See https://www.edsurge.com/news/2019-06-09-a-call-to-remake-the-maker-faire.

pation of learners who have been historically underrepresented based on gender, race, ethnicity, or perceived ability.

Overall, the push has been for learners to develop the skills and competencies that are reflective of the discipline (i.e., professional authenticity). As programs in and out of school continue to develop and provide learners with opportunities to engage in computing experiences, it is essential to consider how the design of these experiences develop interest and competencies for computing. Learners' technology experiences have been dominated by playing and tinkering with commercial games, software, and social media platforms since they first began gaining access to computers in the 1980s (Ito, 2009). Authentic, open-ended learning activities—through project- or problem-based learning and makerspaces—have been offered as an approach to support broader access to STEM learning and can catalyze interests and learning in computing (Calabrese Barton, Tan, and Greenberg, 2017; Capraro and Slough, 2013; Dischino et al., 2011; LaForce, Noble, and Blackwell, 2017; Resnick, 2017). These open-ended experiences are "authentic" in the sense that they are designed to reflect the practices of the discipline; that is, they are close approximations to the work that a STEM professional would engage in. In addition to approximating the work of the professional, there has been increasing attention to designing authentic STEM experiences so that they are connected to real-world problems learners' care about and the challenges they face.

In the past decade, making and makerspaces have emerged as a movement within and outside of learning spaces (see Box 1-2). Whether in formal or informal educational settings, many maker efforts are oriented toward STEM skills and workforce development (Blikstein, 2013b; Martin, 2015; National Science Foundation, 2017; Vossoughi and Bevan, 2014), where making is the vehicle to STEM + Computing (STEM+C) careers or to accessing new opportunities (Fancsali et al., 2019). Within learning spaces, making has been embraced by both in-school and out-of-school communities, in early childhood all the way to higher education (Fields and Lee, 2016; Peppler, Halverson, and Kafai, 2016). Proponents and some empirical research suggest that collaboration (Clapp et al., 2017), interest, content, and practices oriented toward STEM (Kafai, Fields, and Searle, 2014; Sheridan et al., 2014), failure, persistence, and iteration (Maltese, Simpson, and Anderson, 2018; Ryoo and Kekelis, 2018; Ryoo et al., 2015), and a number of other skills are fostered through maker learning approaches and environments (Fancsali et al., 2019).

Research suggests that authentic STEM experiences may foster the development of deep conceptual understanding and skills for STEM disciplines (NRC, 2009; 2014; 2015). That is, through these types of experiences, which may be more intrinsically motivating, individuals learn how to identify a problem or need as well as how to plan, model, test, and iterate

BOX 1-2
Making and Makerspaces

Made visible by MAKE: Magazine and Maker Faires that centered on adult hobbyists and DIYers, the broader maker community has since diversified and expanded, with continued efforts and needs to address equity and cultural relevancy (Calabrese Barton and Tan, 2018; Vossoughi, Hooper, and Escudé, 2016). Within learning communities, there exists a duality to making. Whether or not a dedicated physical space is available, making is recognized as a learning approach (Honey and Kanter, 2013; Petrich, Wilkinson, and Bevan, 2013; Resnick and Rosenbaum, 2013; Vossoughi and Bevan, 2014). Making can and often does happen in physical settings, such as a makerspace, often taking on the contexts of the overarching organizations in which they exist. Although "makerspace" is a commonly used term, not all spaces use that name (FabLabs, creativity studios, and Tinkering Studio), and not all maker learning takes place in dedicated physical spaces well-equipped with technology and supplies. In fact, whether in schools or after-school spaces, museum floors, or library environments, activities and materials may be distributed across multiple areas via cart-based systems, classroom corners with tools, or pop-up programming (Peppler, Halverson, and Kafai, 2016). Dedicated makerspaces may allow for consistent interactions with the physical environment and with a community of peers, families, mentors, and/or facilitators (Brahms, 2014). And making occurs at home as individuals, families, and communities have long fixed and made things out of necessity (Calabrese Barton and Tan, 2018; Danticat, 2013; Vossoughi and Bevan, 2014).

Depending on how maker learning programs or makerspaces are designed, what purposes or values are upheld, what settings and contexts they exist within, and what activities are emphasized, making can be authentic to a learner's personal and individual interests, as well as authentic to a community's collective identity (Blikstein, 2013a; Martinez and Stager, 2013). Learners decide which activities and projects to pursue, based on their passions or curiosities (Wardrip and Brahms, 2016), and much of the teaching and learning is hands-on, open-ended, and learner-centered, scaffolded by educators and facilitators but also driven by self-exploration and inquiry (Clapp et al., 2017; Halverson and Sheridan, 2014). Specific to computing, maker learning programs frequently include digital and analog opportunities that range from e-textiles and paper circuitry to physical computing to digital fabrication to multimedia production, where learners are exposed to and develop computing skills with microcontrollers (LilyPad Arduino, Raspberry Pi, micro:bit), programming languages (block-based programming, Java, Python, HTML and CSS, Processing), 3D design (CAD for CNC machines), and more (Berland, 2016; Blikstein, 2013a,b; Kafai, Fields, and Searle, 2014; Lee and Recker, 2018; Martin, 2015).

solutions, all of which makes their higher-order thinking skills tangible and visible (Bennett and Monahan, 2013). Moreover, emerging research has begun to examine the ways in which these types of activities, rooted in authenticity, have the potential to invite in learners from underrepresented communities (based on gender, race, ethnicity, or perceived ability) in STEM fields, particularly computing (Lim and Calabrese Barton, 2006; Migus, 2014). As such, it is important to understand the ways in which authentic STEM experiences can develop interests and competencies for computing.

CHARGE TO THE COMMITTEE

Sponsored by Google and the Grable Foundation, the Board on Science Education (BOSE) of the National Academies of Sciences, Engineering, and Medicine, in collaboration with the Computer Science and Telecommunication Board (CSTB) convened an expert committee to examine the evidence on the ways in which authentic STEM experiences develop interest and competencies for computing (see Box 1-3). The 16-member expert Committee on the Role of Authentic STEM Learning Experiences for Developing Interest and Competencies for Computing included individuals with expertise in the design and construction of learning spaces in formal and informal educational settings that are aimed at providing opportunities to engage in STEM and computing. The expertise spans the K–12 range in a number of important areas, including disciplinary knowledge in science,

---

BOX 1-3
Statement of Task

An ad hoc committee will explore authentic STEM learning experiences that develop interest and foundational knowledge and competencies for computing. The committee will examine the evidence on learning and teaching using authentic, open-ended pedagogical approaches and learning experiences for children and youth in grades K–12 in both formal and informal settings. The committee will consider a range of pedagogical approaches and learning experiences aimed at cultivating the interest and foundational knowledge and competencies necessary for pursuing careers in computing, with particular attention to engaging participants in authentic, open-ended experiences such as problem or project-based approaches and making/makerspaces. The committee will give particular attention to approaches and experiences that promote the success of children and youth from groups that are typically underrepresented in computing fields. In cases where the evidence base with respect to interest and competencies in computing is not robust, the committee will draw on evidence from research on learning and teaching in science, engineering, and mathematics.

mathematics, and computer science; the development of curriculum; teacher professional learning and development; as well as perspectives on issues around diversity, equity, and inclusion.

STUDY APPROACH

The committee met six times over a 15-month period in 2019 and 2020 to gather information and explore what is known about the role of authentic experiences for the development of interest and competences for computing. During this time, the committee reviewed the published literature pertaining to its charge and had opportunities to engage with many experts. Evidence was gathered from presentations and a review of the existing literature (including peer-reviewed materials, book chapters, reports, working papers, government documents, white papers and evaluations, and editorials) and previous reports by the National Academies (see Box 1-4).

The committee searched for information on a number of different outcomes for computing as well as on the different features of design and the institutional/organizational contexts that can facilitate or hinder learners' participation in authentic experiences. When looking at particular outcomes, the committee focused on a number of cognitive, behavioral, and affective outcomes that included interest, identity/belonging, motivation, self-efficacy, knowledge and skills, engagement, and persistence and retention.

In reviewing the evidence, the committee sought to assemble a set of studies that represented the extent of available evidence. A search was conducted through Scopus requesting studies from the past two decades (2000–2020) and limited to English. The review focused on literature and programs centered around three categories of outcomes: (1) affective (such as interest, identity/belonging, motivation, and self-efficacy); (2) cognitive (such as knowledge and skills); and (3) behavioral (such as engagement, persistence, and retention). Details regarding this search can be found in Appendix A.

Many different types of studies were included in this review: meta-analyses and reviews, qualitative case studies, ethnographic and field studies, interview studies, and large-scale studies. The committee recognized that the literature consisted predominantly of studies that were largely descriptive in nature with few studies that could demonstrate causal effects. As appropriate, throughout the report, the evidence is qualified to articulate the type of research being reviewed and its strength.

Throughout the study, members of the committee benefited from discussion and presentations by a number of individuals who participated in the fact-finding meetings. At the first meeting, the committee had an opportunity to speak with the sponsors to ask questions and get clarity on the

---

BOX 1-4
Previous Relevant Reports by the National Academies of
Sciences, Engineering, and Medicine

Over the past 10 years, there has been a lot of interest in understanding the role of STEM and computing experiences in both higher education and K–12 across a variety of settings (formal and informal). In 2018a, *Assessing and Responding to the Growth of Computer Science Undergraduate Enrollments* examined the potential impacts to the increased demand for computing in higher education, drivers of the current enrollment surge, and the relationship between the surge and current and potential gains in the diversity in the field.

In the K–12 education space, there has been a series of reports that have tackled related issues from a number of different perspectives. The first of these was a pair of reports, *Learning Science in Informal Environments: People, Places, and Pursuits* (NRC, 2009) and *Surrounded by Science: Learning Science in Informal Environments* (NRC, 2010a), that assessed the evidence on science learning across settings and learner age groups and over varied spans of time, providing case studies, illustrative examples, and probing questions for practitioners.

The next pair of reports centered on computational thinking. In particular, the first, *Report of a Workshop on the Scope and Nature of Computational Thinking* (NRC, 2010b), focused on presenting the range of perspectives with respect to the definition and applicability of computational thinking whereas the second, *Report of a Workshop on the Pedagogical Aspects of Computational Thinking* (NRC, 2011a), focused on illuminating different pedagogical approaches to computational thinking.

In an effort to better understand the ways in which individuals' science learning can be accomplished through interaction with digital simulations and games, *Learning Science Through Games and Simulations* (NRC, 2011b) provided a review of the available research on the potential of digital games and simulations to contribute to learning science in schools, in informal out-of-school settings, and everyday life. The final report sought to draw upon a wide range of research traditions to illustrate that interest in STEM and deep STEM learning develop across time and settings. *Identifying and Supporting Productive STEM Programs in Out-of-School Settings* (NRC, 2015) provided guidance on how to evaluate and sustain programs.

---

statement of task. In particular, the committee wanted to better understand the sponsor's stance on authenticity and what could be included in the range of authentic experiences. The committee also had the opportunity to hear more about the framing and state of evidence with respect to equitable access to authentic STEM opportunities.

During the second meeting, the committee considered the ways in which robotics competitions and engineering programs were reaching their participants either through the design of the experiences or through outreach efforts to ensure that girls and learners from minoritized groups had access to these programs. Additional presentations described what is known about hobbies and their relationship to different STEM outcomes and the implications of this research for computing.

During the third meeting, there was a large public workshop that focused on a number of key issues. In particular, the presenters were asked to unpack the state of evidence on (1) the role of STEM learning opportunities, (2) promising approaches and strategies in the development of interest and competencies, and (3) what these mean for the goals, design, and implementation of such experiences for computing. A recurring theme throughout the workshop was the importance of evidence that emphasized the implications for increasing access for learners from minoritized communities.

At the fourth meeting, the committee discussed the draft of the report and reached consensus on a number of key issues (described in the previous section). In between meetings, the committee had in-depth conversations with several youth-serving STEM programs to understand their design and their evidence with respect to impacts on the desired learner outcomes. Additionally, members of the committee conducted structured interviews with several young adults who have pursued or are immediately pursuing computing and technology-intensive postsecondary education.[10] These illustrative cases were intended to provide some longitudinal, retrospective data that could highlight aspects of the individual experiences that led the learners to persist in computing. These cases do not reflect the experiences of individuals who have opted not to persist (for a variety of reasons; see Chapter 2).

At the fifth meeting, the committee reviewed the draft report to ensure that there was sufficient evidence for the claims being made. As stated above, throughout the report, the type of research reviewed, and the strength of research evidence, are clearly articulated. The majority of the committee's final meeting was devoted to discussing the conclusions, recommendations, and research agenda to reach consensus. During these discussions, the committee was careful to qualify and temper the conclusions and subsequent recommendations, based on the type and strength of the evidence presented.

REPORT ORGANIZATION

This report examines the research on authentic experiences in computing for learners in grades K–12 across formal and informal settings. Chapter 2 examines the structural (e.g., racism and sexism) and cultural barriers

---

[10] The committee sought IRB approval from the Institutional Review Board, and it was determined that the protocol qualified for exemption from IRB review, under category 2(i, ii) on March 5, 2020. Pseudonyms are used to protect confidentiality.

(e.g., stereotypes and implicit bias) to participation in computing that exist at multiple levels. These barriers to participation impact the nature of the learner's experiences and their development of a computing identity. Chapter 3 articulates the committee's theoretical framing that describes the varied factors that influence whether and how learning is positioned to develop interest and competencies for computing whereas, Chapter 4 presents the evidence on how individual programs or individual curricula speak to the intended outcomes of interest and competencies. Chapter 3 also describes the need for adopting an ecosystems approach to understanding learner's contexts and motivating factors and how these may lead to continued pursuits with computing.

Chapters 5 and 6 describe the institutional and/or organizational contexts that provide the necessary infrastructure for learners to engage in educator-designed authentic experiences for computing. Chapter 5 focuses on authentic experiences that occur outside of school time and emphasizes the strengths and challenges with respect to ensuring equitable access to these programs. Chapter 6 describes the factors (e.g., school funding, teacher preparation, standards and certifications) that influence whether and how authentic experiences for computing are offered in formal educational contexts.

Chapter 7 then provides guidance on how to design authentic experiences for computing given the evidence and organizational constraints. Chapter 8 presents the consensus conclusions and recommendations that are derived from the evidence provided in earlier chapters and articulates an agenda for future research.

2

Barriers and Supports for Learners in Computing

As computing has become increasingly prevalent in the many facets of our daily lives, efforts have focused on engaging children and youth in computing. A number of initiatives, in and out of school, seek to engage learners in a variety of different computing experiences—many with the goal of fulfilling the needs of the future workforce. As part of these expanding opportunities, there is strong emphasis on increasing the participation of learners from groups that are historically underrepresented in computing compared to their representation in the U.S. population, namely, woman, people of color (i.e., Black, Latinx, and Indigenous learners), individuals from rural communities, and those with perceived differences in ability (e.g., students with learning disabilities). Reaching representational parity is a goal that still remains despite these national efforts to increase participation of learners from underrepresented groups.

The causes of the patterns of underrepresentation in computing are complex (Charleston et al., 2014; National Academies of Sciences, Engineering, and Medicine [NASEM], 2018a; 2020; Scott, Sheridan, and Clark, 2014). A number of factors have been identified, including structural barriers such as access to courses and to technology, cultural barriers related to the norms and practices in the discipline, and stereotypes and implicit biases. Many of these barriers are rooted in racism and sexism and assumptions about who is capable of succeeding in computing.

In this chapter, we examine patterns of participation in computing and discuss the barriers to participation. While it is beyond the scope of the committee's charge to provide a detailed analysis of the historical, cultural, and social factors at play in the patterns of underrepresentation, they are important to understand at a broad level as they shape the learners' perceptions of and experiences in computing. To illustrate how these barriers impact the trajectories of individual learners, we weave personal narratives from youth throughout the discussion.[1]

REPRESENTATION IN AND ACCESS TO COMPUTING

Computing, along with other STEM fields, is a discipline that has long been perceived as being biased toward White men (Charleston et al., 2014). As stated above, there are a number of ongoing efforts to increase the representation of women and people of color. Despite these initiatives, the trends in representation of individuals in computing jobs throughout the past decade have remained relatively stable (see Figure 2-1). In 2019, the total U.S. workforce for all occupations included about 157.5 million workers; 47 percent are women, 12.3 percent are Black, 6.5 percent are Asian, and 17.6 percent are Hispanic. In contrast, as can be seen in Figure 2-1, in the computing workforce 25.3 percent of the workers are women, 10 percent are Black, 16.5 percent are Asian, and 8.9 percent are Hispanic. These data mirror the known patterns of overrepresentation of Asians and underrepresentation of women and Black and Hispanic people (Debusschere, 2018; Funk and Parker, 2018). It is important to acknowledge that Asian is an incredibly broad category with different histories of immigration and exclusion from U.S. society and economies. Although Asians are overrepresented in computing, they are underrepresented in the United States and are subjected to many of the same experiences described throughout this chapter.

These patterns of representation (and underrepresentation) start early. For example, as described in more detail in Chapter 6, access to computing varies by grade, rates of poverty at a school, ethnic make-up of a school, and school size (Banilower et al., 2018). Further, the patterns of who takes computing courses are comparable to the patterns observed in the profession; girls and people of color are less likely to take advanced placement computer science courses (see the section on Equity in AP Computer Science Courses). Additionally, as described in Chapter 5, there are differences in the availability of computing experiences in out-of-school settings (Afterschool Alliance, 2016).

Access to computers and the Internet at home is another factor that may contribute to patterns of underrepresentation. The term "digital divide" is used to refer to differences in access to, or use of, technologies

---

[1] As noted in Chapter 1, these cases are illustrative and reflect the experiences of learners who have chosen to persist in computing. These cases do not highlight the many other examples in which learners do not persist either because they drop out or feel forced out (as discussed throughout this chapter).

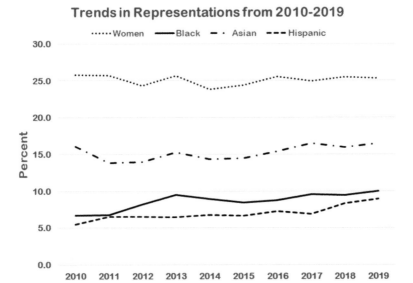

FIGURE 2-1 Trends in representation for computing jobs.
NOTES: It should be noted that the data do not report on Pacific Islanders, Native Americans, or multiracial people. Additionally, the data are flawed in that people who identify as Hispanic are typically not reported as having a race.
SOURCE: Committee generated based on data from the U.S. Bureau of Labor Statistics, Labor Force Statistics from the Current Population Survey. Data tables available at https://www.bls.gov/cps/tables.htm.

across individuals or schools based on race, gender, socioeconomic status, geography, education level, disability status, and first or primary language (Gorski, 2005). One common indicator of this "divide" is inequality in access to computers and the Internet (Gorski, 2002; 2005). Figure 2-2 shows the access to computers in the home for learners broken down by race and ethnicity. Figure 2-3 shows Internet use in the home. During the 7-year period from 2010 to 2017, levels of access and use have remained relatively stable for learners who are White or Asian, while access and use among learners from other racial and ethnic groups has increased. Despite these increases, gaps still remain, particularly between learners who are Native American/Alaska Native and their White and Asian counterparts.

SOCIAL AND CULTURAL BARRIERS IMPACTING PARTICIPATION

While access and opportunity likely contribute to the historical patterns of underrepresentation, social and cultural barriers rooted in racism and sexism play a significant role. Rodriguez and Lehman (2018) stress

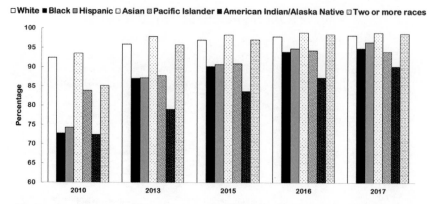

FIGURE 2-2 Percentages of learners ages 3–18 who have access to computers at home, selected years: 2010–2017.
SOURCE: Committee generated based on data from the National Center for Education Statistics; available at https://nces.ed.gov/programs/digest/d18/tables/dt18_702.10.asp?current=yes.

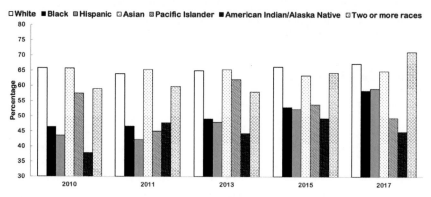

FIGURE 2-3 Percentages of learners ages 3–18 who use Internet at home, selected years: 2010–2017.
SOURCE: Committee generated based on data from the National Center for Education Statistics; available at https://nces.ed.gov/programs/digest/d18/tables/dt18_702.15.asp.

the importance of understanding who is being privileged or marginalized in the system, and how individuals from privileged groups have access to opportunities for success and possess power over marginalized groups. Computing, as a field, has been historically composed of White men, and the values, norms, and practices of the field have been shaped by them (Björkman, 2005; Faulkner, 2001; Rodriguez and Lehman, 2018). These norms, values, and practices are reinforced and perpetuated by those in the discipline with the most power (Rasmussen and Håpnes, 1991) and are communicated to prospective learners (Rodriguez and Lehman, 2018). Thus, in both in-school and out-of-school learning environments, learners are exposed to the cultural norms and assumptions of the field, and this shapes their perception of computing and their own relationship to the discipline (Barkey, Hovey, and Thompson, 2015; Hansen et al., 2017; Rodriguez and Lehman, 2018; Schulte and Knobelsdork, 2007; Wong, 2016; Zander et al., 2009). In some cases, the norms and values of computing may be unfamiliar to individuals who are not White men, and in some cases, they may even be at odds with the norms and values learners bring from their own homes and communities (NASEM, 2016).

When individuals experience overt or implicit racism and sexism, they may perceive an environment as oppressive and hostile (Beasley and Fischer, 2012; McGee, 2016; Naphan-Kingery et al., 2019). Moreover, they may come to feel as if they are "tokens" or representatives of their social group (Kanter, 1977), which has been associated with depression and anxiety (Jackson, Thoits, and Taylor, 1995) and declining performance due to stereotype threat (Steele and Aronson, 1995).

Sense of Belonging and Identity

Across the varied settings of everyday life, as well as in media and popular culture, young people encounter representations of STEM and computing culture and identities. This includes encounters with role models, media depictions, and instructional content that influence how learners value and identify with different activities, practices, communities, and potential occupations. Learners begin to develop mental models about vocational pathways and identities and also develop a self-concept in relation to potential occupational pathways. This influences a learner's sense of affiliation with a professionally authentic computing community of practice (see Chapter 3 for additional discussion of communities of practice). Box 2-1 presents the case of Nathan, who first started out playing Minecraft with friends and, through his continued computing experiences, felt "competent and empowered" as he began to develop an identity as a computing professional.[2]

Research has suggested that one of the reasons women and people of color choose not to participate in computing is a sense that they do not belong in the field (Barker, McDowell, and Kalahar, 2009; Cohoon, 2002; Margolis and Fisher, 2002; Sax et al., 2018). Sense of belonging

---

[2]Four individuals—Nathan (Box 2-1), Raven (Box 2-2), Hermione (Box 2-3), and Antonio (Box 2-4)—and their self-reported formative experiences of authentic experiences for computing are described. Out of consideration of these individuals' privacy, proper names have been changed. Throughout the report, where appropriate, the experiences of these individuals are referenced to illustrate various aspects of the committee's framework (see Chapter 3) with respect to authentic experiences and their potential impact for outcomes related to computing.

BOX 2-1
Nathan

Nathan, a White man in his early 20s, grew up the oldest of three siblings in Texas where the sole computer at home available for child use was a shared family laptop. In middle school, when he had his scheduled turns to use the family laptop, he would often play Minecraft with friends in the neighborhood. Upon learning that players could set up their own server, Nathan and his friends decided that they should create one for themselves that was customized to allow the play styles they preferred. "Completing that installation was my first real experience with debugging and exposure to programming. Even though it took time and involved some problem solving, I felt competent and empowered" because he was able to install a server version of his favorite online game. His interest in the backend of computing piqued, he would later use portions of his time on the shared family laptop to watch online video tutorials that introduced programming basics in the Java programming language. By working on some of these online programming problems, he became exposed to various discrete mathematics and number theory problems that came up with computing.

This led him to search for online solutions and stumble upon online coding communities that posted mathematical coding challenges. He began to complete those challenges and participate in those online communities. By this time, Nathan was in high school and enrolled in computer science courses including the AP computer science course that was offered. "My first classroom computer science teacher was an inspiration" and ended up being an influential figure "who demonstrated a strong understanding of coding and was a highly effective teacher."

Throughout high school, Nathan also maintained an interest in biology and started a high school club around the topic of synthetic biology. In his summers, he worked in a biology laboratory at the local university that he learned about from contacts his parents had, and that too eventually led to some use of his coding skills. After high school, "I wanted to pursue studies in bioengineering at a major research university but decided to add computer science as a second major because I am still really interested in it." Years later, Nathan is still in touch with his first high school computer science teacher through social media and participates in online coding communities and the open source movement.

SOURCE: As told to the committee on April 24, 2020.

---

refers to the extent to which individuals feel like they belong or fit in a given environment and is a fundamental need that drive learners' behaviors (Baumeister and Leary, 1995; Sax et al., 2018; Strayhorn, 2012). As described in the previous section, learners from groups that are traditionally underrepresented in computing (based on gender, race, ethnicity, or perceived ability) experience learning environments in computing differently (Barker, McDowell, and Kalahar, 2009; Margolis and Fisher, 2002; Margolis et al., 2008; Strayhorn, 2012). For example, women may be discouraged from participation in STEM because the typical discourse promotes the narrative that these fields are better suited to men (Blickenstaff, 2005; Haaken, 1996; Raffaelli and Ontai, 2004; Reilly, Rackley, and Awad, 2017). These messages can be conveyed by parents, teachers, and others who have this assumption about computing careers (Eccles, Jacobs, and Harold, 1990; Sadker and Sadker, 1994).

Sense of belonging is important for developing an identity as someone who can succeed in computing. Dempsey et al. (2015) defined a computing identity as the extent to which the learner sees themselves as a computing professional (Rodriguez and Lehman, 2018). There is a strong relationship between having a computing identity, intending to pursue computing as a major (Dempset et al., 2015), and feeling a sense of fit with the field (Lewis, Anderson, and Yasuhara, 2016; Lewis, Yasuhara, and Anderson, 2011). For example, in school settings, learners are less likely to be exposed to teachers of color, which is a missed opportunity to expose learners to role models and pedagogies that are informed by minoritized perspectives and experiences (see Chapter 6, Equity and Access in Computing in Schools section).

In understanding how learners experience computing and how they see themselves fitting into the field, it is important to consider the learner's intersecting identities (Coles, 2009; Crenshaw, 1994; Donovan, 2011; Settles, 2006). That is, for example, how being a woman and being Black or Latina might together create a unique lens through which an individual experiences and perceives the world. In addition, the ways that other people perceive an individual's intersecting identities may contribute to a learner's experience of marginalization (Rodriguez and Lehman, 2018). Despite the importance of intersectionality for understanding learners' experiences and the development of their identities in computing, current research predominately focuses on gender *or* race and ethnicity.

The Role of Stereotypes and Implicit Biases

Stereotypes create associations between occupations, fields, and identity categories such as class, race, and gender. Stereotypes suggesting science and other high-prestige occupations are the province of people who are privileged in society—upper-middle class, White, and male—are pervasive even in school settings (Allen and Eisenhart, 2017; Bang et al., 2013; Carlone and Johnson, 2007; Carlone, Scott, and Lowder, 2014; Tan et al., 2013). For example, researchers have found that stereotypes about the gendered nature of a discipline (e.g., computer science is for men) have a negative effect on whether people not of that gender (e.g., women) have a sense of belonging to that field (Cundiff et al., 2013; Martin, 2004).

Stereotypes about computer science start young and may be more prevalent than stereotypes about other STEM disciplines, such as science and math (for additional discussion, see Chapter 6). For example, researchers found that learners as young as first grade believed boys were better than girls at robotics and programming but did not believe the same about math and science. They also found that girls with stronger stereotyped beliefs had lower interest and self-efficacy in computer science (Master et al., 2017). However, providing girls with experience in programming at this age seemed to confront these trends and reduce gender gaps by increasing learner interest and self-efficacy in computer science.

Models do not come solely in the form of adults. Eckert and McConnell-Ginet (1995) describe learners as making behavioral judgments based on what near peers are doing and what those in the next stage are doing. For example, sixth graders look toward what eighth graders do, and this may then shape the degree to which sixth graders participate in computing experiences.

At the high school level, one study found that negative stereotypes about computer scientists have a detrimental effect on girls' interest and sense of belonging in computer science (Master, Cheryan, and Meltzoff, 2016). Further, these researchers discovered that stereotypes can be communicated by the physical environment (such as images that convey the notion of computer science as geeky on the wall of a classroom) and that physical environments that do not convey these images can have a positive effect on girls' interest. As described above, the tendency to reiterate the lack of women in computer science activates a stereotype threat that negatively influences women's involvement (Naphan-Kingery et al., 2019). As aspirations are impacted by stereotype threat, an effort to change recruiting verbiage and attitude is required at all levels (Shapiro and Williams, 2012).

Box 2-2 provides a case example of Raven, who first developed an interest in computing in elementary school as she used graphic editing tools while working on the school's yearbook.

BOX 2-2
Raven

Raven, a self-identified Latinx/Native American woman in her early 20s living in the southwest United States, had just completed her bachelor's degree in computer science and minors in mathematics and art from a public university in the South when we spoke with her. Her family values the arts, with her grandfather working as a practicing artist and arts figuring prominently in her mother's career and in her sibling's hobbies. "I did not consider myself to be especially strong in the arts until I got involved with computing. I enjoy computing activities that involve designing and developing front-end interfaces and experiences for websites and web services." While artistic expression was a part of what she currently enjoyed

BOX 2-2 Continued

about computing, it was not her initial entry point. Her first memorable exposure to computing was through working on her elementary school's yearbook and using graphics editing tools, although it was her move to middle school that really got her interested in computing. When she began middle school, Raven joined an after-school program offered at her school that would provide students time to work on projects and computer modeling software. As a student in a new school, "my primary motivation for joining the afterschool program was to meet new people and make friends. I did not know other students at my new school, and the program sounded like everyone worked together and could be a way to build relationships while building things with computational technology."

She described her participation in that after-school program as central to her interest and pursuit of computing as an adult. Raven continued with that same after-school program for years and did make good friends through it. Sustained participation led to Raven's eventually becoming one of the mentors in her later years because "the mentors and facilitators in the program were my inspiration." Some came from a technical background and knew more about the tools and technologies that they were using. Some came from an artistic background and championed the creative process for the learners who participated. Through that after-school program, Raven was exposed to multiple computer-based modeling environments, HTML and CSS, paper circuitry, and the Processing arts-oriented programming language. Her growing confidence with technology led her, as a high schooler, to sign up for and participate in local summer programs at a nearby university that introduced her to Arduino and animation-based programming (e.g., Alice). The breadth of exposure helped Raven appreciate that computing was not for a single career or application. Rather, it could be used across industries and one could apply computing in a number of different ways in a number of different professions. Through her participation in these out-of-school activities, she would make small projects as gifts for her sister or to help her sister with school projects. She also pursued options in school to build websites for class projects rather than traditional papers or dioramas. One of her websites went on to win a state award.

When she began college as a computer science major, "I was discouraged by one of my introductory programming courses." Raven described how she struggled with the traditional programming assignments and tests that were given, which were quite different from her experiences in after-school and summer programs. Her professor even told her that computer science may not be the right field for her, but she had enough resilience to decide she was not going to be dissuaded from completing that degree. As a college student, she also continued to mentor—most prominently for a couple years as an after-school computer science teacher for a university-affiliated elementary lab school. There, she introduced younger students to Scratch and the Greenfoot programming environments. Having just graduated with her degree, she is confident that she has skills that are broadly applicable to a range of fields and jobs. She is, to this day, in close contact with her mentors and mentees from the afterschool computing program that she began in middle school.

SOURCE: As told to the committee on June 11, 2020.

Strategies to Address Cultural Barriers

Lack of socially similar (defined as being of the same gender, race, or socioeconomic class) role models has frequently been cited as an important reason why there are few women in STEM and IT (Teague, 2002; Townsend, 1996). Exposure to alternative representations in the media, instructional materials, or through atypical role models exhibiting vocationally relevant dispositions and skills is a way of combating stereotypes (Carter-Black, 2008; O'Keeffe, 2013). Several scholars have found that exposing learners to women in computer science who can serve as role models that are similar to those learners can help them see themselves in the computer scientist role (Asgari, Dasgupta, and Stout, 2012). For example, young women exposed to computer science instructors who are women in high school were more likely to major in computer science in college (Beyer and Haller, 2006).

Box 2-3 describes the case of Hermione, who had exposure to role models who reflected her identity, in multiple settings, all of which allowed her to persist in computing while recognizing that in the field of computing she is "unique" as a Black women. Studies in engineering have also shown a positive relationship between exposure to women role models and persistence in the major (Amelink and Creamer, 2010). However, other scholars have found that role models can have a negative influence if they conform to negative stereotypes. For example, Cheryan et al. (2011) found that when role models conform to the stereotype that computer scientists are "geeks," they did not have the expected positive influence on women's self-efficacy.

Culturally relevant, responsive, and sustaining pedagogical approaches (described in more detail in Chapter 7) have highlighted the importance of settings that recognize the varied backgrounds and unequal resources that young learners bring to STEM experiences (Ladson-Billings, 1995; Scott and Zhang, 2014; Scott, Aist, and Hood, 2009; Scott, Sheridan, and Clark, 2015). For example, research with young women of color in STEM

BOX 2-3
Hermione

Hermione, a college sophomore, is a Black woman who grew up in a large urban center in the Northeast, who always thought she wanted to be a history teacher. Working in the field of computer science (CS) had never crossed her mind. Her first exposure to CS was through an AP CS course, the *Beauty and Joy of Computing*,[a] her sophomore year of high school. At the time, her family did not

BOX 2-3 Continued

own a computer. "The school put me in the class. I had no choice and tried to get out of it. At first, I hated it. I didn't understand it. But I had a fabulous teacher, and I fell in love with it."

The following summer, she had an opportunity to intern through the school district's CS internship program. The paid internship offered 60 hours of on-the-job CS/tech experience and career preparation through a local university that included writing assignments, interview practice, and resume review. Hermione recalled that the internship was transformative in that it exposed her to careers in computing that she did not know existed and also put her in contact with an excellent mentor. This first internship led to a second one the following summer with the district's CSforAll initiative team. Through this internship she learned more about the education side of the industry. While interning, she worked with district staff who designed and implemented the initiative and attended many of the district's professional development offerings for teachers. She met other industry professionals, including software engineers who "blew my mind talking about what they do and how much they love it." Having sparked an interest in CS, Hermione began to attend hackathons outside of school.

These internship experiences led her to apply to a small liberal arts college as a computer science major (with a data science minor), where she has just completed her sophomore year. As a Black woman, Hermione noted that she does not "see" herself in CS at her college. Despite this, she feels supported by her professors and believes they work hard to make her feel included. Her first mentor at her internship was also Black, and she noted that he prepared her for what she would experience in the field of computing. For example, he talked to her about code switching and encouraged her to "be yourself as much as you can."

Though no one in her family worked in CS or knew much about the field, they supported her pursuit of her interests. In addition to her AP CS course teacher and her mentor at her internship, Hermione points to several CSforAll school district staff whom she met through her internship (including several who are women, Black, and Latinx) as a constant source of motivation and encouragement to stay in CS. To this day, they continue to check in on her, send her emails, and invite her to attend summer professional development sessions.

Hermione's career goal now is to combine computer science and statistics in some way, perhaps in biocomputing. She wants to "take data and tell a story with it." Her summer internship following sophomore year in college was cancelled due to COVID-19, so instead she made plans to take an online bootcamp course to learn blockchain in C.

SOURCE: As told to the committee on May 12, 2020.

---

[a]The *Beauty and Joy of Computing* course is a computer science Principles course developed for high school juniors that is designed to meet learners where they are. Snap! (an easy-to-learn blocks-based programming language) is used to cover the big ideas and computational thinking practices in the CS principles curriculum framework (Ball et al., 2020).

programs has highlighted the importance of creating programs grounded in learners' identities and life experiences, equipping learners from minoritized groups to be change agents who can challenge dominant practices and cultures (Ashcraft, Eger, and Scott 2017; Ashford et al., 2017; Scott and Garcia, 2016). These counter spaces are a way of making STEM and computing relevant and authentic to learners who are marginalized in the dominant cultures of STEM, and have been shown to increase their engagement and interest (Barron et al., 2014; Erete, Martin, and Pinkard, 2017; Lee et al., 2015). Box 2-4 presents the case of Antonio, who had multiple opportunities with computing in a number of different settings; through these experiences he had opportunities that allowed him to further develop his interest in programming and robotics.

ROLE OF AUTHENTIC EXPERIENCES

The committee sees authenticity as central to learners' creation of a computing identity and authentic experiences as a vehicle for addressing the structural and cultural barriers inherent in computing. Throughout this report, the committee puts forth two senses of authenticity: *personal authenticity*, which describes activities in which learners find personal meaning and interest, and *professional authenticity*, which describes practices that are like those used by professionals in computing. Learning environments designed for professional authenticity exhibit features of problem solving, creation, experimentation, and inquiry that mirror or are directly connected to the culture, practices, and communities of computing professionals. We use the term "personally authentic" when the activity is personally or culturally meaningful in the mind of the learner.

Authentic experiences in computing come in many variations from coding an app for a service-learning project to crafting/sewing e-textiles with a caregiver to playing video games with friends. All of these might be considered authentic experiences, but they might vary in the degree to which they are personally or professionally authentic.

The committee recognizes that there might be a perceived tension between personal authenticity and professional authenticity. But this tension dissipates when personal and professional authenticity are understood as separate dimensions rather than as oppositional to each other, or as two ends of a single continuum. Instead, the committee considers personal and professional as each representing their own continuum, and an experience can be more or less personally and/or professionally authentic on each spectrum. An experience that learners find personally motivating may not be grounded in professional practice, just as an experience that a learner recognizes as reflecting professional practice can also be grounded in per-

BOX 2-4
Antonio

Antonio is a Latino high school senior living in the mountain west who has been accepted to the college of engineering at a major research university. Although he has yet to decide on the specific major he will study, the ones he is considering are all computing and technology intensive. Three years prior, when Antonio was in his first year in high school, his family immigrated from Mexico, where he was born and raised. In Mexico, Antonio's primary exposure to computing was through his school's computer literacy courses, which emphasized learning keyboarding skills and productivity software, and through his own smartphone, which he had received when he had been in the fourth grade. He had found his Mexican school's exposure to computing to be uninteresting. His preference at that time was to focus on popular video games. "My friends and I would search for online videos on how to hack some of those games." Besides that, he freely explored and customized settings on his smartphone because "I wanted to figure out how things worked, and I was curious how I could modify the different settings."

After moving to the United States, he discovered that the local public library had a makerspace and was offering workshops and classes for free. He began to attend those regularly, going up to twice a week to the library makerspace, and learned how to program an Arduino, operate a 3D printer, build robots, and laser cut objects. "The staff and instructors really encouraged and motivated me as I programmed games, made miniature light sabers, and built webpages." Over the years, his participation in library makerspace programs escalated to the point that he became one of the mentors there. He also began participating in workshops that were hosted by the local university, some of which his mother had learned about and shared with him and some that were implemented through the library makerspace.

In school, when his schedule had room for electives during his junior and senior years, Antonio began taking some courses on programming and robotics to further his interest. He also took courses in media editing software, which improved his ability to make custom videos. "The classes were more enjoyable than some of my other classes because the teachers were more fun and entertaining." Most recently, Antonio participated in programming internships with local organizations. He considers himself to be quite interested and competent in technology and computing, and attributes this in large part to the library makerspace, technology classes at school, and some workshops offered at his university, as well as the enthusiastic support and encouragement from his immediate family.

SOURCE: As told to the committee on April 9, 2020.

sonal interests. But experiences can be designed to be both professionally authentic and personally authentic.

In it important to recognize, however, that professional practice in computing reflects a history and disciplinary culture that tends to exclude women and other marginalized groups such as Black, Latinx, and Indigenous learners. Therefore, an experience that is "professionally authenticity" may inadvertently exclude some learners. Although educators can work to create learning experiences in computing that foster personal authenticity by incorporating cultural elements and practices of groups traditionally underrepresented in the field, the professional world may also need to evaluate and address policies and practices that create barriers to diversity and inclusion.

SUMMARY

Many authentic learning environments in computing have strong associations with a culture of science and technology that has historically been dominated by White men. What feels authentic to those who reflect the dominant culture of computing may feel exclusionary to women, people of color, and those with differences in perceived ability. As articulated throughout this chapter, women and minoritized learners experience multiple barriers to participation in computing. Some barriers are technological and economical, while others are social and cultural, including racism, sexism, stereotypes, and implicit bias. These barriers can in turn influence computing identity and a sense of belonging to STEM and computing in particular. Providing learners with authentic experiences that attend to both professional and personal authenticity may be a mechanism for addressing some of these barriers.

3

How Learning Happens in Authentic Experiences for Computing

Many types of experiences in a young person's life contribute to whether they later exhibit interest or competence in computing. These experiences can be formal or informal and can involve exposure to individuals who will help shape the relationship that a young person will later have to computing. Messages will also be communicated in both explicit and tacit ways to a young person, which they internalize about how well suited they are for a future in computing. Larger systemic factors, such as the availability of educational programs, technologies, courses, and skilled educators, also play a role. Prior consensus reports established the groundwork for the ways these influences apply to science and to science, technology, engineering, and mathematics (STEM) education broadly (e.g., see National Research Council [NRC], 1999; 2009; National Academies of Sciences, Engineering, and Medicine [NASEM], 2018b). In this chapter, the committee presents a learning and development framework for understanding the many influences on a young person's choice to pursue computing, and the factors that place them in a position to be receptive to these influences, whether it is through advanced study, active participation in computing practices, or career.

The chapter begins with a discussion of this framework, which articulates the underlying learning and development processes that are revealed in existing theories and conceptual models. Following this, the committee further elaborates on the framework, looking at both "internal" and "external" factors. The committee begins by describing the "internal" psychological and individual influences relevant to authentic experiences; in particular, interest (which can be both an outcome and an individual mediator) and competencies for computing. The committee then delves into "external" social and cultural influences, calling attention to sociocultural and situated learning theory. This is followed by a discussion of the ways in which culture and personal relevance influence professional identity. The chapter concludes with the committee's articulation of the ways learning happens over time and across settings (i.e., an ecosystems approach), which the committee believes holds promise for the development of interest and competencies for computing. Although this discussion is primarily theoretical and conceptual in nature, examples are used to illustrate how some of these relationships have been studied in research on computational identity, interests, and competencies.

FRAMEWORK FOR LEARNING AND DEVELOPMENT IN CONTEXT

The committee's investigation focused on how engagement in authentic experiences embedded in meaningful social and cultural contexts is linked with specific affective, behavioral, and cognitive outcomes. For example, how might the computing experience be tied to a young person's sense of self and agency in a way that nurtures computing interests and competencies and, eventually, participation in the world of computing as a professional? The four learner examples described in Chapter 2 illustrate the interwoven nature of influences that expose learners to computing and support the development of computing interests and competency. These include recreational pursuits that learners engage in with peers such as playing and tinkering with video games, activities supported in informal learning institutions such as libraries and after-school groups, as well as formal learning experiences in school. All four learners had "authentic" experiences in that they were embedded in valued social and cultural contexts, were personally meaningful and interest-driven, and included tools, skills, and practices that computing professionals engage in. Raven (Box 2-2) learned how to create artistic objects and gifts for her sister. Nathan (Box 2-1) figured out how to set up a Minecraft server with friends. Antonio (Box 2-4) programmed light sabers and robots for fun in his makerspace community. Hermione (Box 2-3) engaged in hackathons and now wants to use computer science to tell stories with data.

These influences and outcomes are intertwined, and their relationships are multidirectional as well as multidimensional, taking place across multiple settings and over significant spans of time. These profiled experiences also illustrate the multifaceted and unplanned nature of how learners are exposed to and develop computing interests and skills, and the dynamic and complex way in which learners build a long-term interest in computing. The relationship between experiences of tinkering, making, and programming and long-term interest, skills, participation, and persistence in computing is influenced by a wide range of experiences at home, school, online, and in the local community as well as by individual factors such as identity. Given this complexity, the committee took a first step in building an organizing framework: identifying learning and development dynamics based on existing theories and conceptual models.

This learning and development framework rests on the committee's interpretation of "authentic experiences" as reflective of professional communities of practice (professionally authentic) and personally meaningful contexts (personally authentic). The committee recognizes the importance of the culture and practices of computing as an important reference point for authenticity, and participation and belonging in these professional communities of practice as a key outcome. Thus, the framework takes into account experiences beyond those in formal education to consider out-of-school time learning environments as well as sites of play with peers, and community engagement where learners find personally meaningful ways of engaging with computing. The committee also emphasizes the bidirectional relationship of affective, cognitive, and behavioral outcomes with authentic learning contexts, which can also serve as key mediators that influence how learners identify with cultures and practices of computing and develop interests and a sense of belonging.

Authentic experiences, conceptualized in this way, are vehicles for learners to develop interests and identification with computing practices. As described in Chapter 2, the culture of science and technology has been historically dominated by White men.[1] This suggests, that many professionally authentic STEM, including computing, environments have strong gender and cultural associations. Therefore, what feels authentic to those who reflect the dominant culture of computing may feel exclusionary to women and other minoritized groups such as Black, Latinx, and Indigenous learners as well as those with differences in perceived ability. Moreover, these groups experience barriers (i.e., racism, sexism, stereotypes, implicit bias, and lack of representation in communities of practice) at every level of social and cultural influence. These barriers, described in Chapter 2, can in turn influence identity and self-efficacy in relation to STEM, broadly, and computing, in particular. This chapter describes findings from theoretical and empirical research that has examined strategies for overcoming these systemic challenges. What follows is a discussion of what is known with respect to developing interest that promotes the motivation to develop competencies in computing.

---

[1] It is important to acknowledge that Asian is an incredibly broad category with different histories of immigration and exclusion from U.S. society and economies.

INTEREST AND COMPETENCIES IN COMPUTING

In STEM, researchers have traced learners' motivation to learn and learning outcomes to three factors: (1) their personal interest in—or fascination with—the topic; (2) their perception of the value and use of the topic; and (3) their development of competence while engaging in the practices and community of the discipline (Bathgate and Schunn, 2017) as discussed more fully below. Key to understanding how authentic experiences may influence interest and competencies in computing is understanding how learners develop interest and the mechanisms that promote interest and motivation to learn. That is because these outcomes can also be individual mediators. In this section, the committee reviews theory and research on how interests develop over time and the mechanisms that foster and mediate interest and competencies. Because the literature specific to computing is limited, this section also draws on literature from STEM disciplines more broadly.

The Relationship Between Interests and Competencies

Interest is a key influence on learning and the development of competencies. When learners are interested in a topic, they have greater attention spans, are intrinsically motivated to learn, and see greater achievement (Hidi and Renninger, 2006; Nye et al., 2012). As interest develops, individuals are more likely to re-engage with content, which can lead to deeper interest and knowledge (Mehta and Fine, 2019). Understanding how interest develops provides insight into the types of experiences and interventions that can foster interest and competencies in computing.

Hidi and Renninger (2006) postulate that interest develops sequentially through four stages, beginning with externally supported situational interest and deepening to more intrinsic and stable interest. The first phase is *triggered situational interest*, defined as "a psychological state of interest that results from short-term changes in affective and cognitive processing" (p. 114). For example, interest may be sparked by unexpected or novel information, or personal relevance of the topic to the individual. Novelty, challenge, choice, active participation, and group work have been noted as key factors in triggering learners' initial situational interest (Renninger and Hidi, 2011). Situational interest is often fostered by community-specific opportunities in professionally authentic computing communities.

The second phase, *maintained situational interest*, "involves focused attention and persistence over an extended episode in time" (p. 114). Once interest is sparked, it can be supported or sustained by repeated engagement that is initiated by the individual or promoted by outside factors, resulting in deeper interest. This can lead to the third phase, *emerging individual interest*, where learners may actively seek out and choose to re-engage with the content or tasks of interest. As their interest deepens, learners gain more knowledge about and value for the topic or task. Finally, emerging individual interest may lead to the fourth phase, a *well-developed individual interest* that is characterized by continued engagement with content over time. At this phase, learners may show more persistence and ability to continually participate and engage with a topic and more self-regulated behavior. This can lead them to become more central practitioners in the computing community, even though the form and nature of their participation can vary (Azevedo, 2011). Although this model appreciates that engagement stems from interactions between individuals and their environment, it does not properly account for the diversity of people's environment or how history, a sense of future, or interactional goals might supersede their interest development (Azevedo, 2013; Pinkard et al., 2017)—contexts and learning environments will be discussed in more detail below.

Researchers have found that activities that trigger initial interest can be different from those that maintain it over a longer period of time. For example, Mitchell (1993) found that group work and interaction with puzzles and computers in mathematics classes triggered initial situational interest, while personal relevance of the content and active participation fostered and maintained longer lasting interest. As reviewed in *How People Learn II: Learners, Contexts, and Cultures*, choice can also increase interest, engagement, and persistence (NASEM, 2018b).

Finally, it is important to note that interest has a reciprocal relationship to other factors, such as goals, self-efficacy, self-regulation, knowledge, and value (Renninger and Hidi, 2011). For example, competence can lead to a sense of accomplishment, and in turn, fuel interest (Allison and Cossette, 2007). On the other side of the coin, lack of knowledge may lead to lower self-efficacy, dampening interest (Schmidt, 2014). Below the committee summarizes the theory and research behind these mechanisms.

Mechanisms That Promote Interest and Competency

Researchers have identified several factors that are characteristic of authentic experiences that can promote and mediate the development and deepening of interest. This includes the internal disposition of identity (discussed in this section) and the external influences (inputs) of role models, programs and practices, and communities of practice (described in the next section).

Most scholars describe three components of identity: a sense of belonging to a group, a sense of achievement within the norms of the group, and particular behaviors associated with belonging to a group (Carlone and Johnson, 2007; Cheryan, Master, and Meltzoff, 2015; Erikson, 1968; Lave and Wenger, 2002; Tajfel and Turner, 1986). Put more simply, identity in a community, such as computing, is about whether you see yourself and are recognized by others as someone who understands and uses the practices of that community (as set up in Chapter 2 and described in more detail later). Researchers have argued that it is through social processes and shared experiences that people gain a sense of identity (Boaler, William, and Zevenbergen, 2000; Lave and Wenger, 1991).

Studies have linked the presence of a STEM identity with interest and persistence in STEM education and careers. For example, science identity has been found to predict learners' interest in science, persistence in a science discipline, intention to pursue a scientific career, and decision to pursue graduate work in science (Merolla and Serpe, 2013; Merolla et al., 2012). Studies exploring the disproportionality of women and of Black, Latinx, and Indigenous individuals in STEM fields have also pointed to identity as a key factor. For example, Jones, Ruff, and Paretti (2013) found in a study of women that a strong STEM identity was related to greater persistence in the field. Stets et al. (2017) found that learners at Historically Black Colleges and Universities (HBCUs) with a strong STEM identity were more likely to enter into a science occupation following graduation.

Kim, Sinatra, and Seyranian (2018) argue that an under-acknowledged factor in STEM identity development for females is their social environment—their caregivers, friends, peers, and teachers. Specifically, in their review of the literature, they found support for the idea that women receive many signals from their environment that they do not belong in STEM. This environment impedes women's motivation to pursue and persist in STEM coursework, ultimately reducing the likelihood that they will pursue STEM careers. Further, Kim et al. notes that STEM identity is also influenced by other social identities including one's race, ethnicity, age, socio-economic status, and gender, to name a few.

As introduced in Chapter 2, Rodriguez and Lehman (2018) recognized a need for an enhanced, intersectional computing identity theory that could allow for deeper understanding of how learners come to understand themselves as computer scientists. This theoretical framing could unpack why women and underrepresented learners continue to have difficulty identifying as computer scientists even when efforts are designed to be more inclusive. Thomas et al. (2018) interviewed 11 Black women in an effort to characterize the factors that influenced their continued participation in computing. The researchers noted that personal and professional goals, effective mentors, and familial inspiration were called out as factors that helped the women overcome adversity, which included experiences of discrimination, unrealistic expectations (either too high or too low), isolation, sexism, and racism.

Taken together, the broader theoretical and empirical literature on the development of interest and competencies in STEM suggest links between interest, identity, and continued persistence in STEM fields. For communities often underrepresented in STEM, such as women, racial and ethnic minorities, and those with disabilities, research is still ongoing. This is in part because an important aspect of the research is consideration of the individual nested within a broader context of social and cultural influences. What follows is a discussion of these "external" factors and the implications within the committee's learning and development framework.

SOCIAL AND CULTURAL INFLUENCES ON AUTHENTIC LEARNING

To elucidate the kinds of contexts that support authentic experiences, the committee drew from two different conceptual and theoretical literatures. The first is sociocultural and situated learning theory, which has developed a conceptual model for understanding how professional communities of practice support learning and belonging. The second body of research centers on how culture and personal relevance influence professional identity, including the role of place-based and problem-/project-based learning in shaping what young people view as personally relevant and authentic.

Situated Learning and Communities of Practice

Many longstanding approaches to instruction presume that learners will transfer what they are learning in one context to other future contexts. However, this idealization of the transfer process has been challenged in empirical studies (e.g., Gick and Holyoak, 1980). Although some conditions can better facilitate transfer (NRC, 1999), knowledge and understanding are largely rooted in particular contexts. For instance, grocery shoppers were effective at figuring out best-buy calculations at the supermarket but performed poorly when given similar problems in a paper-and-pencil mathematics classroom-like task (Lave, 1988). Studies such as these have led to the recognition that learning is situated in specific settings, with specific tools, and around specific practices (Brown, Collins, and Duguid, 1989).

Consequently, learning is now viewed as a process of enculturation within a community of practice. Through documentation of learning via apprenticeship in a variety of settings, Lave and Wenger (1991) established a theory of situated learning in which novices develop competencies through a process of legitimate peripheral participation. That is, novices begin by observing, taking on some peripheral tasks, and increasingly assume greater responsibility over time within the community such that they become more central participants in the community. For instance, Antonio's participation in his local library makerspace began with his peripheral participation, but over the years and with continued visitation, led to him becoming one of the youth mentors in that space. Raven progressed from being a newcomer at an afterschool computing group to eventually serving as a mentor both in the group and in an elementary school when she was in college.

This turn toward recognizing the situated nature of knowing and learning has contributed to interest in learning experiences that are authentic relative to professional communities of practice. Learner practices in designed learning experiences that are comparable to practices of professionals are central to authentic learning experiences in STEM broadly and computing more specifically (Chinn and Malhotra, 2002; Crawford, 2012; Kapon, Laherto, and Levrini, 2018). Importantly, these authentic approximations of professional practice can serve to enculturate learners to professional communities of practice. Rather than presenting various decontextualized scientific principles in a classroom lecture, a more authentic approach positions learners as novice scientists and has them engage in versions of learning activities that better approximate professional scientific inquiry (Edelson, 1998). In an out-of-school-time learning space, this could involve a learner doing work with robotics that includes more experimentation, tinkering, and exploration akin to what an engineer would do, rather than simply assembling a robot from a kit by following a set of written instructions (Bevan, 2017).

Moreover, authentic experiences that approximate professional practice provide access to tools used in professional communities of practice, albeit sometimes designed to ensure that they are accessible for more novice users (Edelson and Reiser, 2006). This was the case for Antonio, who had the opportunity to use high-end, expensive fabrication equipment to support his developing interest in technology. Mastery of these context-specific tools is thought to lead not only to increased competence in the discipline but also to an increased sense of identity as a person with special expertise.

Linking Communities of Practice to Developing Interest and Competencies

Some researchers argue that by structuring learning activities and environments so that they better approximate professional practice, the distance between practices in designed learning experiences and professional practice is greatly reduced (Edelson and Reiser, 2006). This results in the need to facilitate only near transfer between the learning context and the context where those practices are used professionally. The learning that takes place in the authentic experience therefore has greater relevance and utility for future use, which makes the competencies that develop from participating in an authentic experience more directly applicable to subsequent professional practice. In considering motivation and interest, the increased relevance of the knowledge and practices to be learned relative to professional practice increases the utility value of the learning experience, which in turn increases the subjective task value and motivation to develop competencies in the STEM domain (Eccles and Wigfield, 2002, Jacobs et al., 2005; Wang and Degol, 2013; Wang and Eccles, 2013). The greater relevance drives an increase in motivation to learn and thus develop greater competence. This seemed to be the case for Raven, whose motivation grew as she saw connections with the computing skills and languages she was learning and a range of professions and industries where they could be used.

Moreover, researchers posit that over time, and with greater participation in authentic versions of the practice, learner identities shift such that they see themselves and are seen by others as more established practitioners in the target community (Simpson and Bouhafa, 2020). This takes place as part of the transition a novice makes from "newcomer" to "old timer" and from "peripheral participant" to "central participant" in the community (Lave and Wenger, 1991). This appeared to be the case for Nathan and his participation in online communities. While first a consumer of existing media (programming videos), he eventually went on to become a participant in some online programming communities in high school and later an active contributor to the open source coding community in college. There, competency develops as status in the community changes. As part of this shift in learner identity, the features of the practice that engender interest by professionals are thought to be recognized and valued by participants as they become further enculturated in the community (Glaze-Crampes, 2020). Interest in the professional practice develops as an identity as a competent practitioner develops.

Additionally, it is believed that participation in activities that are authentic relative to professional STEM practices promotes situational interest, which in turn promotes a deeper sense of belonging within a community of practice (Moallem, Hung, and Dabbagh, 2019). As stated above, situational interest refers to the momentary state of interest that is cued by a specific activity or feature of the setting or environment; as the learner continues to re-engage with content over time this promotes deeper and more engaged learning, which in turn contributes to competency development (Hidi and Renninger, 2006). This was the case for Nathan, who had his interest piqued by bugs encountered in game server installation and later went on to explore programming. The greater authenticity of the learning environment leads to more overlaps between the features of the learning environment and the professional practice that are found interesting, thus promoting continual re-engagement and the development of competencies.

Lastly, an underlying assumption of learning through enculturation is that learning is inherently a social activity. Learners benefit from exposure to more established practitioners and to role models that facilitate the development of new competence and the assumption of new identities (Lockwood,

Marshall, and Sadler, 2005; Marx and Roman, 2002). Exposure to these role models can increase interest in the discipline by providing a plausible image of a professional position in the discipline that the learner can attain (Lockwood and Kunda, 1997; Marx, Stapel, and Muller, 2005). Role models also provide mentoring, access to professional networks, and forms of informal teaching that help learners develop practice-specific competencies on a just-in-time basis (NASEM, 2019). Raven had this through her after-school program, Hermione through an internship, and Antonio through his local library makerspace. Near peer mentoring, with older learners serving as mentors for younger learners, is one example of how interest in computer science can be developed (Clarke-Midura et al., 2018).

Exclusion from Communities of Practice

Engagement in communities of practice, activities, and programs also provides occasions for young people to encounter role models and representations of computing. Different types of exposure and influence are most effective at different developmental stages. Interventions targeted toward younger learners are often centered on exposure, and as learners grow older, they are able to develop skills through activities, and eventually they can participate in professional communities (Callahan et al., 2019). Of special interest for educators is the influence that authentic experiences can have on computing interest, competencies, and engagement with communities of practice.

Although the concept of communities of practice helps to explain some of the means through which young people begin to establish active patterns of participation in computing, it also raises concerns about equity and access, and reveals social and cultural influences on authentic learning in STEM and computing more specifically. New membership in communities of practice is largely defined by those who are already established practitioners (Wenger, 1998), and professional computing has a history of excluding individuals on the basis of gender, race, ethnicity, or perceived ability (see Chapter 2). Despite a desire to promote greater diversity in computing, barriers to participation remain; these barriers include (but are not limited to) implicit biases (Cheryan et al., 2013; Steinke, 2017), systemic barriers (Margolis et al., 2008; 2017), and other detriments to cultivating feelings of belonging (Stout and Wright, 2016).

As discussed above, shared interests and affinity fostered by overlapping learning and professional practices are powerful drivers of learning, engagement, and belonging within a community, but they are also exclusionary to those with dissimilar backgrounds and identities (Ito et al., 2018). Furthermore, within established communities of practice, members of socially marginalized groups begin in more precarious positions (Van

Laar et al., 2019). Some are even actively discouraged from pursuing computing, as had been the case for Raven in her introductory computer science course in college.

Research on situated learning also shows that the social interactions that take place and relationships that develop in communities of practice appear to be an important driver for engagement and for continued participation (Azevedo, 2011; 2013; Lee, Fischback, and Cain, 2019). Members of minoritized and non-dominant groups are often more uncertain of the quality of their social bonds within the community, and thus more sensitive to issues of social belonging (Walton and Cohen, 2007). This means that for those members of historically excluded groups who have been able to begin participating in a community of practice, there is still an ongoing disadvantage for maintaining and eventually increasing that participation.

One way to disrupt these exclusionary processes is through affinity-based mentorship in programs where marginalized learners form relationships with peers and mentors who both share their background and are part of a high-value field or career path (Ben-Eliyahu, Rhodes, and Scales, 2014; Pinkard et al., 2017; Raposa et al., 2019). For instance, research suggests that middle and high school girls' engagement with mentors can add significantly to the information girls have about future career paths and can improve self-confidence with regard to STEM (Kahle and Meece, 1994; Nightingale and Wolverton, 1993). This impact was demonstrated in Hermoine's and Raven's cases; however, creating counter space (or safe spaces) does not erase the need to address systemic practices such as racism, sexism, and unequal access to opportunities that create the need for affinity groups in the first place.

Culture and Personal Relevance

As acknowledged in *How People Learn II* (NASEM, 2018b), "a learning environment is structured to promote particular ways of engaging in a specific set of activities, and the features of every learning environment reflect the cultural context in which it is situated" (p. 138). Moreover, learners bring their own individual cultural meaning derived from their out-of-school experiences in homes, neighborhoods, and communities to the learning environment. A learners' funds of knowledge[2] can be used as a valuable resource as part of the learning experience (NASEM, 2018b). When STEM learning is connected to familiar and personally meaningful cultural referents, places, and social relationships, it can support a sense of relevance and authenticity. Moreover, it could also support the development

---

[2] Moll et al. (1992) have described funds of knowledge as the valuable understandings, skills, and tools that youth maintain as part of their identity.

of connected knowledge, so that learners could then apply their knowledge to other situations (NRC, 2012).

Problem-, project-, and place-based learning are a number of different strategies linked to promoting the engagement of learners as they are more learner-centered, require that learners take more responsibility for their learning, have choices, and are provided with opportunities to participate in real-world tasks that are meaningful for them (NASEM, 2018b). This suggests that experiences designed in this way are deeply motivating to students due to their personally authentic, iterative, and collaborative nature (Kolodner et al., 2003). Some of these approaches, such as place-based learning, are a subset of culturally relevant and sustaining pedagogies (see Chapter 7's Content and Pedagogy section for more discussion of these approaches). Researchers such as Lim and Calabrese Barton (2006) have adopted equity-oriented approaches to these strategies to transform disciplinary content from abstracted knowledge to local knowledge that is related to communities' cultural practices (Gruenewald, 2003).

Place-based education engages learners in activities within and about their communities to highlight disciplinary concepts that are embedded within local systems, organizations, histories, and interactions and advance meaning making (Smith, 2002; Sobel, 2004). Siebert-Evenstone and Shaffer (2019) investigated the impact of authenticity in a simulated place-based learning environment. The environment was a simulation of a city that was local to some learners and not to others. Their study found that learning outcomes were better when learners engaged in the place-based simulation about their own local setting, suggesting that place plays a critical role in the impact of place-based education.

Youth development benefits of place-based pedagogies include increased engagement in school and motivation for achievement (Athman and Monroe, 2004; Duffin, Powers, and Tremblay, 2004; Falco, 2004; Powers, 2004). Place-based pedagogies can increase workplace skills such as leadership, persistence, taking responsibility, teamwork, developing plans to reach a solution, managing time, motivating others, and dealing with unexpected challenges (Duffin, Powers, and Tremblay, 2004; Glenn, 2001); and development of an action-taking orientation and action competence (Barratt and Hacking, 2011; Mogensen and Schanck, 2010). In addition to academic and youth development benefits, a substantial body of research links place-based education with outcomes in the literature on social-emotional development. Impacts of place-based education on social-emotional development include increases in self-esteem, increase in one's sense of empowerment and agency, greater social interaction and social skills, increased social capital, and improved awareness of cultural diversity (Billig, 2000; Robinson and Zajicek, 2005; Schusler et al., 2009; Schusler and Krasny, 2010); increased sense of community attachment and community consciousness (Barratt and

Hacking, 2011; Harrison, 2011); and increased civic engagement, involvement, and responsibility (Duffin, Powers, and Tremblay, 2004; Flanagan and Gallay, 2014; Gallay et al., 2016; Schusler et al., 2009; Volk and Cheak, 2003). In engineering, studies of place-based pedagogies have documented the disproportionate involvement of women learners in community-based and service-learning engineering programs (Amadei and Sandekian, 2010; Coyle, Jamieson, and Oakes, 2006; Litchfield and Javernick-Will, 2014; Ruth et al., 2019).

LEARNING OVER TIME AND ACROSS EXPERIENCES: AN ECOSYSTEMS APPROACH

Developing both interest and competencies in computing-intensive activities, or any STEM field for that matter, can be a long-term process that may play out over years and in multiple settings. Therefore, no single short-term experience alone is likely to change a person's life course or, at a systems level, to dramatically increase the participation of learners that have been underrepresented based on gender, race, ethnicity, or perceived ability working in computing. Recognizing this, researchers have articulated the importance of taking an ecosystems approach and examining the ways in which different kinds of experiences and supports in multiple settings over time reinforce each other to either build or undermine the development of interest, identity, and competency in a field of endeavor (Azevedo, 2018; Azevedo, diSessa, and Sherin, 2012; Barron, 2006; Bell et al., 2012; Bevan et al., 2010; Bransford et al., 2005; Crowley et al., 2015; Falk and Needham, 2011; Falk et al., 2015; Ito et al., 2013; Krishnamurthi et al., 2013; Mehus, Stevens, and Gringholm, 2010; NRC, 2015; Rahm, 2008; Traphagen and Traill, 2014).

To illustrate, recall in Chapter 2 some of the descriptions of how actual youth active in computing came to their current level of interest and competence. Nathan, for instance, participated in gaming communities, online programming communities, formal high school courses, and in clubs. Gaming led to initial opportunities to begin some work with backend computing, which led to discovery of online programming communities, which also contributed to participation in formal course selection and so on. It was not any single activity alone that led to his pursuit of a computer science degree. The combination of all, distributed across time and space, contributed. Similarly, Raven went from participating in an after-school program to then pursuing summer programs related to computing and then eventually a major in computer science. The combination of those activities was additive with respect to her growth in interest and competence in computing, even sustaining her when she was discouraged from maintaining that path in college.

As illustrated above, conceptualizing development of interest and competencies in computing would involve explicit recognition of the ecosystem of opportunities and supports that are available to learners. A number of initiatives (e.g., CSforALL,[3] CIRCL,[4] and STEM ecosystems[5]) have been developed to expand and explore the implementation of ecosystems. Where learners connect in the ecosystem may vary. For some learners, their interest in computing begins with enjoying and playing video games. For others, it could be an after-school opportunity to become acquainted with new people working in computing and build relationships while building tools. And for others still, the entry might be highly engaging, personally meaningful project experiences in school that relate to computing, such as in Hermione's experience.

Barron (2006) employed this ecosystems approach in a study of "learning histories" for individual young people's acquisition of interest and fluency in using computer technology. Barron stressed the importance of multiple contexts of fluency development related to technology that range from home, school, work, peers, community, and distributed resources such as online groups. In some of Barron's case profiles, school experiences stimulated learners to seek technology learning experiences outside of school; in other cases, learning outside of school provided the impetus for a young person to take computing courses in school. The combination of learner initiative and broader support networks that included brokers to new opportunities contributed to the creation of technology learning opportunities.

Crowley et al. (2015) used retrospective interviews to document the reported pathways taken by 69 scientists and science professionals and to track how interest was developed and involved in their eventual positions as professional scientists. Across their sample, the majority of participants (86%) reported interests being sparked during childhood. Out-of-school science experiences played a significant role in supporting interest in nearly half the participant sample (45%). School experiences were reported by 28 percent as positively related to their interest development. For those who felt their formal schooling contributed positive experiences that led to their current interest in science, enthusiastic teachers, independent study, after-school clubs, and specific hands-on activities were noted as important. Another more recent retrospective study by Hecht, Knutson, and Crowley (2019) confirmed these patterns in a study of interest development among

---

[3]For more information about the ways in which CSforALL is providing opportunities to connect formal and out-of-school time providers, see https://www.csforall.org/out-of-school-time-providers.

[4]For more information about the Center for Innovative Research in Cyberlearning, see https://circlcenter.org.

[5]For more information, see https://stemecosystems.org.

naturalists. Different combinations of school, family, and out-of-school learning experiences triggered and mutually supported interest development over time. These retrospective accounts are suggestive of how prior experiences shape subsequent interest and STEM identity.

Studies of the Digital Youth Network compiled by Barron and colleagues (2014) have further illustrated how the combination of experiences and movement between school, community, home, and online provided a mix of technology-related engagements that led to development of technology interests and competencies. The prominence of early and ongoing experiences in family contexts in many of these longitudinal or retrospective studies, underscores the equity concerns raised throughout this report. Hermione is an interesting case in that her interest was not sparked by family, out-of-school settings, camps, etc. Her interest was sparked in school and relatively late in life and was nurtured through multiple in-school and out-of-school experiences. Moreover, it is likely that these experiences were arguably personally and professionally authentic. As such, this indicates that interest does not have to be sparked early, or through family or informal experiences. Young people from groups underrepresented in STEM and computing fields are less likely to grow up with authentic experiences that are both personally, culturally, *and* professionally relevant (Cheryan et al., 2016; Rodriguez and Lehman, 2018).

An ecosystems approach challenges the dominant metaphor of a workforce "pipeline" that must be strengthened in order to increase participation in computing. A web of experiences over time and across settings that spark new interests and connect with existing personal interests, coupled with positive relationships with caring adults and peers working in those settings (Ito et al., 2020), has thus appeared to be the main driver of interest and participation in computing. Moreover, it is not simply the presence of a multitude of experiences and a network of caring peers and adults that will lead to long-term professional participation in computing.

Through a series of coordinated studies, the Connected Learning Research Network has documented that when learning is embedded in meaningful relationships, and connected to interests and home cultures, it is uniquely relevant and resilient (Ito et al., 2020). For example, Sefton-Green, Watkins, and Kirshner (2019) collaborated to investigate "the last mile" that connects education and careers. They found that success hinges on building an extensive, interconnected, and diverse network of relationships to supportive peers, mentors, and organizations that create new opportunities for youth, as observed in the case of Hermione. Following Ito and colleagues (2020), this ecosystems approach in research suggests the need to consider models of network and capacity building. The importance of building social capital and relationships may be particularly important for connecting personally authentic learning experiences to professionally authentic computing opportunities (Martin, Simmons, and Yu, 2013; Martin, Miller, and Simmons, 2014).

This ecosystems approach has important implications for equity and access to authentic learning experiences and computing fields. A growing body of research has documented personally relevant STEM learning experiences such as making and mathematics in the home culture and communities of groups underrepresented in STEM (Eglash et al., 2013; Nasir et al., 2006; Peppler, Sedas, and Dahn, 2020). These studies also note that these practices are not commonly connected or legitimated in dominant STEM educational practices. Gutiérrez and Rogoff (2003) have described the efficacy of an asset-based approach that engages "repertoires of practice" across home and school contexts as a way of addressing this disconnect. Researchers have described how girls from underrepresented groups may benefit from mutually enhancing experiences that connect STEM experiences in home and school to engage and develop STEM identities (Calabrese Barton, Tan, and Rivet, 2008; Calabrese Barton et al., 2013; Kang et al., 2019). Research on the Digital Youth Network documented how, when provided with supports that spanned school, after-school, and online settings, Chicago learners from economically disadvantaged middle-schools developed tech interests and skills on par with tech-privileged youth growing up in Silicon Valley (Barron et al., 2014).

Altogether, studies such as these and those from the STEM literature more broadly suggest that an ecosystems approach for computing education experiences may be warranted (NRC, 2015). Experiences and activities that are personally authentic to youth can be a critical entry point for eventual long-term participation in computing, but the entry point alone is not enough to count on long-term computing participation. The growing body of evidence described above (Barron, 2006; Crowley et al., 2015) suggests that when young people experience validation and support for connecting personally relevant computing experiences across the settings of home, school, and community, this can reinforce their sense of belonging and interest. That is, it is important to consider the ways in which learners participate in *multiple* communities of computing practice over time and the various forms of authenticity emphasized in those communities. Individually, these communities may not be in direct alignment with professional communities of practice. In the aggregate, they support and lead to the eventual participation in professional computing communities.

SUMMARY

In an attempt to understand the role that authentic experiences play in developing interest and competences for computing, the committee began with a review of the evidence on learning. The committee introduced a framework that illustrates how the influences and outcomes are intertwined and takes place across multiple settings and over significant spans of time. The chapter then characterized the relationship between interests and competencies. To understand how authentic experiences may influence interest and competencies in computing, it is important to understand how learners develop interest and the mechanisms that promote interest and motivation to learn.

Moreover, the framework focuses on the underlying learning and development dynamics that are based upon existing theories and conceptual models, specifically, calling attention to sociocultural and situated learning. In particular, the committee recognized the ways that the situated nature of knowing and learning has contributed to interest in learning experiences that are authentic relative to professional communities of practice. The committee then discussed the role of culture and personal relevance, describing the evidence on problem-, project-, and place-based learning. The chapter concluded by articulating the need for an ecosystems approach, notably an understanding that learning happens over time and across settings. That is, the development of expertise requires time, and no single short-term experience is likely to be enough to develop the competencies and skills needed for computing. Moreover, different kinds of experiences and supports in multiple settings over time reinforce each other and may serve to build an interest in future computing endeavors.

4

Authentic Experiences for Computing: Reviewing the Impact

T he charge of this report was to investigate the promise of authentic learning experiences for computing in developing interest and competencies that would support K–12 learners' future endeavors in computing. This chapter focuses on the outcomes identified in Chapter 3—knowledge/skills, interest, motivation, self-efficacy, belonging, engagement, and persistence— and reviews the evidence that authentic experiences can support them. The committee draws heavily on its review of the literature, which sought to identify studies, interventions, or programs that incorporate authentic approaches. Broadly construed, that is, the focus was on programs that incorporate hands-on, problem- or project-based approaches (see Appendix A for a discussion of the committee's search strategy and studies identified). Whenever possible, we highlight studies that specifically examined the impacts of these experiences on learners who have been traditionally underrepresented in computing based on gender, race, ethnicity, or perceived ability.

It is important to acknowledge that the interventions and programs reviewed in this chapter and throughout the report cannot be identified as professionally or personally authentic as defined by the committee. This is especially true given that personally authentic experiences require a perception by the learner of being personally relevant, and it cannot be assumed that this would be uniform for all learners in an experience. However, it is valuable to understand what is currently known about the impact of authentic experiences in computing more broadly, given current attention to these approaches.

Many of the studies reviewed are still in exploratory or early stages of the research. Studies of this type help establish initial connections between authentic experiences and outcomes of interest, but they support inferences about *associations* among the factors, not inferences about *causation*. In other words, the findings may show that there is a *connection* between the experience and changes in the outcome, but they do not provide insights about ways that the experience might *cause* changes in the outcome measure. Moreover, many of the studies do not measure change. Nevertheless, preliminary conclusions can be drawn from the well-designed studies.

What follows are sections summarizing the evidence for cognitive (knowledge and skills), affective (interest, identity/belonging, motivation, and self-efficacy), and behavioral (engagement, persistence, and retention) outcomes, respectively. It should be noted that the studies reviewed may not capture the full range of settings, including home and online communities. Moreover, within the research and evaluation literature, there is a tendency to focus on individual programs or individual curricula in ways that do not reflect an ecosystemic view of outcomes. As such, there are limitations to the generalizability.

COGNITIVE OUTCOMES

In this section we focus on two cognitive outcomes: knowledge development and skill development. Knowledge outcomes measure what is generally thought of as the *theoretical or practical understanding of a subject* or field. Knowledge development involves the accumulation of new knowledge as well as the integration of knowledge into conceptual frameworks. The acquisition of knowledge is important because it increases the speed and accuracy with which people can recall and retrieve knowledge and complete tasks (National Academies of Sciences, Engineering, and Medicine [NASEM], 2018b, p. 90). The integration of knowledge into mental structures is the basis for expertise in domains (NASEM, 2018b, p. 85).

Skill outcomes measure skills—the *development of proficiency in the application of knowledge* through training and/or practice. Skills can be further categorized as technical, such as computer programming skills, or professional and interpersonal, such as critical thinking, creativity, problem-solving, flexible/adaptability in thinking, and collaboration. Many of the studies reviewed presented changes in knowledge or skills or a combination of both.

Knowledge

In this section, the committee considers studies that examine how and to what extent authentic experiences in computing support development and improvement of knowledge outcomes. The interventions and programs studied used different platforms, and different types of technology (e.g., game design activities within online platforms, unplugged computer activities utilizing classroom materials, computer-aided design [CAD] activities, and specialized IT camps). Knowledge outcomes measured included awareness of computing-related fields, definitional knowledge, and other domain-specific content knowledge. Whenever it was difficult to discern whether an outcome involved knowing how to do something versus the practice of doing something (a skill), the discussion was moved to the section on skill outcomes.

Current understanding of how computing knowledge develops is hampered by the lack of consensus about the components of computational thinking and of validated assessments of computing concepts. As pointed out by Tran (2018), although some recent studies have started to assess computing, there continues to be a lack of research. Few studies sought to assess learner growth in knowledge of computing and awareness of the career opportunities afforded to those with computing skills. The studies examined were largely exploratory and did not seek to assess the efficacy or effectiveness of the intervention using experimental studies. While the reviewed studies point to various ways to increase knowledge and awareness through engaging learners in computing practices on and off the computer, caution is needed when linking knowledge and awareness to preparation for computing fields. That is, knowledge of computing concepts and awareness of career opportunities are likely not sufficient to prepare learners for computing careers.

Three studies reported gains in knowledge outcomes associated with participation in authentic experience for computing. The gains were evident in learners' knowledge of definitions of key computing concepts (e.g., computational thinking, algorithm, sequence, branching, iteration, variable, abstraction, clarity, correctness, and efficiency, data collection, data analysis, data representation, problem decomposition, parallelization). Two of these studies integrated unplugged computer activities into the regular school day classroom (Folk et al., 2015; Ouyang, Hayden, and Remold, 2018).

For example, Ouyang, Hayden, and Remold (2018) describe the "Quest CT" intervention that aimed at helping upper elementary school (fifth and sixth grade) teachers integrate computational thinking concepts through unplugged computing activities within science lessons. Following an intensive summer professional development experience, teachers co-developed then field tested unplugged, integrated computational thinking lessons with learners in a summer camp. The following academic year teachers implemented the activities in their regular school day classrooms. There were 327 matched pre-post surveys administered: approximately half of the learners in the study were women, 34 percent were English learners, and roughly 34 percent were significantly behind grade level in reading. Gains from pre- to post-test were statistically significant for both the assessment as a whole and the sub-scores in two categories: awareness of computational thinking (i.e., given a scenario, identifying the computational thinking process being used) and computational terms (e.g., data collection, data analysis, data representation, problem decomposition, parallelization, and algorithms and procedures). Even though statistically significant gains were found for all learner groups analyzed, boys showed slightly higher scores at both pre- and post-test as well as larger gains between pre- and post-test.

In another study (Jenson, Black, and de Castell, 2018), a game design intervention was used to increase students' programming knowledge. Participants' previous programming knowledge was a factor that produced differential outcomes—multiple regression analysis showed that pre-test programming knowledge accounted for 25 percent of the variance in post-test scores.

Studies also examined learners' awareness of skills needed for participation in STEM fields and awareness of the fields themselves. High school learners' (n = 95) perceptions of the need for creativity and problem-solving skills in STEM fields, particularly engineering, increased somewhat after a 2-week summer camp featuring experiences with modeling in 3D CAD software and printing 3D artifacts (Bicer et al., 2017). There were no statistically significant differences between changes among learners with different ethnic backgrounds (Asian, Black, Hispanic, White, and Native American) or between men and women.

Similarly, results of the SPIRIT program (Harriger, Magana, and Lovan, 2012), a week-long, residential, summer camp for 75 high school learners at a Midwestern university, indicated increased awareness of careers in computing. The goal of the program was to educate learners about career opportunities for people with IT skills. The intervention included hands-on experiences using the Alice storytelling environment and learning about the work experiences of IT professionals. Learners completed a survey 10 months after attending the program. Findings from learners' self-reporting showed that the program raised learners' awareness of computing opportunities.

Denner et al. (2012) studied 59 middle school girls who participated in a voluntary after-school computer game–making club over a period of 14 months, including 3 weeks during the summer. The club was focused on "programming, documenting and understanding software, and designing for usability" (2012, p. 242). Each of the girls created between two and five games, working in pairs for 1 hour of coding time. The rest of the time in the club was spent on other tasks such as writing in an online science journal and taking field trips to local colleges and IT schools. The primary results from the study were that game making can contribute to understanding computational concepts; and further, for novices to coding and game making, "extensive" instructional support is necessary.

Skills

In this section, the committee considers evidence on the extent to which authentic experiences support skill outcomes related to computing. In reviewing this literature, an outcome was considered a skill if it pertained to the practice of *doing something* rather than *knowing how something was done*. The distinction between computing skills and computational thinking skills is not consistent across the studies reviewed; some authors considered computing skills as a component of computational thinking whereas others view computing and computational thinking as independent topics.

Elementary-age Learners

Kazakoff and Bers (2012) examined computing skills in 58 kindergarten learners (ages 4.5–6.5) who participated in 20 hours of instruction during the regular school day using a robot programming system. The system allows learners to use interlocking wooden blocks or corresponding onscreen representations and to go back and forth between the two. In the quasi-experimental study, the experimental group showed greater positive change from pre-test to post-test in a picture sequencing assessment. Sequencing is considered a component of computational thinking.

Moore et al. (2020) studied young learners' representation and translation between representations (including computational representations) as a precursor to algorithmic reasoning. They reported that learners in grades K–2 engaged with and moved among multiple representations as they managed the cognitive demands of various computational tasks. Through a series of case studies, they found that learners were able to translate among representations by constructing intermediary representations such as gestures and placing objects in the environment to represent current state, an early form of simulation, to manage cognitive load.

Allsop (2019) investigated the ways computational thinking could be evaluated in a classroom environment for 30 primary school learners (ages 10–11) in London in the context of a computer game design and development intervention over a period of 8 months. Outcomes of interest included computer programming, computational concepts, metacognitive practices, and learning behaviors. Participants developed metacognitive skills related to computational thinking. These included planning and choosing appropriate strategies for a solution; monitoring their work and thinking about how to improve it; and evaluating their work in terms of checking for errors. Additionally, participants were able to use programming constructs such as sequences, loops, parallelism, conditionals, operators, and event handling in making their games.

Adolescents

Fronza, El Ioini, and Corral (2015) described the design and implementation of a short course during summer school to teach computational thinking to 11th and 12th grade learners (n = 19). Participants designed and developed mobile apps using AppInventor. Use of computational thinking skills (data collection and analysis, data representation, problem decomposition, abstraction, algorithms and procedures, automation, and simulation and parallelization) was assessed through an analysis of the quality and functionality of the learners' final projects. The results suggest that learners, regardless of their background, can exercise the computational thinking skills to walk through the process of identifying a problem to solve in the form of a functional product.

In a study of high school learners, participating in two summer academies with computational thinking enhanced maker activities. Yin et al. (2019) examined changes in computational skills and dispositions. The Assessing Computational Thinking Maker Activities (ACTMA) project developed maker activities and formative assessments that promote physics and engineering learning, and computational thinking skills and dispositions in makerspaces. The maker activities included electronic circuits, e-textiles, makey-makey, breadboards, and arduino microprocessors. The effectiveness of the activities was evaluated by comparing the pre- and post-test scores across four computational thinking skill dimensions (i.e., abstraction, decomposition, algorithmic thinking, and pattern generalization) and across the five activity types. A self-reporting portion of the survey asked learners to report on their frequency of using computational thinking skills and to provide their assessment of their computational thinking skills. The assessment also asked learners to perform activity-related tasks such as diagramming of circuits and supplying missing code snippets to program a blinking pattern on an Arduino. The results suggest that learners' scores improved significantly on all the measures (i.e., computational thinking-integrated achievement test, frequency of using computational thinking, self-rated maker activity knowledge, and self-rated computational thinking skills).

Pohner and Hennecke (2018) researched learners' learning of problem-solving in the context of robotics. In an exploratory case study, they analyzed the use of problem-solving strategies of teams participating in the World Robot Olympiad, an international robotics competition. Participating teams used the LEGO robotics set to build and program a robot to complete a novel task specified by the competition committee. Typically, the learner teams completed their projects over the course of 4 months. The aim of their research was to determine how successful and less successful teams differ in their problem-solving strategies. Their problem-solving process model encompassed four aspects: conceptual aspects describing issues with the general design of the robot (hardware, theoretical); algorithmic aspects describing issues with the development of algorithms or solution approaches of the given problem (software, theoretical); construction aspects describing issues with the construction of the robot (hardware, practical); and implementation aspects describing issues with the implementation within a programming language (software, practical). The two teams that were the basis for the case studies achieved different results. Each team's diaries were analyzed using descriptive statistics and qualitative content analysis. The successful team invested more time in the theoretical aspects (conceptual and algorithmic), capped off construction at week 15, and reserved the duration of the time for the implementation aspects, whereas the less successful team interwove construction and implementation until nearly the end of the 28-week period. In addition to evidence of problem-solving in the robotics domain, teams completed projects that required algorithm development and programming.

Several studies described outcomes associated with the development of skills related to computer science such as programming, debugging, and code commenting skills. Denault, Kienzle, and Vybihal (2008) described a 5-day computing summer camp for high school learners (grades 10 and 11) held on a university campus. The goal of the intervention was to motivate the learners to consider computer science as their future field of study. Computer game development was the context for learners to exercise problem-solving skills. Through code analysis and analysis of responses to an evaluation questionnaire, the researchers concluded that the camp had a positive impact on learning. They reported a steady growth in the code complexity over the first 4 days and restructuring and commenting of code on day five. An increase in the number of if statements on the fifth day was seen as evidence that learners made improvements to their decision trees.

Evidence of skills outcomes in authentic programs was seen in interventions of different types: game design and development, app development, makerspaces, robotics, computer aided design, and augmented reality in the context of camps, competitions, and afterschool clubs. Outcomes in the computational thinking skills category included using computational thinking, recognizing computational thinking, and identifying problems to be solved through computational thinking, whereas outcomes in the computing skills category included computer programming, debugging, and commenting; analyzing technical requirements; and designing for interaction. Meta-cognitive skills such as planning and choosing appropriate strategies for a solution; monitoring one's work and thinking about how to improve it; and evaluating one's work were also reported. Several studies focused on outcomes related to the development of computational thinking skills at different ages suggest that these skills can be nurtured in school-age learners in age-appropriate ways. The evidence base is limited—few programs attempted to assess learner skills development and those that did were not utilizing common assessments and common definitions of computational thinking skills.

Summary

Overall, the evidence of outcomes in knowledge and skill development is emergent. Most studies we reviewed were exploratory and took a design-based research approach to refining curricula and/or pedagogy to enhance learner engagement or were early pilots of such interventions. Few studies applied rigorous approaches to evaluating the efficacy of effectiveness of interventions on learners' learning.

AFFECTIVE OUTCOMES

Individuals' decisions about subject areas to study and careers to pursue are influenced by a host of affective and contextual factors (Dou and Gibbs, 2013). For example, early STEM interest appears to be a predictor of later STEM interest and eventual choices of careers in STEM. Beyer (2014) documents the connection between interest, self-efficacy, and subsequent college-level computing course-taking. Similarly, Denner et al. (2014) showed relationships between affective factors and course-taking at the community college level.

This section reviews the findings from the literature on affective attributes hypothesized to be important outcomes of authentic experiences for computing, specifically interest, identity/belonging, self-efficacy, and motivation. The discussion of each outcome addresses the measurement issues as well as how participation in authentic experiences in computing affect these outcomes. It is important to note that most of the studies reviewed had sample sizes that ranged from 10 to 100 students; however, a few self-efficacy studies noted larger sample sizes.

Interest

In the studies reviewed, interest was typically measured through the use of self-report surveys that asked participants direct questions about their perceptions of the experiences and their inclinations to pursue future computing activities. Questions asking participants to agree/disagree with statements such as, "I could see myself pursuing a career in computing or computer science" are typical. Sometimes, data are collected from observers or through more open-ended mediums such as journal writing and feedback from camp instructors.

All experiences, programs, and activities in these studies took place in out-of-school settings. The most common setting was in summer camps that lasted between 5 days and 2 weeks. In some instances, the summer camp experience was combined with after-school sessions for 21 weeks or combined with Saturday sessions for about 2 years (i.e., Ladeji-Osias, Partlow, and Dillon, 2018). The duration of the authentic experiences in computing were highly variable. In some cases, experiences included bi-weekly 2-hour sessions for 4 months; five Saturday sessions for 3 hours/session; 1-day workshops; and 30–45-minute sessions. This variability makes it difficult to evaluate program effects.

Many of the studies reviewed reported no significant change in interest from pre- to post-activity (Bugallo, Kelly, and Ha, 2015; Denault, Kienzle, and Vybihal, 2008; Krayem et al., 2019). However, in some cases, it is possible that no change in interest is related to a ceiling effect (Bugallo, Kelly, and Ha, 2015); that is, participants already had a high degree of interest and even if participants enjoyed the activity, there is no way to be able to measure this possible change.

Use of wearable technologies and e-textiles is one approach researchers are exploring for engaging learners in computing and increasing their interest (Buechley and Eisenberg, 2008; Buechley et al., 2008; Merkouris, Chorianopoulos, and Kameas, 2017; Qiu et al., 2013). For example, Lau et al. (2009) examined outcomes for 25 middle school learners in a workshop-style summer camp activity that lasted 5 days and covered electronic circuit theory, t-shirt circuit design, integrated circuits, and programming. The overall task for participants was to make their own interactive garment, wear it, and present how they built it to their peers. Feedback from camp instructors as well as results of a pre-/post-survey of participants indicate that although learners did not develop interest in learning about electrical theory, they did develop interest in computing. In particular, participants became excited about the wearables, which led them to further experiment on their own, and the learners indicated the intention to participate in future computing courses.

Importantly, a few studies focused explicitly on girls and learners from minoritized racial/ethnic groups (Gardner-McCune et al., 2013; Jageila et al., 2018; Ladeji-Osias, Partlow, and Dillon, 2018). However, across the studies, the findings were mixed.

In a study of 22 girls (ages 13–18) who participated in five 3-hour workshops across consecutive Saturdays, Jageila et al. (2018) did not observe significant changes between pre- and post-program responses about participants' interest in a career in computing. This may be due to participants' high levels of interest at the start of the program.

Gardner-McCune et al. (2013) reported on a program aimed to engage 9th–12th grade African American and Latina learners in research and design activities (85% of participants were girls in these underrepresented groups). Sixty-four learners were enrolled in the program at some point; however, not all of them participated in all phases of the program. The program was divided into three 5–7-week phases during which participants were taken through a series of activities to help them learn how computers work and process information and how to develop proposals for new applications or devices. They learned about development environments and creation of innovative devices and applications. Learners exhibited and presented their work through showcases, public competitions, and research poster sessions at technical conferences. While data are not available for all of the participants in the program, the available data indicate that slightly over half of the participants have majored in or intend to pursue a STEM or computing major.

Ladeji-Osias, Partlow, and Dillon (2018) reported on a program for middle-school-aged African American boys, which involved a 4-week summer program and 10 Saturday sessions during the academic year. The long-term goals of this project were for participants to create products using 3-D modeling software and printers, develop software and embedded applications, enhance computational thinking skills, and pursue related entrepreneurial ventures. Data were collected through a participant survey and observations by an external team. The results from the survey revealed an increase in participants' responses to the question "I understand how to use software to create an app" as well as interest in pursuing "a career in app development." However, only 30 out of 38 participants completed the final survey.

Identity/Sense of Belonging

As highlighted in Chapter 2, development of a computing identity is related to a sense of belonging to the field (Dempsey et al., 2015; Rodriguez and Lehman, 2018) and influences interest and persistence (Brickhouse, Lowery, and Schultz, 2000; Carlone and Johnson, 2007; Rodriguez and Lehman, 2018; Seyranian et al., 2018; Vincent-Ruz and Schunn, 2018). Interest, motivation, and participation in computing may ebb over time, especially if learners develop a sense that they do not belong in the field, whether STEM in general or computing in particular. In this section, we talk about the outcome commonly referred to as STEM identity or belonging, which is how a person views oneself in terms of being a mathematician, scientist, engineer, or perhaps a computer programmer.

Identity development can involve multiple components including change in perception of who should pursue STEM fields and change in perception of an individuals' own fit in STEM. Studies that examine identity as an outcome used a variety of data collection strategies including observations, online activities, video and audio recordings, semi-structured interviews, and researcher reflections. Sample sizes for the studies ranged from 17 to 93 learners.

Ahn et al. (2014) conducted a longitudinal study on an after-school program for middle school students called Sci-Dentity.[1] The program utilized science storytelling and news media to engage learners in STEM ideas and examined learners' development of personal STEM identity over an 18-month time period. Some of the activities related to computing and influence computing-related outcomes. Using case-study methodologies (e.g., video recordings of each session that they participated in, observations notes, audio recordings of conversations with these learners, artifacts produced by these learners, and researcher weekly meeting reflections), the researchers mapped the identity trajectories for the two Black boys who participated. One of the boys expressed a desire to become a "game designer or scientist." He disclosed that he knew of particular game design companies in his home state that he aspired to work for and had also done independent, online research to identify colleges that had game design degree programs. The other boy did not get the same benefit from Sci-Dentity. He said he participated in the program because it gave him a connection to his friends, and shared that he probably will not go to college.

Two studies focused on the Digital Youth Divas project, an out-of-school program that seeks to engage young girls (predominantly Black and Latina learners) in design-based engineering and computing activities. This program includes four components: (1) a curriculum clustered into three project units—e-fashion, e-paper, and e-dance that combines computational and digital artifacts to produce creative artifacts; (2) video narratives featuring racially diverse women characters that parallel the project activities in the units (e-fashion, e-paper, and e-dance); (3) a private online social learning network used to share and showcase their work and interact with adult mentors who pretend to be these fictional narrative characters; and (4) distributed online and offline mentorship—diverse in-person mentors encourage participation and completion, and online mentors offer feedback and advise the girls on the next steps.

One study of the results of this program included 29 girls who participated. Through a pre- and post-program survey that measured access, interest, experience, and perception, the researchers found that the participating girls identified stereotypical descriptions of those who should pursue STEM fields (people who are good in math and science). At the post-survey, these stereotypes declined as three times more girls ranked people who are artistic in the top three as people who can pursue STEM careers. The

---

[1] The research described the program as being implemented in a large, urban school district where approximately 90 percent of students come from minority groups and nearly 77 percent qualified for free and reduced meal (FARM) programs.

study reported there was no change in girls' perception of their own place in STEM, however.

In another iteration of this work, Pinkard et al. (2017) worked with 17 Latina and Black girls at two elementary schools serving low-income populations, where they examined the connection between the co-designed narrative materials created and identity development. Through qualitative analysis of in-person observations of the design sessions, summaries of the girls' online activities, and semi-structured interviews with the participating girls, the researchers found evidence that narratives motivated girls to continue with challenging STEM activities and STEM identity development. The details presented through the characters in the narratives created opportunities for the participants to reveal their stereotypes and awareness of limiting gender, racial, and intersectional and multiple identities in the narratives' storylines.

Choudhury, Lopes, and Arthur (2010) reported findings from experiences with an IT Career Camp developed in partnership with several businesses and corporations. The camp was designed for high school learners with the goal of helping them view IT/information systems work as exciting and creative. Each day of the camp included a visit to the businesses and corporations where learners took part in a hands-on activity to solve a problem involving IT, as well as a competition between teams to solve such problems. The learners also worked on a service-learning project. Teachers and counselors served as advisors during the camp. Through pre- and post-camp surveys and interviews, the researchers found that the learners' perceptions of IT professionals changed significantly. Many learners began the camp with a very stereotyped, unfavorable image of IT professionals (i.e., "[they] work in a 'back closet' and are 'very pale, with glasses'"), and were reluctant to share with their friends that they were attending an IT camp. At the end of the camp, their opinions toward IT professionals were more positive (i.e., "I thought IT was something of a nerd thing, but my opinion has changed."). However, the camps did not significantly influence participants' decisions to pursue an IT career or IT major.

Motivation

Self-determination theory posits that there are two main types of motivation: intrinsic (motivated by internal factors) and extrinsic (motivated by external factors or influences). This report focuses on studies that measure intrinsic motivation (Ryan and Deci, 2000; 2017), as researchers have stressed the necessity of cultivating intrinsic motivation to counter ongoing challenges of novice programming (Pinkard et al., 2017).

Change in motivation can be captured in multiple ways, including a desire to learn more about computing or an intention to take computing courses in the future or pursue a career in computing (or cybersecurity). A few different types of methods were used for data collection: self-reported surveys administered pre- and post-treatment; a survey administered only post-treatment; and triangulation of data from observations, semi-structured interviews, focus groups, and field notes. Researchers' findings on change in motivation in each study varied, ranging from no change in motivation (such as in Bugallo, Kelly, and Ha, 2015) to an increase in motivation (such as in Jin et al., 2018; Klopfer, Yoon, and Rivas, 2004; Lau et al., 2009; Scott and White, 2013).

Bugallo, Kelly, and Ha (2015) developed a 2-week summer camp for high school learners that provided rigorous instruction and hands-on engineering tasks designed to solve everyday problems. Some of the engineering tasks included building a line-following robot and fabricating a fiber optic voice link. Results of a pre-/post-survey of 38 participants in the camp showed no significant change in learners' career motivation in electrical and computer engineering.

Jin et al. (2018) report on a 1-week GenCyber summer camp that involved 181 high school learners. Slightly over half of participants (51.3%) were Black and Latinx, and there were about twice as many men as women. The camp is modeled on game-based learning and hands-on lab experience. Participants engaged in four different modules:

1. A social engineering and information security module to raise general awareness of social engineering scams;
2. A secure online behavior game that allowed learners to handle email messages, text messages, weblinks, and phone calls appropriately, using various computing devices such as school computers, mobile phones, laptop computers, and networked game consoles;
3. A Cyber Defense Tower Game that allowed learners to protect their virtual computer server from the different cyber-attacks;
4. A computerized version of a physical card game about cyber-security. The computer-based card game is a single-player version of the physical one.

Each GenCyber camp day consisted of four 90-minute sessions with two 15-minute group discussions. On a post-camp survey completed on the last day of camp, 154 participants indicated that game-based learning for cybersecurity motivated them to pursue higher education and careers in the field of cybersecurity.

Scott and White (2013) reported on a culturally responsive multimedia program called COMPUGIRLS that holds sessions after school and during the summer. For this study, 41 Black and Latina girls, aged 13–18, from high-needs districts participated.[2] COMPUGIRLS utilizes multimedia activities as a means of developing computational thinking, enhancing socio-technical analytical skills, and providing a dynamic, learning environment that nurtures the development of a positive self-concept. Through the course of the project, the girls created a digital product using various tools and a research paper, which included research questions, peer-reviewed references, primary data, analysis, and implications of their findings.

Qualitative data were collected in the form of field notes from observation, focus groups, and interviews. Two primary themes emerged from the qualitative data: (1) girls were empowered by the challenge of learning and mastering the technology; and (2) manipulation of the technology and engagement in the learning experiences became a form of self-expression and exploration, which encourages the enactment of a social justice agenda and a way to inform their community and peers.

Self-Efficacy

As described by Bandura (1997), self-efficacy comprises an individual's belief in their ability to perform and successfully complete a task. Self-efficacy is important because it can promote interest and motivation and shape career aspirations. It has been shown to correlate with academic achievement (Aivaloglou and Hermans, 2019; Dunn and Kennedy, 2019). Researchers have used various instruments to measure self-efficacy in K–12 STEM education; across studies the results seem to strongly suggest that self-efficacy is related to learner persistence in STEM pathways (Brown et al., 2016; Concannon and Barrow, 2010).

Change in self-efficacy was captured in ways that were specific to the context of the program studies and the specific activities: in electronics, circuitry, coding, and programming self-efficacy; in performing robotics and cybersecurity-related tasks; and comfort in using newer technology. Data were collected via self-reported pre- and post-treatment surveys; cybersecurity engagement and self-efficacy survey; weekly learner journals; and observation. Several of the studies reported increases in learner self-efficacy following participation in a variety of hands-on, potentially authentic, computing experiences (Amo et al., 2019; Barker et al., 2018; Jagiela et al., 2018; Nugent et al., 2016; 2019; Stapleton et al., 2019). The results for gender differences

---

[2] As Scott and White (2013) describe, "In the contextualized aggregate, these districts represent the typical characteristics of an urban school. Except for one of the high school districts, the other two host students who for the large part qualify for free or reduced lunch (82–90%), disproportionately serve racial and ethnic minority students (African American 10%, Latino 62%, White 19%, and Native American 3%), and have less than 50% of high school students passing statewide assessment" (pp. 662–663).

were mixed (Loksa et al., 2016), and differential impacts on learners from underrepresented racial and ethnic groups were rarely examined.

Qiu and colleagues (2013) investigated the impact of a 12-hour project-based computational textiles curriculum on learners' technological self-efficacy. The researchers were particularly interested in this approach as a means to diversify the computing community by drawing upon non-traditional applications that might interest a broader group of learners. Computing concepts and practices targeted included abstraction and modularity, computer architecture, variables, control flow, functions, data structures, debugging, and iteration. Evaluation results indicated a positive impact on students' technological self-efficacy as well as interest in programming and electronics.

Nugent et al. (2019) examined the WearTec intervention, an electronic textile curriculum delivered to upper elementary learners, primarily in formal classroom settings. The sample size was large, with 800 learners participating in lessons and activities utilizing LilyPad Arduino programmable microcontrollers along with conductive thread, LED lights, motors, and switches to create a textile-based product of their design. Overall, participants' self-efficacy increased over time. Interestingly, although e-textile interventions are commonly described as appealing particularly to girls, boys had significantly higher self-efficacy following the WearTec intervention, even after controlling for pre-treatment scores and despite no gender differences in knowledge outcomes. Learners from minoritized groups had similar increases in self-efficacy as compared to their White peers, although they made up only approximately one-third of the participants.

Nugent et al. (2016) examined how multiple versions of their robotics program across 8 years—delivered through summer camps, academic year clubs, and robotics competitions—supported middle school learners in STEM learning and motivation. They reported results from 6 years of data collected from 1,825 campers, 3 years of data from 458 competition participants, and 2 years from 126 club participants. Participants were from 23 states in the United States, 70 percent were boys and 30 percent were girls. Participants completed a survey that measured four constructs:

1. task value: perceived value of science, mathematics, and robotics;
2. self-efficacy: confidence in performing robotics tasks;
3. workplace skills: teamwork and problem-solving; and
4. career orientation: interest in STEM careers.

The researchers also included a quasi-experimental study that compared results from the summer camp to a control group composed of learners identified by regional educational service units as those with interest in technology and robotics.

The researchers highlight two results. First, the camp data showed more positive results in the increase in interest in engineering. There were increases in learner interest in engineering careers in 2 of the 3 years of competition data, but not in science, technology, or mathematics. The clubs did not show any increases in learner interest in pursuing STEM careers. Participation in robotics camps, clubs, and competitions tended to increase learner self confidence in performing robotics tasks. Participants showed gains in self-efficacy as they accumulated experience in writing programs to control their robot's actions effectively.

Summary

Overall, the evidence for affective outcomes appears to be mixed, despite showing promise in some areas. With respect to interest, most of the studies were still in the exploratory/early stage phase and suggested little change. The same is true for motivation with most of the studies exploring themes that may contribute to enhancing motivation through STEM experiences. The research for identity and self-efficacy was more promising. Findings suggest that prolonged exposure to STEM experiences lead to significant increases in self-efficacy.

BEHAVIORAL OUTCOMES

There is widespread belief that a necessary condition for expanding participation in careers and majors in computing is broadening exposure to and engagement with computing (Folk et al., 2015). As the reasoning goes, engaging in computational thinking—in the contexts of technology use, computing, or more general STEM applications—can help build the skills needed to understand and work effectively with computers. Adding direct, hands-on experience can further build these skills and can also foster interest and comfort with computing. These experiences, in turn, can then increase the likelihood of pursuing—and persisting in—computing studies and careers.

The literature describes a wide range of strategies for ensuring that K–12 learners are exposed to opportunities to engage in computing. In some cases, the strategies entail use of technology and other times not. They generally target learners in the middle and high school age range, and have been designed for a variety of settings, ranging from traditional classrooms to small-group workshop-like settings. Most of the studies reviewed were exploratory or in early stages with a subset including evaluations of impact. As such, very few studies have taken the extra step of examining the effects of these strategies on improving engagement in computing; there is even less evidence on strategies that promote persistence. These studies are discussed below, organized by outcome focus.

Engagement

Participating in authentic activities in STEM, and computing more specifically, is believed to be helpful in fostering continued engagement in the activities themselves (see Chapter 2). In turn, this greater engagement, coupled with the skill-building focus of the activities may encourage learners to pursue STEM careers, including computing and computing-related career tracks. Whereas there is a robust literature describing the nature and logic of the myriad strategies designed to increase engagement in STEM activities and/or course taking, there is a dearth of research on the effectiveness of authentic experiences for computing in promoting engagement in computing specifically.

Several exploratory studies examined descriptively the level of learners' engagement in various types of programs but did not attempt to assess whether participation in a given program affected the likelihood or level of engagement relative to what it would have been absent the program (Folk et al., 2015; Gardeli and Vosinakis, 2019; Wanzer et al., 2020; Weston, Dubow, and Kaminsky, 2019). For example, Folk et al. (2015) focused on a program designed to infuse middle and high school science classes with exercises designed to build computational thinking skills applicable in a wide range of settings. This program, *Discover Science through Computational Thinking*, did not entail the use of technology. Rather, it involved enhancements to instructional modules that required learners to develop algorithms or follow explicit logic trees to solve problems. The study, which focused on 16 middle and high school teachers and their learners, used pre- and post-tests of learners and qualitative feedback from teachers, and learners to judge the impact of the program on learner engagement and learning. The evaluators concluded that the strategies were successful in engaging the learners in the computational thinking exercises. However, they also noted that learners often needed prompting to engage with the task and frequently needed support to complete the tasks.

Two studies explored descriptively the effectiveness of game-based strategies for promoting engagement in computing and computational thinking. One of these, *ARQuest*, is a mobile augmented reality game for middle-school learners. *ARQuest* blends game play and game design activities with real-time feedback intended to build computational thinking skills (Gardeli and Vosinakis, 2019). The study focused on 26 learners ages 9 and 10 across two schools. Based on observations of the game play during a single session (25 minutes for three groups of learners and 1 hour for the fourth group), the evaluators judged that the game successfully engaged learners meaningfully in computational thinking. They did not examine whether the game led to higher levels of engagement in computational thinking or whether participants were more likely to enroll in computing courses or majors later on.

The other study of a game-based learning strategy examined the use of the mobile game, *Meleon* (Klein, 2013). This game was designed as a structured mobile game environment intended to promote computational thinking and skill-building by inviting learners to play the game on their own using their local environment as the environmental inputs. The evaluation of *Meleon* is based on the experiences of 15 10- to 15-year-olds in a youth play club. The evaluators observed learners playing the game for an average of about 20 minutes each. Based on observations and semi-structured interviews with learners, the author concluded that learners were highly "immersed" in the game and able to reflect on their actions during play. However, like the study of ARQuest, there was no comparison group and no evaluation of the impacts of *Meleon* on more distal outcomes.

Two of the studies identified looked at the impact of the program on engagement in computing activities. Amo et al. (2019) conducted a randomized controlled trial of a 60-minute hands-on workshop in networking ("cyber detectives") for learners in middle school and from low-income families. The study found no growth in cyber awareness as a result of their participation in the exhibit (n = 79).

The other impact evaluation study (Kloper, Yoon, and Rivas, 2004) examined whether there were differences in levels of engagement and skills development of learners who played games—*Virus* and *Live Long and Prosper*—when delivered via Palm Pilot devices supported simulations versus using wearable Tag-based simulations. Tag-based simulations involved participants wearing a small computer that allows them to become agents in the simulation, whereas Palms involve participants using a personal digital assistant. In a randomized controlled trial that included 188 11- to 16-year-olds in three schools, the evaluators found no difference in learner engagement between those using the Palm- versus the Tag-supported simulations. The study did not include a no-treatment control group and, thus, by design, did not estimate impacts on engagement per se.

Persistence and Retention

To meet the workforce demands of the future as forecasted by the Bureau of Labor Statistics (2020), it is critical to increase computing literacy among the population, as well as to have greater numbers of individuals prepared for computing careers. Moreover, Dee and Gershenson (2017) highlight that it is important to promote equitable access to computing careers among underrepresented groups. There are too few learners exiting high schools with the skills required to pursue computing majors in college, and many who have the skills lack the interest and/or self-confidence to enter computing majors. This suggests the importance of finding ways to increase the likelihood that more of those who gain exposure and have predispositions to engage in computing majors and careers persist in preparing for them.

A recent observational study explored predictors of the decisions of high school girls with interest in computing to act on that interest by persisting in computing majors during college (Weston, Dubow, and Kaminsky, 2019). This study surveyed learners who had demonstrated an interest in computing by registering on the Aspirations in Computing Award website when they were in high school. Using data from a 3-year follow-up survey, the study showed that the strongest predictor of persistence was having taken an AP computing course in high school. Notably, participating in tech-related workshops, internships, or after-school programs was negatively associated with persistence in computing majors.

The other study identified in the literature search examined the impacts of a particular web-based learning platform for teaching beginning programming, *EarSketch*, on intentions of high school learners to persist in computing (Wanzer et al., 2020). The program was developed to foster persistence in computing among diverse population groups (i.e., learners not identified as White or Asian race/ethnicty) through a variety of applications, including brief workshop settings, summer camps, and even in full-semester courses. Two of the Wanzer et al. (2020) studies focused on high school learners who had taken a computing class that incorporated *EarSketch* (DRK studies of a 2015–2016 and a 2016–2017 cohort). Both studies had a treatment and a control group and measured impacts by comparing the difference between learners' self-reported intentions to persist in computing before and after the *EarSketch* experience. Both treatment groups had higher average gains in their reported intentions to persist in computing than their control-group counterparts. However, in neither case were the gains large or significantly higher for the treatment group.

Summary

Overall, the studies reviewed with respect to engagement suggest that the findings were generally mixed and/or insignificant. Only one study (Folk et al., 2015) reported positive impacts on long-term learner engagement; the others only showed short-term impacts (Gardeli and Vosinakis, 2019; Klein, 2013) or none at all. Many of these studies did not include control groups or measure more long-term impacts. For retention, the findings suggest that engaging in computing courses (such as AP computer science) or computing experiences may lead to persisting in computing, although more research is needed to further interrogate these findings.

SUMMARY

In this chapter, the committee reviewed the literature on the relationships between authentic experiences for computing and desired outcomes, such as improvements in knowledge and skills about computing, changes in interest in computing, and motivation to pursue future activities in computing. The results were limited and, in some cases, suggested positive impact. However, many of the studies were exploratory and were not designed to establish causal conclusions about the relationships between the interventions and changes in the outcomes. Additionally, unlike the evidence described in Chapter 3 that discussed connections across settings and time (see section Learning Over Time and Across Experiences: An Ecosystems Approach), these examples mainly examine programs in isolation. Nonetheless, they provide a foundation for future studies.

This discussion of research on the outcomes of authentic experiences in computing lead to several insights. There is substantial variability in the settings and measures making standardization in terms of measures and interventions difficult. For example, measures of cognitive outcomes (knowledge and skills) were typically designed to measure specific learning outcomes directly related to a given curriculum, programmatic activity, or course. Most of these were not standardized measures or based on large-scale assessments (at the state, national, or international level), rather they were developed by the program designers. Affective outcomes involved measuring engagement, interest, self-efficacy, and the development of an identity as a computational thinker; outcomes that can be difficult or impractical to measure. These limitations in measurement likely contribute to the lack of significant findings.

Despite the limitations in the research base, the past decade has seen an increase in research and development activities related to computing. Future research includes developing programs to expose learners to authentic experiences for computing as well as better articulation between the goals and objectives for the programs and design mechanisms to evaluate the extent to which they have been reached. This alignment is needed to better understand how the program leads to the intended outcomes. Overall, more research is needed.

5

Learning Spaces Outside of School Time

Out-of-school time (OST) spaces comprise a vast range of environments and situations, including youth development programs, museums, libraries, zoos, botanical gardens, higher educational institutions, science centers, and community centers, as well as home-based and online communities. Given the substantial breadth and variability of these activities, this chapter focuses primarily on community-based organizations, museums, and public libraries, which are considered "educator-designed settings" of informal learning environments (National Research Council [NRC], 2009). This chapter discusses the potential roles and ways in which OST settings strive to provide authentic experiences that develop interest and competencies for computing to learners in grades K–12.

Community-based organizations often support a diverse set of initiatives that are core to their missions. Learning and engagement within these programs occur outside of school hours and may be held on school campuses, near school campuses, or elsewhere. The learning environments and experiences generated by these organizations are quite varied. Some of these programs are supported by a national umbrella organization or headquarters with a network of multiple sites (e.g., 4H, Boys & Girls Clubs, the Clubhouse Network, *FIRST*®, the SMASH Academy, and YWCA and YMCA to name a few). Other programs are single-site, unique, and stand-alone, sometimes tied to an overarching organization or funder (e.g., Mouse in New York City, DIY Girls in Los Angeles) and certain K–12 programs hosted by colleges and universities. Whether the programs have a national or state office or overseeing leadership structures, the programs on the ground take the shape of the region, community, and participants.

Whereas community-based organizations often provide a mixed suite of services for the community, it is not uncommon for their youth-serving efforts to be oriented toward science, technology, engineering, and mathematics (STEM), whether as a primary focus or integrated into their overall design. Less common and only recently introduced are youth programs from community-based organizations specifically focused on computing outcomes in their offerings. For example, Girl Scouts of the USA (GSUSA) released a large set of new badges and computing opportunities (e.g., Cybersecurity and Coding for Good).[1] Another national organization, 4-H, created a 4-H CS Pathway that aims to support 4-H educators and facilitators, especially those in rural communities or areas with limited access to technology and computing resources, to teach computer science skills and coding projects.[2]

Museums—including science and technology centers, children's museums, art museums, history museums, and even zoos, aquaria, arboretums, and botanical gardens—have evolved as institutions whose focus has shifted from curation or preservation to include a focus on learning and interactivity (Crowley, Pierroux, and Knutson, 2014; Falk and Dierking, 2018). Through educational programs, curricula, and exhibition topics, museums work to reach diverse communities, whether by geography, race and ethnicity, and/or socioeconomic level.[3] Museums offerings are varied, including a combination of any of the following: collections and galleries, exhibits, school field trips, family workshops, teacher professional development, volunteer programs, summer camps, online content, etc. Although they are predominantly considered as informal/out-of-school space, museums have strong relationships with school institutions by aligning content with state and national standards (Center for the Future of Museums, 2014). Museums create a substantial amount of content as well, whether curricula, videos, games and apps, and/or other work related to research and evaluation efforts, often accessed and used globally by other museum settings, classrooms, professional development, and even directly by learners (Center for the Future of Museums, 2014).

In recent years, museums have begun to offer a range of computing-oriented programming, often embedded within their STEM portfolios and sometimes as a standalone effort. These programs may occur within a museum's physical space or as part of community partnership work and

---

[1] For more information, see https://blog.girlscouts.org/2019/07/big-news-42-new-girl-scout-badges-to.html.

[2] For more information about the initiative, see https://4-h.org/media/4-h-google-expand-access-to-free-computer-science-education-to-one-million-youth-across-the-country. This includes efforts to introduce students to computer science: https://about.google/stories/google-4h as well as considering pathways: https://4hcspathways.extension.org.

[3] For 2018 information, see https://www.aam-us.org/2018/01/20/museums-and-public-opinion.

include opportunities such as timed workshops, hands-on activities within interactive spaces on the museum floor (such as makerspaces or labs), classes coupled with field trips, outreach programs for specific youth, and/or collaborations with local institutions, including schools and after-school programs. For example, in San Francisco, the Exploratorium's Tinkering Studio has developed activities and led workshops on Computational Tinkering.

Like museums, public libraries have evolved to meet the needs of their communities, including the K–12 population.[4] In terms of programming[5] and services for youth, two target populations are included: children (ages 11 and under) and young adults (ages 12–18). Public libraries offered 503,334 young adults' programs and 2.85 million children's programs in 2016 (Institute of Museum and Library Services [IMLS], 2019). IMLS (2019) also reports that the more rural the library is, the more children and young adult programs are offered. Libraries are deemed capable of filling the gap that schools are lacking in terms of providing opportunities related to computing, which may result in broadening the participation for youth of color in computing (Braun and Visser, 2017). It is important to note that public libraries vary tremendously in size, staffing structure, availability of resources, opportunities for professional development, and access to community partners, among other distinctions (IMLS, 2019; Real and Rose, 2017).

A variety of technology-enabled programs that leverage learner's interest and promote equitable opportunities to use and experience technologies have been happening in public libraries for more than a decade (Braun et al., 2014; Subramaniam et al., 2018). A recent trend has been to offer programs tailored to the development of interest and competencies in STEM (Garmer, 2014; Martin, 2017) and to computing more specifically (ALA, 2019). The type of computing programs include topics such as robotics, gaming, making, learning specific coding languages, and app development, as well as other unplugged programs that are integrated into existing programs such as story times and reading programs. These programs may leverage design principles of the connected learning framework (Hoffman et al., 2016; Ito et al., 2013; Subramaniam et al., 2018) that strive to be authentic to youth, interest-driven, fun, and different from in-school settings. Based on available scholarship and data, some libraries (especially small and rural libraries) are likely contributing to cultivating interest and competencies for pursuing careers in computing by using authentic experiences (Phillips, Lee, and Recker, 2018); however, there is limited published empirical evidence.

---

[4] It should be noted that although the committee is focusing on library programs outside of school settings, an important setting that could help with broader reach is computer labs in public schools.

[5] The committee utilizes the phrase "library programs" or "library programming" to reflect the programs and activities offered in libraries. This is a common vernacular in library scholarship.

In its discussion of the ways in which these OST settings and their present and potential impact on interest and competencies for computing to learners in grades K–12, the chapter will emphasize the strengths and challenges that these settings face with respect to:

- access, equity, and cultural norms;
- duration and the format of programs;
- space and/or facility issues;
- learning facilitators; and
- measuring outcomes.

It is worth stating that the intention is not to address *all* types of computing programs (e.g., unplugged, game making) throughout the sections, but to use the available data and select examples to explain each of the above-mentioned factors by making connections to how these types of programs provide authentic experiences for computing. Moreover, when possible, the examples will focus on "authentic" experiences. However, a limitation of the available literature is understanding what is considered "authentic" in these contexts; in these cases, the committee draws from the broader literature.

ACCESS, EQUITY, AND CULTURAL NORMS

It is important to consider the degree to which the various settings afford opportunities to engage learners in authentic experiences for computing. However, it is worth noting that there are limitations to access and engagement beyond financial cost and access to resources (discussed below). For example, the learners' home and family environments can have an impact, as when the presence or absence of supportive and/or knowledgeable family members can significantly impact learners' experiences (Ito et al., 2020). The learner may have the resources to attend an OST program, but may have caregivers who are not willing to support the experience, or vice versa. Some learners must maintain an after-school job or care for their siblings. Moreover, informal experiences have affordances and constraints that play a specific role. What follows is a review of the ways in which issues related to access, equity, and cultural norms may facilitate or hinder the participation of learners in authentic experiences for computing and the ways in which OST institutions can potentially attend to these issues.

Distribution and Quality of Opportunities

Previous work has suggested that families from high socio-economic backgrounds spend nearly seven times more money on OST enrichment activities than families from low socio-economic backgrounds (Duncan and Murnane, 2011; Lopez, Caspe, and McWilliams, 2016). It is clear that the distribution of these opportunities and the quality of opportunities are tied to various factors such as socio-economic status and geography. Although institutions such as public libraries (IMLS, 2019), 4-H, and others have substantial reach and offer quality programming for youth in rural areas, the strengths, challenges, and availability of resources in programs serving rural communities are distinct from those experienced by programs serving suburban or urban communities (Hartman, Hines-Bergmeier, and Klein, 2017; Ihrig et al., 2018). Differences in broadband access, physical space, and the socio-demographic characteristics of learners will undoubtedly affect the types of programs that facilitators can or choose to offer (Davis et al., 2018).

Moreover, across all settings, OST educational programs vary in terms of access and are inequitable, impacting minoritized communities who may need them most (Afterschool Alliance, 2014; 2016). For example, the Afterschool Alliance, a national non-profit organization that supports and advocates for quality after-school opportunities, notes in the 2014 (and 2016)[6] *American After 3PM* report that access to and supply of quality after-school programs is highly uneven for different communities and populations. There is a higher rate of participation and higher demand, though often unmet, for after-school opportunities among low-income households, African American families, and Hispanic/Latinx families, than compared with high-income households and White families. However, as suggested above, it is important to consider whether the learners' home and family environments also serve as a potential barrier to participation.

Time, Cost, and Transportation

Significant barriers to accessing authentic experiences for computing include time availability, cost, and transportation. For example, Sirinides, Fink, and DuBois (2016) show that some public libraries' hours of operations provide access challenges to families that work during the day and cannot get to the library until night—this is despite approximately 311 million people living with a public library service area (LSA) with free library programs. Some branches do not have regular evening hours during the week, and some smaller libraries change hours frequently. Some families opt to make a longer commute (if they can) to get to the central library, which may offer better resources, programs, and staff to work with or assist them than the local branch library (Sirinides, Fink, and DuBois, 2016).

---

[6] See http://www.afterschoolalliance.org/press_archives/CCP-African-American-NR-083016.pdf.

In addition to the hours of operation, financial and family time commitments can be a major constraint in the opportunities afforded to learners. In a 2019 article, the National Conference of State Legislatures (NCSL) clearly states:

> Only one dedicated federal funding stream, the 21st Century Community Learning Centers Program, is available for afterschool programs. Although 24 percent of the children in afterschool programs live in communities with concentrated poverty, federal funds cover only 11 percent of program costs. Therefore, the burden of funding such programs often falls on states, communities, and parents. (p. 1)

As an example, traditional Scouts programs require a substantial amount of voluntary time, and often money and resources, from families and caregivers. Troop leaders have been characterized as willing, impassioned caregivers, leading and supporting efforts on a volunteer basis, and troops may expect all families to contribute time, service, and resources.[7] These norms and expectations, as well as the types of activities that troops engage in (e.g., campouts, community service, hiking, crafts, and sales), are reflective of the dominant culture, and access can be limited for those with different abilities, different schedules or availability (i.e., working an evening shift or weekend hours), different family units, and different values.

To offset some of the costs, institutions of interest, such as museums, often support complimentary admissions, reduced-price tickets, free school field trips, and a variety of other programs and services that support accessibility or learning needs. Organizations such as the Association of Science-Technology Centers (ASTC) have occasionally provided small grants to museums and science centers to subsidize the cost of providing transportation to enable youth to attend. Libraries have also found ways to confront this issue by obtaining bus passes or bringing programs to more accessible locations for learners such as community centers (Garmer, 2014; Zhou et al., 2019).

Technological Resources

The programs across the different settings are not always equipped with technologies that can facilitate authentic experiences for computing (e.g., computer or learning lab, a makerspace, a studio) and support (e.g., curriculum, materials) that may develop learners' interest and competencies in computing (Hoffman et al., 2016). Some centers impose time limits on

---

[7] See Pack 296 Cubs, Oakland, CA (2018). Available at http://www.pack296cubs.org/documents.

the use of tablets and computers. As a result, learners who do not have access to these technologies or only have mobile access at home may have to take a few days to complete their computing projects. These may result in learners falling behind in competency development or losing interest (Braun and Visser, 2017).

Families and learners living in poverty are more likely to visit a library than any other community venue, such as a museum (National Center for Education Statistics, 2015; Swan, 2014). This may be because nearly all public libraries offer free access to computers and wifi (American Library Association [ALA], 2019). Libraries also have ventured into unplugged programs to help learners understand computing concepts (see Box 5-1).

There are some potential approaches to offset lack of access to techno-logical resources, beyond offering unplugged programs. A potential com-mon strategy employed by libraries is to partner with organizations that

---

BOX 5-1
World's Slowest Computer at the Seattle Public Library

Inspired by game designers Kaho Abe and Ramsey Nasser's creation of the Slowest Computer on Earth, Seattle Public Library (SPL) created *World's Slowest Computer* program. The program was unplugged and targeted for teens ages 11–16. The goal of the program was to provide opportunities for teens from low-income communities to learn about computing (i.e., computational thinking) as well as to obtain leadership skills.

This program ran once a week during summer 2019 and once a week after school in fall 2019. In the program, teens attend a session (typically about 120–180 minutes) to build and program the slowest computer in the world using sponges, sticky notes, markers, and tapes. The teens are directed on how to initially order the sponges (10 × 10 with the yellow facing up), build the axis on two sides using tape making the shape of L, and write 0–9 on the masking tape for both the columns and rows. The 16 sticky notes are arranged in two rows of eight right below the sponges—each labeled with a letter A through P. The grid of sponges is the screen, and every sponge is the pixel, which can be turned off (yellow side) and turned on (green side). The arranged sticky notes serve as the computer memory, and each sticky note is a cell within the memory. The teens obtain a set of instructions that contain seven commands that allow them to build the slowest computer on Earth, which include plot (which means flipping a sponge at the column and row given by two memory cells), set (write a value to a memory cell), jump, greater than, plus, minus, and less than. Working in groups, they com-pete on who can work through the instructions and reveal the graphic the fastest, which is an element of gamified learning. Such team efforts allow them to develop teamwork and perseverance.

SOURCE: Based on personal communication with Juan Rubio.

can provide the physical and intellectual access needed to design, develop, and implement authentic experiences. Collaborators can include local after-school programs, higher educational institutions, state libraries that provide technical and staff assistance to libraries within the state, makers in the community, local schools, other informal learning spaces such as museums, businesses, non-profits, authors, and individual community members with technical expertise such as animation, coding, game design, and filmmaking (Subramaniam et al., 2018). Urban libraries may have a more extensive portfolio of partners to tap into than rural libraries, which often have trouble designating a partner (Davis et al., 2018).

Cultural Norms

OST settings also vary, as expected, in their norms and values, which are often drawn from the communities they serve and/or exist within. In some cases, OST programs may uphold cultural norms and values that are exclusionary, especially given the often private nature compared to the public nature of schools.[8] However, in other instances as observed in the Clubhouse Network (originally known as the Intel Computer Clubhouse Network), these environments can "provide a creative, safe, and free OST learning environment where young people from underserved communities work with adult mentors to explore their own ideas, develop new skills, and build confidence in themselves through the use of technology."[9] As with any learning community, the members and actors of the clubhouse help to set the values, norms, and culture (Michalchik et al., 2008). Art—defined broadly, whether through music and rap, animation and video, poetry, drawing, or fashion design, just to name a few—is a way to express their own interests, identity, culture, and personality. Technology is specifically called out as a tool for expression, as the "tools provide an opportunity for learning of complex skills and, at the same time, the possibility of applying these skills in authentic situations across one's life" (Michalchik et al., 2008, p. 32).

Museums and libraries have been engaged in debates for a long time around which communities and cultures they represent and how those are represented in their collection, programming, artifacts, and galleries showcased, and how they respond when there is a specific need in their communities (Gibson et al., 2017; 2020; Watson, 2007). Through new and refined initiatives addressing diversity, equity, accessibility, and inclusion in the museum and librarianship field overall, museums and libraries are examining their own practices, making clear the work needed for combating

---

[8] In some instances, these programs may also have religious ties and uphold narrow views around topics such as gender (e.g., Boy Scouts).

[9] For more information, see https://theclubhousenetwork.org.

implicit bias and enabling systemic change at all levels, and recognizing the need to remain relevant, responsive, and reflective of the communities in which they exist (see Box 5-2; ALA, 2019; American Alliance of Museums, 2018).

In addition, thinking about how communities are represented in their collections, museums and libraries also attend to how they can use their collections, spaces, and resources to serve members of those communities. Attending to the local communities can be achieved by leveraging the knowledge that program facilitators have about the learners in their communities gained through everyday interaction: for example, learners' interests, their current challenges, the technologies they use, what they learn

---

BOX 5-2
Science Museum of Minnesota: Making Connections

Supported by the National Science Foundation, the Science Museum of Minnesota initiated an ambitious participatory research project in 2013, called Making Connections, that released a practitioner guide in 2018. The guide addressed the cultural relevance of its maker activities and projects by critically examining internal staff culture and language and by developing trusting, vulnerable, and sustained relationships with members of racially non-dominant communities in the metropolitan area to inform its museum maker activities and approaches. In the guide, Bequette et al. (2018) writes:

> All communities have Makers, but not all communities have been actively included in the more recently branded Maker movement. While for years science centers and museums throughout the United States have identified a need to increase the diversity of their audiences, they have struggled to make significant headway toward this goal. The Making Connections project aimed to contest the homogeneity of the Maker Movement, which has a primarily White, male, and middle/upper-middle class following. Recognizing the museum's historical underinvestment in relationships with members of communities of color and American Indian communities in the Minneapolis/St. Paul metro area, we also sought to develop more intentional relationships with family groups who identified as such. (p. 4)

Alongside the many community meetings, workshops, and showcases, the project members also committed to extensive dialogue, iteration, and reflection. Upon conclusion, in addition to institutional and individual changes, the project resulted in more than 25 co-designed Play, Tinker, Make activities that respected the authenticity of the cultural and historical traditions, as well as unique expressions of the idea of making. All were carefully informed and modeled by community members (Bequette et al., 2018).

SOURCE: Committee generated based on Bequette et al. (2018).

BOX 5-3
Seattle Public Library: *TechTales*

Zhou et al. (2019) designed a family-centered, culturally expansive science, technology, engineering, arts, and mathematics (STEAM) learning experience called *TechTales*, developed in partnership with learning scientists, Seattle Public Library staff, informal science education staff, and staff from Native American community organizations. *TechTales* involved more than 65 families across 13 iterations of the program, implemented in the Seattle Public Library, telling a range of culturally relevant stories that are deeply rooted in the place, identity, lives, and desires of these participating families. Stories run a gamut of their personal histories from "stargazing out of the window of a cabin at a 'family camp,' racing goats on a family reunion trip to Ethiopia, an epic family move from Arizona to Washington" to "becoming a family on 'adoption day'" (p. 57). These families come to *TechTales* with fraught relationships with technologies, as these "technologies have served to erase, make invisible, or assimilate their communities" (p. 62). Families use Scratch and robotics to create and animate their stories and identify and explore new or prior interests and competencies in multidisciplinary forms of work such as art, robotics, computing, and electrical engineering.

SOURCE: Committee generated based on Zhou et al. (2019).

in school, and challenges their families face. For example, the Los Angeles Public Library System offered Scratch programming workshops at 11 libraries serving underserved populations across the system (for a description of Scratch, see Box 7-7). Librarians reported learner interest in hip-hop, skateboarding, vampire and monster romance novels, Ninjago, Minecraft, etc. The fascination with hip-hop was incorporated into the design of the Scratch programming that the library offered. Learners used Scratch to combine and remix hip-hop dance moves by photographing themselves performing stop motion dance moves and remixing these moves with some of their friends' movements in their Scratch projects (for another example, see Box 5-3).[10] Another emerging way to design authentic experiences for computing is to incorporate "youth voice" in the design of such programs; this is a set of participatory design techniques derived from child-computer interaction research (Druin, 1999; Subramaniam, 2016; Yip, Lee, and Lee, 2019). Rubio (2017) uses the term "youth voice" to highlight and advocate for the partnership of younger learners and adults, built to facilitate deep participation in library programs and progressively build trust with underserved communities.

---

[10] For more information, see https://scratch.mit.edu/codingforall.

DURATION AND PROGRAM FORMAT

Duration, frequency of visits, and overall accessibility to authentic experiences for computing have implications for how to design and implement these flexible and adaptable experiences across designed settings. As will be discussed in Chapter 7, it is important for designers and educators to take into consideration the quality and outcomes of an experience when learners may engage from 5 minutes to 60 minutes (or more), may engage independently or in a highly-social and collaborative manner, may be visiting the space for the first or fifteenth time, may come with deep knowledge and interest or little experience, and more. This can also include experiences across different settings. When there is variation in how much time is spent—and possible variation among learners as to the amount of time each spends—the facilitation, structures, and activities must remain flexible and adaptable. Moreover, the timeframe of a program—when in the year a learner might attend—may affect the learning or effectiveness as well. Some programs, such as the SMASH Academy program offered through the Kapor Center, are extensive in how long and consistently they engage with their participants (see Box 5-4).

The programs offered by community-based organizations, museums, and libraries can occur in various formats—such as in the form of summer or spring break camps, weekend programs, weekly programs that extend the whole year, season, or several weeks, and special one-time programs (see Box 5-5 for an example). Some of the programs may require mandatory attendance, though drop-in programming remains the most prevalent. For programs that have mandatory attendance, pre-registration is typically required, whereas for drop-in programming, educators may not necessarily know who will attend, how long they will stay, what prior knowledge they may bring, and how they will engage with other learners in the space. Drop-in programs may be able to expect a certain level of regularity, though regularity may look quite different from one program to another: twice a week for 2 hours each time, or every day for 30 minutes, or once a month on Saturdays for 3 hours with their families. This is important as learners have different reasons or motivations for engaging in authentic experiences.

Social interaction and peer learning are critical parts of authentic STEM experiences (NRC, 2009). For example, research focusing on museum experiences has suggested that socially engaging encounters are important in connecting the immediate experience to relevant interests and prior knowledge as well as transferring knowledge gained in the present to future experiences, regardless of how learners interact with others (Falk and Dierking, 2018). Research has also suggested that it is unlikely that meaningful social interaction can occur if learners are engaged in one-time classes or on a drop-in basis (Rubio, 2017), which may be a limitation

---

BOX 5-4
Kapor Center: SMASH Academy Program

SMASH Academy is free and specifically designed for a long duration of engagement. For early high schoolers who are typically underrepresented (gender, race, ethnicity, or socioeconomic status) in computing, the SMASH model includes a 3-year program, year-round academic courses and support, a 5-week summer residential program on university campuses, coursework and community building that support STEM skills and life skills, and more. The extended, in-depth, and culturally relevant nature of the SMASH intervention aims to overcome race and gender barriers in the STEM workforce. SMASH Academy focuses on computing, emphasizing professional authenticity to develop its participants' skills, knowledge, and interest in these areas, and has found that 83 percent of its alumni intend to major in STEM, compared with a national average of 45 percent.

Findings of a study focused on the SMASH Academy program found that women of color had significantly lower interest and engagement in computing at the beginning of, as well as 1 year into, the program. Those gender differences evened out by the third year when there were no differences in the enrollment and completion numbers of the AP Computer Science A course. However, differences appeared again in college, where 79 percent of the program alums who majored in computer science were men, compared with 21 percent for women. Gender continues to be a factor in computing pursuit and success, compounded by race (Scott et al., 2017). Here and with any learning experience or environment, sociocultural influences are critical to consider, and time spent is only one of many parameters or factors to design for.

SOURCE: Based on Koshy (2017).

---

of some programs in particular settings (e.g., museums and libraries). To accommodate this, some libraries have begun to offer the same program multiple times a day during the week or extend it for longer hours so that learners and their families have opportunities to participate when they are available, especially when the curriculum involves authentic experiences where deep engagement with content is warranted (Lopez, Caspe, and McWilliams, 2016; Zhou et al., 2019).

Some libraries have proposed other efforts to provide opportunities for and maintain the much-needed deep engagement in authentic experiences. These include (1) providing meals and snacks; (2) encouraging regular participation while offering additional sessions such as "booster days," which are drop-in sessions when learners and families who have attended the mandatory sessions can attend to extend their learning (Zhou et al., 2019); (3) offering bus passes to ensure that learners can attend a program

---

BOX 5-5
Providence Public Library (Rhode Coders 2.0)

Rhode Coders 2.0, which was launched in 2016, provides a foundation for web-development programming and coding, conducted by the Providence Public Library (PPL). Students ages 12–18 meet for 2 hours twice a week (a total of 25 sessions per semester) to learn web development such as HTML, JavaScript, and CSS (among others). The courses are offered as part of the Rhode Island Department of Education's Advanced Course Network. Most students have no or minimal coding experience and are recruited through an after-school program arranged by the Providence Afterschool Alliance at local schools in Providence. Participation in the program offers a pathway to college and computing, particularly for students who have limited to no access to the Internet/computers at home and/or have access via mobile phone with restricted data service.

The program culminates with the creation of a website that is presented and showcased to the community using a Science Fair style. Upon completion of this program, students have the opportunity to earn 0.5 high school credits. Through the Providence Afterschool Alliance, the students can earn digital badges (rewarding them for perseverance, teamwork, engagement, communication, critical thinking) that will prioritize them for summer employment through the city of Providence.

SOURCES: Based on personal communication with Kate Aubin and Karisa Tashjian.

---

regularly (Garmer, 2014; Zhou et al., 2019); and (4) designing a program or a curriculum that allows for a particular participant to get up to speed when several sessions have been missed (Martin, 2017). Another important strategy promoted by an ecosystems approach may include brokering the connections across settings as it is important to not only engage learners for longer periods of time in a single setting, but also broker to and from different environments.

However, it is worth acknowledging that the research is mixed as to whether the amount of exposure (whether in duration or in frequency) or how that time is spent (the quality of the activities and engagement) has an impact on learning at all (Lauer et al., 2006). Specific programs do show that increased "dosage" is associated with increases in academic achievement and test scores (Wai et al., 2010) or other outcomes such as science interest (Noam et al., 2014). Ultimately, the goals of the learning experience are critical to consider when planning the expected duration or frequency of learning.

SPACE AND/OR FACILITY ISSUES

Physical space and facilities vary widely within and across the different designed settings.[11] The National Clearinghouse for Educational Facilities notes that characteristics of academic facilities, such as ventilation and air quality, lighting, acoustics, temperature, and more, may have impacts on teacher and student performance (Schneider, 2002). These aspects are equally important to consider for OST spaces and facilities, though they may be more diverse and inconsistent in nature, from outdoor spaces in nature for environmental programs to computer labs and workshops. For authentic experiences that increase interest in computing, access to and availability of appropriate devices or tools, Internet and sufficient bandwidth, and electrical power capacity are critical factors.

The spaces for programs led by community-based organizations can vary in a number of ways: consistency (the same space is available every week); type of space (e.g., local fairgrounds, an enclosed community room at the community center, or shared multipurpose space when programs compete for time and access); and resources available in the space (e.g., spaces with working and maintained equipment and plentiful materials, compared with spaces with folding chairs and irregularly donated items). Moreover, some community-based programs may take place on school campuses in classrooms, gyms and cafeterias, higher-educational institutions, libraries, and makerspaces, such as *FIRST*® Lego League or *FIRST*® Robotics, as well as a number of multipurpose after-school programs that support academics and provide enrichment opportunities.

Museums also vary significantly in size and type of facility in part due to the ways in which they receive monetary support (i.e., government support at local, state, and federal levels; earned income; donations or endowments; and grants) and in part because they exist in and serve communities of every size and shape (IMLS, 2019). The physical footprint of museums ranges significantly. Physical space notwithstanding, museum facilities, resources, and capacity vary as well, whether related to dedicated access to tools and equipment for development of exhibits, or materials and supplies available to visitors, or opportunities to develop novel or innovative programs (see Box 5-6 for variations on makerspaces in museums).

Brick and mortar libraries continue to have a presence in communities, according to a survey conducted by the Pew Research Center (Zickuhr, Rainie, and Purcell, 2013). Libraries have evolved from quiet places to active learning places that encourage play-based learning, gaming, and interaction (Hassinger-Das et al., 2020). Some libraries have dedicated teens/children sections, while some have learning labs, computer labs, makerspaces, and

---

[11]It is worth noting that much of this discussion predates COVID-19.

BOX 5-6
Museum Makerspaces and Variations

In recent years, museum-based makerspaces have revealed creative approaches to working within or around space and facility issues, while simultaneously continuing to work within the expectations and parameters of any programming. Because the physical environment is important to learning, issues of space and facilities—not necessarily the size or resources available but rather the design and utilization of—are critical. Brahms and Crowley (2016) note, "As the field of informal learning embraces making as an essential aspect of the museum experience, designers, educators, and evaluators must reconsider . . . the ways in which the designed environment must change to support such learning" (p. 18). Makerspaces also bring in new design elements to consider, such as power availability, tool use, safety guidelines, bandwidth needs, and highly facilitated programming. The Fort Worth Museum of Science and History (Fort Worth, TX), like other museums, employs a pop-up model for its maker programming, utilizing existing spaces to offer new and unique programming once a month. Serving early learners, the Bay Area Discovery Museum (Sausalito, CA) created a Try It Truck, an "engineering lab-on-wheels," that can deliver programming outside of its museum walls, reaching new audiences at other educational institutions and community organizations.

SOURCE: Committee generated. For more information on the Fort Worth Museum of Science and History program, see https://www.fwmuseum.org/learn/make. More information on the Try It Truck program is available at https://bayareadiscoverymuseum.org/school-community-programs/visits-to-your-school/try-it-truck.

---

recording studios; these spaces vary tremendously as potential learning environments that support authentic experiences (see Box 5-7 on Chicago YOUMedia). While some libraries have received funding from IMLS and/or their states, many do not; hence the space for learners often varies based on funding, support, and the size of the libraries. Some libraries have used their limited spaces creatively for computing opportunities for youth, conducted programs at partner organizations' sites, or brought programs to the places where youth already go, such as community centers, juvenile detention centers, etc. (ALA, 2019).

In 2012 and 2013, IMLS and the MacArthur Foundation funded the design, development, and implementation of Learning Labs in museum and library spaces around the United States.[12] These dedicated spaces were

---

[12]For more information on the Learning Labs program, see https://www.imls.gov/assets/1/AssetManager/LearningLabsReport.pdf.

BOX 5-7
Chicago YOUMedia

The trend of setting up learning labs was inspired by the learning lab site, Chicago YOUMedia, which began as a teen digital learning space at the central library branch and is now available at 23 locations across the Chicago Public Library System and Chicago high schools. Funded by John D. and Catherine T. MacArthur Foundation, Pearson Foundation, Chicago Public Library Foundation, and City of Chicago, YOUMedia offers a "hangout," "messing around," and "geek out" space for teens to develop skills in digital media, making, and STEM (Larson et al., 2013). Using funding from IMLS, more learning labs in libraries were established across the United States. These new sites are intended to replicate Chicago's YOUMedia in some manner, but are also designed to make unique contributions to the learners in the respective communities.

SOURCE: Committee generated. For more information on the Chicago YOUMedia program, see Larson et al. (2013) and https://www.chipublib.org/programs-and-partnerships/youmedia.

---

focused on supporting a community of learners engaged in collaborative, hands-on, interest-driven learning across many types of media, all based in the principles of connected learning. The physical spaces that were created are representative of the thinking and repurposing that a lot of museums and libraries do anyway—renovations of meeting rooms, corners of bike shops and makerspaces, old computer labs developed into places for teen communities. Libraries are often used more as a physical space for experimentation or intervention rather than to develop an intellectual space offering authentic experiences (Garmer, 2014).

LEARNING FACILITATORS

Alongside with the learners and the setting, facilitators are critically important to any authentic learning experience for computing. These are the people who help to shape and foster learners' interests and competencies for computing. What follows is a discussion of the facilitators for each designed setting separately.

Community-Based Organizations

Educators working at community-based organizations draw from a varied set of backgrounds, experiences, and goals. Already, they navigate many of the aforementioned challenges of time, access, technology, and duration that influence the engagement of their learners, and their responsibilities may span a wide range of expectations, from homework help to enrichment to STEM programming. Due to the fragmented nature of the sector (Afterschool Alliance, 2014; Huang and Dietel, 2011; Lauer et al., 2006; Little, Wimer, and Weiss, 2008), the professional development, preparation, and support for instructors and facilitators in community-based organizations is varied and inconsistent as well, and educators do not always have related academic degrees, content-specific knowledge, or education-specific training (Bouffard and Little, 2004; Costley, 1998). Many of these positions are part-time, seasonal, or volunteer opportunities, and some are used as career growth or transition steps, which can result in educators staying only for short tenures (Bowie and Bronte-Tikew, 2006; Fleming, 2012).

In recent decades, marked by an increasingly important role played by OST programming, newer professional development and credentialing programs are being developed for after-school educators. Reports from the National Institute on Out-of-School Time (NIOST) share findings from multiple states on the development and impact of credentialing systems and core competency frameworks. In 2002, the Academy of Educational Development (AED), which had led the National Training Institute for Community Youth Work (NTI), developed the *Advancing Youth Development: A Curriculum for Training Youth Workers* (*AYD*) program. A summary report of an evaluation of its National BEST (Building Exemplary Systems for Training Youth Workers) Initiative, which created a citywide network and professional development systems to support youth workers, was releaased. The report noted that training affected both the pedagogical understandings and practices of facilitators, and that continued, ongoing professional support of facilitators may help to increase the overall positive perception and professionalization of the field. In turn, educators at these community-based organizations feel more connected, more valued, and more likely to remain in their positions with opportunities for professional growth and sustainment.[13]

Museums

Similarly, museum educators come to the profession from a diverse set of backgrounds, sometimes with educational training, sometimes with a degree in a specific field of study related to the museum's focus (e.g., art, history, science), sometimes with a combination of the above. However, often many do not have museum-specific training nor computing-specific backgrounds. Across the wide variety of museum settings, educators vary

---

[13]For more information, see http://scs.fhi360.org/publications/best.pdf.

widely in their practices, do not necessarily have the same set of responsibilities or roles, do not often have a shared pedagogical background or training, and may even conceive of learning differently from one another or from the educators—both inside and outside of the museum—with whom they work (Bevan and Xanthoudaki, 2008; Tran, 2006; Tran and King, 2007). Many studies show that museum educators are often basing their teaching and guidance on their own experiences, which are typically drawn from school settings (Crowley, Pierroux, and Knutson, 2014).

In addition to the complexity of educator roles in the museum profession, it is important to note *who* is involved in the delivery of such authentic experiences (Crowley, Pierroux, and Knutson, 2014; Hooper-Greenhill, 2013). Leaders and staff members of museums and cultural institutions are often unreflective of the demographics of the populations with respect to race, ethnicity, and socioeconomic status they serve or are striving to serve. Jacobs (2019) stated that people of color were far from being represented in internal positions (evidence by a 2018 study[14] that surveyed New York City institutions, such as the Metropolitan Museum of Art) and that the city required city-funded museums to put plans in action to address the problem.

Without a doubt, museum education is its own field of research and study, and much work continues in understanding and clarifying its practices, interrogating its representation, and developing opportunities for professional development. That being said, there have long been opportunities and partnerships for museum educators to support and provide professional development opportunities to other after-school and in-school educators. Numerous museums around the country support curriculum integration and professional development at schools in their regions[15] and more recently around computing (see Box 5-8).[16] An interagency, cross-sector collaboration between IMLS and the Department of Education, which began in 2014 and expanded in 2019, supports science and children's museums to provide curriculum, training, and resources to 21st Century Community Learning Centers (21st CCLC) across the country.[17]

Public Libraries

As highlighted earlier in this chapter, public libraries are venues whose potential for offering authentic experiences for computing could be fur-

---

[14]The study was commissioned by the administration of Mayor Bill de Blasio.

[15]For example, see https://makered.org/making-spaces.

[16]For example, see https://www.hopkinsschools.org/district-news/news/science-museum-embeds-computational-thinking-elementary-curriculum.

[17]For more information on this initiative, see https://www.imls.gov/news/imls-announces-19-million-investment-stem-making-education-underserved-youth and https://y4y.ed.gov/stemchallenge/imls.

BOX 5-8
Museum of Science, Boston

Two examples of research-based computing opportunities in museums involve exhibit design and curriculum development, both coming out of the Museum of Science, Boston. The *Science Behind Pixar* traveling exhibition, which opened in 2015, is one such instance; it was developed as a collaboration between the Museum of Science, Boston and Pixar Animation Studios with support from the National Science Foundation. Development of the exhibition involved a 3-year research study that informed how certain elements and activities engage visitors to develop computing (including computational thinking) and problem-solving skills, interest, and exposure. The overall exhibit showcased the process of filmmaking and the diversity of skills and concepts that filmmakers consider and practice such as storytelling, animations, computational thinking, and math modeling (Mesiti et al., 2019; National Science Foundation, 2015).

Another emerging STEM resource that connects museums and computing is the Museum of Science, Boston's Engineering is Elementary (EiE) curriculum and program for grades preK–8. Started more than 15 years ago and used in all 50 U.S. states and globally, EiE's services include curriculum, professional development for educators, and research and evaluation. Its content is project-based and drawn from constructivist approaches, it promotes problem-solving and other critical 21st century skills, and it is aligned with Next Generation Science Standards, Common Core, and other standards. EiE continues to draw parallels between skills inherent to both engineering and computing, such as problem-solving (NRC, 2012; Whitehouse, 2019).

SOURCE: Committee generated. For additional information on EiE, see https://eie.org/about-engineering-is-elementary-EiE.

---

ther developed. The *Re-envisioning the MLS* report called for "facilitating learning in libraries through making, STEAM, coding, and a range of other activities. This not only promotes information organizations as essential to learning and education, but also enhances youth learning" (Bertot, Sarin, and Percell, 2015, p. v).

There are approximately 140,000 librarians in the United States. Many librarians have a master's degree in library and information science (MLIS)[18] from an ALA-accredited program. However, not all librarians hold a MLIS or hold a MLIS from an accredited institution. IMLS (2019) reports that just over two-thirds of full-time-equivalent librarians hold an ALA-accredited MLIS degree. Libraries serving larger populations had a higher percentage of ALA-accredited MLIS librarians (78.98%) than

---

[18]There is a slight variation in the degree names depending on the institution, including Master's in Library Science, Master's in Information Science, etc.

libraries that serve smaller communities (10.21%) (IMLS, 2019). Library staff also may hold other degrees or, conversely, may not have any higher education.

When it comes to providing authentic experiences to learners in STEM or computing, librarians play a central role. In a nationwide interview and focus group study with 92 public library staff serving youth, Subramaniam and colleagues (2018) found that many librarians already leverage one or more of the connected learning design principles to create their programs because of the typical structure of library programs that often strive to be authentic to youth, interest-driven, fun, and different from "school." There have been calls for librarian preparation programs to train future librarians in these areas. For example, Taylor et al. (2018) calls for the integration of computing in preservice librarian training and examines the nature of such integration in selected preparation courses. This requires a significant change in mindset about what librarians can contribute to the development of interest and competencies in STEM generally, and computing in particular.

Librarian preparation programs are providing training in connected learning, media mentorship, youth learning, and facilitation of STEM programs. This follows the recommendation of the two divisions within the ALA (Association for Library Services for Children [ALSC] and Young Adult Library Services Association [YALSA]) that have developed new competencies for library staff serving learners (see ALSC, 2015; YALSA, 2017). These divisions also provide professional development webinars, short courses, conferences, training, and published guidelines for librarians serving learners in public libraries—some free and some for a fee. But while some librarian preparation programs have included such content and some institutions are in the process of doing this, such integration is not prevalent.

Another primary challenge is that library staff members who interact with learners may not have received any training in working with these populations. Another pervasive problem is where libraries provide access to technologies (Davis et al., 2018; Subramaniam et al., 2018) but are not used to provide or facilitate authentic experiences for computing that promote the success of learners typically underrepresented in computing. This can happen when library staff are not aware of the connected learning principles to create technology-enabled learning environments or are unable to connect with other networks that support such endeavors (Ito et al., 2020).

In the face of these challenges, library staff often assume the following approaches when they lack the training or background needed to provide authentic experiences to learners: (1) developing partnerships with institutions and individuals that have expertise, such as science centers, universities, and industries (Garmer, 2014; Zhou et al., 2019); (2) developing skills in mentoring, rather than being an expert who teaches STEM or computing skills by embracing roles such as facilitator and co-learner (Clegg and Subramaniam, 2018; Ito et al., 2020; Tripp, 2011); and (3) training and encouraging peer mentorship and near-peer mentors (Martin, 2017; Vickery, 2014).

MEASURING OUTCOMES

Recently developed efforts focused on evaluation and assessment of learning outcomes in and across museums, libraries, and makerspaces have been pushing research to address many of the evolving questions and needs emerging in these spaces. These projects include development of frameworks (Cun, Abramovich, and Smith, 2019; Wardrip et al., 2016) and observational tools (Martin et al., 2019), as well as investigation of documentation (Byrne and Louw, 2020) and portfolio practices (Peppler, Keune, and Chang, 2018).

Community-based organizations with large national networks and headquarters may have evaluators and program designers on staff, but for educators and facilitators, measuring outcomes is not often a priority, nor do on-site staff have sufficient training or support to gather data and interpret it for their own use (Murchison et al., 2019). Programs also vary widely in their focus (STEM and computing versus academic support) and the rigor of their methods, varying from program to program and location to location, so determining effectiveness is not consistent across the whole field (Lauer et al., 2006; McComb and Scott-Little, 2003; Scott-Little, Hamann, and Jurs, 2002). A RAND Corporation analysis on *The Value of Out-of-School Time Programs* reports that examining program effectiveness writ large can be flawed because "programs are often grouped together without regard for their goals (e.g., improve academic performance, promote positive social skills, or decrease substance use), content, or the measurable outcomes programming might produce" (McCombs, Whitaker, and Yoo, 2017, p. 2).

High-quality research and evaluation studies are limited. Specifically with regard to STEM and computing programs based in community organizations, the quantity and quality of peer-reviewed research is small, especially compared to the evidence base within the formal K–12 system, in part because the OST sector is fragmented. Significantly, there is also far less funding available for research and evaluation, compared to that available for the K–12 school settings (Fredricks and Eccles, 2006; Krishnamurthi, Ballard, and Noam, 2014; Lauer et al., 2006; Weinberg, Basile, and Albright, 2011). The body of research and evaluation on STEM outcomes is continuing to grow, as community-based organizations and the national networks that connect them (e.g., Afterschool Alliance, National Institute for Out-Of-School Time, National Afterschool Association, among others) support development of frameworks, review and report more consistently on program impacts, and offer guidance and tools to train and elevate evaluation for program providers. For example, *FIRST*®, in partnership with Brandeis University, is in its fifth year of a longitudinal study to measure and understand outcomes related to STEM, including interests, attitudes, career trajectory, and workforce skills (Melchoir et al., 2019).

The programmatic efforts, outcomes, and research on community-based organizations focused specifically on providing authentic experiences in computing are expanding and evolving. As noted in the K–12 Computer Science Framework, released in 2016, "informal education organizations are essential to the CS education ecosystem and should be included as critical stakeholders in state and district implementation efforts" (pp. 167–168). But a resource guide from the Afterschool Alliance,[19] does not mince words when it says

> Computer science education of course requires access to technology, internet connectivity, and funding. But beyond that, we know that it's especially challenging to find qualified staff and curriculum specifically designed for the out-of-school time environment. The same levels of professional development and variety of quality curriculum just don't exist for computer science in the same way it does for the other STEM topics like science and engineering. (p. 1)

Clarified definitions and outcomes, reports and guidance, curriculum and activities, professional development and coaching, and funding are being developed by researchers, OST staff, and professional organizations to support the design, implementation, and evaluation of such efforts, ultimately ensuring computing experiences are readily available, accessible, and of high quality.[20]

Museums and libraries take different approaches to establishing and measuring learning outcomes. There is little consistent evidence and research in museum settings specific to interest, outcomes, and trajectories related to computing. Research on museums over the past few decades still seeks to better understand and clarify the complex nature and outcomes of learning that may happen within and in connection with museums (Falk and Dierking, 2018). Though there have been museum studies in the past decade looking broadly at STEM learning experiences and learner outcomes, they are often focused on short-term programming, commonly related to museum visits and field trips, and evidence generally related to STEM, such as attitudes, content knowledge, and skills (Chi, Dorph, and Reisman, 2015).

---

[19] Available at http://afterschoolalliance.org//documents/AfterschoolCS_ResourceGuide_2017.pdf.

[20] For more information, see http://afterschoolalliance.org/documents/Growing_Computer_Science_Education_2016.pdf.

Some museums have their own internal research and evaluation teams or departments (e.g., The Exploratorium, Children's Museum of Pittsburgh) and lead research or research-practice partnerships to better investigate key questions in the field and the impact of their own programming and designs (Association of Science and Technology Centers, 2020; IMLS, 2008). The informal science education field is also supported by the Center for the Advancement of Informal Science Education (CAISE), which originated in 2007 and is funded through the NSF Advancing Informal STEM Learning (AISL) Program. With regard to evaluation, CAISE provides a wealth of resources and guidance for evaluating informal science education efforts.[21]

Libraries have a compounding problem of measuring outcomes, due to the lack of standardization of duration and format, the complexity of assessment of connected learning in the design of authentic experiences (Ito et al., 2020), and the skills that librarians need to design evaluation plans to capture these much-needed outcomes. Information shared by librarians in practitioner literature attests to the importance of libraries as sites where authentic experiences in STEM and computing occur. Libraries continue to count activities and use attendance as a measure of their use and effectiveness in this digital era. However, the Aspen Institute (Garmer, 2014) calls for librarians to think about the long-term public library sustainability by "becoming more skilled at measuring outcomes rather than counting activities." Libraries use surveys and focus groups to assess participants about the content and goals of specific programs. The Capturing Connected Learning in Libraries team has developed some sample case studies of evaluation of connected learning programs with large public library systems and with small and rural library branches, and have created tools such as observations, talk-back boards, and staff surveys (Allen et al., 2020; Penuel, Chang-Order, and Michalchik, 2018). These evaluation case studies are a start toward capturing outcomes resulting from authentic experiences; however, these evaluation studies are not relatable to small and rural libraries that often serve communities that lack resources.

EXPERIENCES THAT CUT ACROSS SETTINGS

The committee recognizes that learners exist within an ecosystem of relationships, opportunities, and contexts; no learning experience is completely isolated from others. It is important to consider some of the genres that can occur in and outside of school spaces within this ecosystem. This section is intended to signal the committee's recognition of topics that were beyond the scope of the charge to review in depth and in some cases lacking a robust research base. The committee calls attention to the fact that

---

[21] See https://www.informalscience.org/what-evaluation-0.

educational research, particularly studies of learning outcomes in home and online youth-driven settings, is sparse. The research that does exist tends to center on social and cultural studies of media, Internet, and youth culture, rather than educational research. What follows is a brief review of online gaming and creative communities and STEM competitions.

Online Gaming and Creative Communities

Even as engineering, coding, and computer science have made inroads into the K–12 curriculum and after-school and summer programming, children's exposure to technology is dominated by their recreational experiences playing computer games and engaging in digital platforms such as YouTube, Instagram, TikTok, and Snapchat.[22] Studies have documented how youth have developed coding and digital creation skills and interests in authentic communities of practice by tinkering MySpace profiles (Perkel, 2010), modding games (Kow and Nardi, 2010; Kow, Young, and Tekinbas, 2014), creating online videos (Lange, 2014), and "geeking out" in varied communities of interest online (Ito et al., 2018; 2019). Exposure to and sustained interaction with augmented reality through apps such as Pokémon Go may also provide opportunities to develop interest in computing; however, Layland et al. (2018) point out that White women as well as Black men and women have limited opportunities to participate. Given the limited lifespan of mobile apps, there continues to be a need for social justice in digital leisure activities (Layland et al., 2018).

Many entertainment-oriented games are explicitly designed to encourage digital making, algorithmic thinking, coding, and remixing. This genre of game was piloted by games such as SimCity, Rollercoaster Tycoon, Civilization, and the Sims, where players can tinker with worlds and algorithms to "grow" cities, theme parks, and families. Studies have documented how commercial games in these genres have fostered technical interests and skills (Ito, 2009; Squire, 2006). More recently, games such as Little Big Planet, Minecraft, and Roblox offer both tools and platforms for communities to make, code, and play together (Dezuanni, O'Mara, and Beavis 2015; Rafalow and Tekinbas, 2014; Ringland et al., 2017). In recent years, these gaming platforms that support player-level making, coding, and tinkering have become increasingly central to young people's growing up.

Many digital games and platforms have engaged youth who may feel excluded or disengaged from STEM or computing in school or other educator-led settings. This genre provides contexts that foster personally authentic computing experiences for youth who may not connect to pro-

---

[22]For more information about teen use of media, see https://www.commonsensemedia.org/research/the-common-sense-census-media-use-by-tweens-and-teens-2019.

fessionally authentic experiences in school. At the same time, youth-led settings of play often reproduce existing cultural and gender divisions and status hierarchies in young people's peer networks. It is widely recognized that tech-savvy gaming communities are more often unwelcoming to women and girls.

These large-scale digital creation, play, and coding platforms and communities are dominated by commercial tools, with at least one notable exception. The Scratch platform (see Box 7-7), launched at the MIT Media Lab and now stewarded by a non-profit with more than 50 million registered users, has been used to connect from homes, schools, and community organizations. Learning institutions have also adopted and adapted commercial tools and platforms such as SimCity, Civilization, Minecraft, and Roblox, seeking to build bridges between recreational pursuits and the interests and skills that young people are developing in their home (Takeuchi and Vaala, 2014).

STEM Competitions

Competitions for young learners are a prominent feature within STEM and computing, coming in a great variety of forms, with substantial differences in intended audience, goals, organizational structure, rules, and atmosphere. Competitions are an important part of many learning ecosystems, crossing as they do between various physical and performative domains, and mediating between different disciplines and modes of learning. Some research exists on a number of different competitions (Hendricks, Alemdar, and Ogletree, 2012; Nugent et al., 2016; Veety et al., 2018; Woszczynski and Green, 2017). The committee offers here a brief overview of the competition landscape for learners, with a particular focus on how competitions engage with the challenges of authenticity, equity, and learning outcomes.

The concept of "competition" is not uniform, even among contest organizers; the lack of consensus and the differences in conceptual framing and terminology have implications for equitable access, inclusivity, and authentic experience. Psychologists, sociologists, and educational theorists—among others—have long explored whether and how competition may foster or hinder learning and other positive youth development outcomes, with findings that support various suppositions based at least in part on the nature and setting of a given competition (Dillenbourg, 1999; Johnson and Johnson, 2009; Kochanek et al., 2019; Torres and Hager, 2007).

Miller, Sonnert, and Sadler (2018) concluded that "students who participate in STEM competitions are more likely to express interest in a STEM-related career at the end of high school than are students who do not participate," and, as a result, "competitions are an effective way to foster career interest in specific STEM careers" (p. 95). However, it is worth pointing out that this may not be surprising as competitions typically include learners who self-select and have the resources to opt into these experiences. One concern observers have raised is that formal competitions may serve as gatekeepers, privileging those who have deeper educational and financial resources and perpetuating dominant forms of authenticity and STEM/computing culture (Mabey, Lande, and Jordan, 2016; Schank, 2015; Zimmer, 2016).[23] By contrast, a study of the Air Force's Cyberpatriot program indicated active engagement by learners whose families have lower incomes (Brough, 2016), suggesting opportunities to design competitions that attract a more diverse set of youth.[24] There does not appear to be much research to determine how best to meet such concerns, especially with respect to learners from minoritized communities.

It is important to note that there may be distinct differences relating to inclusivity and authenticity even *within* a given competition, for instance, *between* its various levels and cohorts. Suggesting what might need to be changed, one recent study of robotics competitions by Witherspoon et al. (2016) found that

> in the youngest groups/entry-level competitions, girls were heavily involved in programming. Unfortunately, in older/more advanced competitions, girls were generally less involved in programming, even after controlling for prior programming experience . . . While robotics competition experiences may motivate students to learn more programming, gender gaps in programming involvement persist in these learning environments and appear to widen as students grow older and enter more advanced competitions. Therefore, addressing gender imbalances in programming will likely require greater attention to particular curricular and pedagogical characteristics of robotics competitions that support girls' interest and involvement in programming. (p. 18)

Partly as a response to perceptions that traditional science fairs may be too rigidly structured and too tightly knit to existing STEM norms, in the past two decades a host of other competitive formats have emerged, including hackathons, game jams, maker faires, and tech showcases. Examples include Games for Change Student Challenge, Emoti-Con run by The Hive NYC Learning Network, hackathons run by Black Girls Code, S.T.E.A.M.

---

[23] For more information by Education Development Center on Taking Science Fairs to the Test, see https://www.edc.org/putting-science-fairs-test.

[24] It should be cautioned that some of these programs have been compared to school-based pathways such as career and technical education, in that these programs may reach more diverse learners but may lead to lower-wage pathways into computing. Moreover, it should be acknowledged that there are criticisms surrounding the military's role in STEM education, particularly when targeting minoritized communities (i.e., learners of color and those with lower incomes) (Vossoughi and Vakil, 2018).

Achievers Purpose Hackathons, Regeneron International Science & Engineering Competition, the Academy of Applied Science's Young Inventor competitions in northern New England, and Technovation's global competitions for families and for girls.

The newer formats emphasize collaboration, learner- and/or community-based identification of the challenge to be addressed, and open-ended, design- and engineering-oriented processes for meeting the challenge. Many of the newer formats include young learners generating ideas for the competition and serving as competition (co-)organizers, peer mentors and judges; many actively reach out to families whose members have never or only very seldom participated in competitions of these sorts. The newer formats do not eschew competition but stress the team element of the contest and emphasize the shared competition against the external challenge (e.g., create and program together a sensing device that will help your school's physical plant use less energy) and against the clock (e.g., do so within this specified 8 hours).

Given the novelty and wide variety of game jams, hackathons, and the like, relatively little research has yet been done to discover what works best and why, and how best practices might be replicated, specifically for young learners and with a focus on authenticity and equity issues. Some initial findings from small sample sizes (including from collegiate settings that may nevertheless apply to secondary environments) include increased interest and retention in computing and tech-related subjects, resulting from students' increased sense of community and their opportunity to craft for themselves an identity within STEM and/or computer science (Arya et al., 2019; Fowler et al., 2016; Lara, Lockwood, and Tao, 2015; Munro, 2015; Pe-Than et al., 2018; Porter et al., 2017; Trainer and Herbsleb, 2014).

SUMMARY

Exposure to authentic experiences for computing occurs in a variety of settings, including youth development programs, museums, libraries, STEM competitions, and home-based and online communities. This chapter presented what is known about the role of educator-designed OST settings—particularly community-based programs, museums, and libraries—in fostering access to authentic experiences for computing.

Although OST experiences have the potential to provide broad access to authentic experiences for computing, there are a number of different barriers and constraints to participation. For example, there are inequities associated with the distribution and quality of OST experiences, which include time availability, cost, and transportation, in addition to lack of resources. A number of programs have sought ways to offset costs, offer programs over multiple sessions, and include low-technology or unplugged opportunities. Differences are also observed across the settings in terms of the duration and format of programming, the preparation of program facilitators, and the outcomes being measured. Moreover, although there has been increasing emphasis on access to authentic programs, the links to computing have been less emphasized and are limited.

Overall, programs are beginning to be more intentional in the outcomes being measured in an effort to ensure that programs are effective and that equity-oriented goals are being met. In an effort to reach learners, a number of programs (e.g., Beam Camp, The Clubhouse Network) have attempted to provide authentic experiences for computing that are developed to capitalize upon the shared and personally relevant interests of learners. Some of these activities occur in settings such as online gaming and creative communities as well as STEM competitions. Unfortunately, across all of the settings discussed throughout this chapter, problems remain with reaching learners who have been excluded based on gender, race, ethnicity, or perceived ability. The most prominent limitation to understanding what is happening in these spaces and how these programs are attending to reaching learners from the aforementioned marginalized communities is the lack of programs measuring and *publishing* outcomes.

6

Computing Experiences in Schools

Schools are potentially powerful settings for infusing authentic learning experiences in computing. Learners are required to attend school, which means schools are a setting that reach a broad swath of students. The compulsory nature of schooling, however, can also make it difficult to create opportunities that balance both professional and personal authenticity.

In this chapter, the committee considers computing education in schools in the United States. We begin with an overview of how computing fits into the landscape of the K–12 curriculum and identify concerns about equity and access. We then consider each level of schooling—elementary, middle, and high school—separately, discussing both the current status of computing education at each level and exploring how authentic experiences could be supported. As teachers are the lynchpin for successful computing education, the final sections of the chapter discuss teachers' learning needs for supporting learning in computing.

In describing current trends in education for computing, the committee drew on the 2018 National Survey of Science and Mathematics Education (NSSME+). This survey is one of the few nationally representative, longitudinal surveys of science and mathematics education in the country. For the 2018 data collection, computer science (CS) was added as one of the subjects that representatives of school systems and teachers were asked about (Banilower et al., 2018).[1]

---

[1] For more information on the sampling methods and sample sizes, see Appendixes A and B of the Horizon report. The final sample for CS teachers consisted of 289 teachers.

OVERVIEW OF COMPUTING IN THE K–12 CURRICULUM

The past decade has seen expansion of access to instruction in computing in schools. The report *State of the States Landscape Report: State-level Policies Supporting Equitable K–12 Computer Science Education* (Stanton et al., 2017) tracks progress toward 10 policy priorities that are seen as central to broadening participation in computer science education. According to this report, in 2017 seven states had publicly accessible K–12 standards for CS content. Eight additional states were engaged in the standards development process. Nine states have dedicated state-level funding to K–12 CS education in fiscal 2016–2017. At least four states had also allocated funding to CS for fiscal 2018–2019. Four states required all public high school to offer at least one CS course. Twenty-three states and DC required that CS be allowed to fulfill a core graduation credit.

A more recent analysis (2019) of state policy in CS education suggests an increase in attention to CS. This analysis reports that 19 states require all high schools to offer CS, and 4 states require CS of all levels to be taught in all public schools. This report also highlights that 34 states have adopted CS learning standards, with another 5 states actively developing learning standards (Code.org, ECEP, and CSTA, 2019).

At all grade levels, instruction in computing can be offered both through stand-alone courses and by integrating computing experiences into courses in other subjects. Teachers' reports suggest that integrating computing into mathematics and science classes is rare (see Table 6-1). At all grade levels, 70 percent or more of mathematics and science teachers report never integrating coding into their courses. While coding is just one aspect of computing, these results to do not provide strong evidence for the presence of computing in science and mathematics classes.

There are disparities in access to learning experiences in computing. Results of the NSSME+ reveal differences in learning opportunities by grade, rates of poverty at a school, and school size (Banilower et al., 2018). Specifically:

- 26 percent of elementary schools offer instruction in computer programming,
- 38 percent of middle schools offer instruction in computer programming,
- 53 percent of high schools offer one or more courses in CS,
- High-poverty high schools (26%) were less likely to offer instruction in CS than low-poverty high schools (46%) (by quartiles), and
- Large high schools (43%) were more likely to offer instruction in CS than small high schools (23%).

TABLE 6-1 Mathematics and Science Classes in Which Teachers Report Incorporating Coding into Mathematics Instruction, by Grade Range

	Elementary	Middle	High
Mathematics			
Never	74 (2.0)	86 (2.1)	89 (1.0)
Rarely (e.g., a few times per year)	15 (1.7)	11 (1.6)	9 (0.9)
Sometimes (e.g., once or twice a month)	7 (1.1)	3 (1.3)	2 (0.4)
Often (e.g., once or twice a week)	3 (0.8)	0 (0.3)	1 (0.2)
All or almost all mathematics lessons	0 (0.3)	0 (0.1)	0 (0.1)
Science			
Never	71 (3.4)	81 (1.9)	89 (1.2)
Rarely (e.g., a few times per year)	16 (2.0)	14 (1.8)	6 (0.9)
Sometimes (e.g., once or twice a month)	11 (2.8)	3 (0.8)	4 (0.8)
Often (e.g., once or twice a week)	3 (0.7)	1 (0.5)	0 (0.1)
All or almost all science lessons	0 (0.0)	0 (0.3)	0 (0.0)

SOURCE: Banilower et al. (2018).

Recent shifts in state approaches to computing education might increase the number of schools that are offering computing education for all learners as part of the core educational curriculum (see Box 6-1).

Knowing whether instruction and courses are available does not provide information about the nature of the students' learning experiences. Course names and descriptions do not always reflect the content of school coursework in computing or the skills of the professional discipline (Margolis et al., 2008). Further, there is variation in the pedagogical preparation of classroom teachers to teach computing and to connect learners to computing in engaging, culturally relevant, and personally meaningful ways. This makes it difficult to know the extent to which students' learning experiences in computing reflect professional and personal authenticity as described by the committee.

The conditions of school facilities, as well as whether learners have access to technical resources at home, also impact CS learning and instruction independently of the particular course or learning experience. One major obstacle in supporting teaching and learning in CS concerns the technology, including devices and connectivity, needed to support learners learning CS. Though 94 percent of school districts meet a minimum speed of Internet access, 6.5 million students, primarily in rural schools, are without access (Mathewson, 2017). Data from the Federal Communications Commission (2015) show that rural areas are less likely to be wired for broadband service

BOX 6-1
Moving Computer Science into the Core of
Chicago Public Schools

Not all policies that support and embed CS instruction into the core curriculum are at the state level. Chicago Public Schools, the third largest school district in the nation, has evolved as the leader in creating systems-level changes to realize the aspiration of providing all learners a CS education. In fact, beginning with 2020, all learners in high school are required to successfully complete an introductory CS course in order to graduate. This course requirement has reflected a decade of collaborative leadership in the district among teachers, district leaders, higher education, computing educational organizations, and city officials.

A decade ago, computing education opportunities were scarce in most schools, and when learning opportunities were offered, they were in selective STEM schools in the district. In 2008, a group of Chicago teachers were attending a Computer Science Education conference in Oregon. They independently attended a panel discussion of the Association for Computing Machinery's Education Policy Committee about the need to expand and broaden K–12 CS education. One of the teachers stood up and asked who he might work with to address this issue in Chicago, connecting him with other Chicago teachers in the room, the Computer Science Teachers Association community, and ultimately, higher education faculty with shared visions of expanding an equitable vision of CS for all. Members of this growing local community of educators attended the Exploratory Computer Science (ECS) professional development offered for Los Angeles teachers in 2010, and deciding that it was an ideal fit for Chicago Public Schools, successfully obtained a series of grant awards from the National Science Foundation to initially offer, then scale, this course and associated professional development in Chicago. The leaders of this movement note that the failures allowed for learning that systemic change requires trust and the need to develop relationships along the way.

Along with this bottom-up approach led by educators and centering on curriculum and professional development, creating systemic change also required the support of city and school district leadership. In announcing an initial partnership with Code.org in December of 2013, the mayor and Chicago Public Schools CEO established a 5-year goal to provide CS learning pathways in high schools. Along with this goal to scale ECS courses to each high school, a robust CS education district team has been created to support and sustain these district-wide teaching and learning efforts while expanding learning pathways into K–8 classrooms. Leadership also elevated computing to a "core subject" district-wide. Galvanizing this top-down institutional and political support has been critical for realizing the wide-scale vision that was initially sparked by a group of Chicago teachers.

With the majority of all learners taking CS, the school district, evaluators, and researchers are collecting additional data on the supports and impact of systemic changes in computing education that will further the district's stated equity goals of reaching "for all" (Dettori et al., 2018).

SOURCES: Committee generated based on Reed et al. (2015) and Dettori et al. (2018).

and tend to have slower connectivity compared to other areas of the country. Given that computing education often depends on digital devices, disruptions in access to using the Internet or other technology tools and supports has a profound impact on the instruction for learners. In fact, high school CS teachers reports that lack of reliable access to the Internet (19% of teachers), lack of support to maintain technology (34% of teachers), and lack of functioning computing devices (27% of teachers) have a negative impact on their instruction (Banilower et al., 2018). Further, teachers also report that security measures, such as school restrictions on the Internet, also inhibit their instruction of CS (37% of teachers). Given the remote learning challenges that were starkly exposed by the COVID-19 pandemic, having access to devices and steady Internet, in any learning setting, is essential for student learning.

In addition to instruction and courses that are part of the curriculum, schools offer a range of activities during the school day and after school to engage students in computing. Results of the NSSME+ offer a window into the kinds of activities available and how their availability varies by grade level (see Table 6-2). These activities are another setting for providing access to authentic learning experiences in computing. They also offer opportunities to foster connections between students' computer learning experiences in and out of school.

COMPUTING IN ELEMENTARY AND MIDDLE SCHOOL

In both elementary and middle school, learning experiences in computing can be offered through both stand-alone classes and integration of computing in classes in other subjects. That said, as indicated in the previous section, integrating computing into mathematics and science appears to be relatively rare. However, there are projects at both the elementary and middle school levels that show the promise of integration.

Elementary School

As noted in the previous section, only 26 percent of elementary schools report offering instruction in computing (Banilower et al., 2018), suggesting that most learners in the United States do not encounter computing education in elementary schools. In fact, widespread efforts to provide computing experiences in the elementary grades are relatively recent. As a result, there is limited research on students' learning experiences in computing in K–5 classrooms. But the research and reports that do include elementary school teachers shed important light on the features and availability of computing education for younger children in schools.

A school-wide study of computing education at a high-poverty elementary school shows the potential of an integrated approach. The school com-

TABLE 6-2 School Programs and Practices to Enhance Students' Interest and/or Achievement in Computer Science, by Grade Range (percentage of schools)

Programs/practices	Elementary	Middle	High
Holds family computer science nights	15 (2.0)	8 (1.5)	5 (1.0)
Offers after-school help in computer science (e.g., tutoring)	14 (1.8)	20 (2.1)	31 (2.8)
Offers formal after-school programs for enrichment in computer science	21 (2.3)	21 (2.6)	15 (1.8)
Offers one or more computer science clubs	22 (2.4)	25 (2.3)	29 (2.2)
Participates in Hour of Code	38 (2.8)	34 (2.8)	27 (2.6)
Participates in a local or regional computer science fair	11 (1.9)	13 (2.1)	12 (1.5)
Has one or more teams participating in computer science competitions (e.g., USA Computer Science Olympiad)	6 (1.3)	10 (1.5)	15 (1.6)
Encourages students to participate in computer science summer programs or camps offered by community colleges, universities, museums, or computer science centers	38 (2.9)	44 (3.3)	51 (2.6)
Coordinates visits to business industry and/or research sites related to computer science	14 (2.3)	22 (2.8)	30 (3.0)
Coordinates meetings with adult mentors who work in computer science fields	14 (2.0)	18 (2.1)	22 (1.9)

SOURCE: Banilower et al. (2018).

mitted to integrating computational thinking into instruction school-wide. Seven teachers and two administrators were chosen as focal cases for the study; four were classroom teachers and three taught special subjects (i.e., art, technology, library/media). All four participating elementary classroom teachers in the study chose to integrate computing lessons into science and mathematics curriculum (Israel et al., 2015a). The teachers suggested that the primary reason they successfully integrated computing education in their classrooms was because integration did not require additional instructional time already designated for other subjects. In contrast, the instructional specialists focused more on discrete computing skills, using CS unplugged activities, Code.org resources, and Scratch tutorials.

Adopting an interdisciplinary approach to teaching computing can encourage teachers to draw upon their existing content knowledge to make connections to computing-related concepts and skills. In fact, teachers are eager to know more about effective ways to integrate computing into other

K–5 subjects (Roberts, Prottsman, and Gray, 2018). While teachers might be able to begin imagining these interdisciplinary connections, however, a qualitative study of teachers from one school district reveals teachers' concerns about integrating computing into their teaching due to limited class time and having difficulty identifying instances in which connections could be made between computing and science and computing and mathematics (Rich, Yadav, and Schwartz, 2019). Another potential obstacle is the perceived mismatch between the accepted best practices across disciplines.

Even with these impediments, elementary teachers point to benefits they appreciate for their learners as a result of teaching CS, including their learners' interest in computing, capacity in problem-solving, improvements in learners' attitudes and confidence, and an increased resilience to stick with problems, even after missteps or iterative failures (Rich et al., 2019). Similarly, a study probing elementary computing education paired together preservice teachers and undergraduate CS learners to collaborate with elementary classroom teachers to design and deliver 10 hours of instruction, over 10 weeks, in two districts chosen due to their "suburban and rural settings with participants from culturally diverse and economically disadvantaged backgrounds" (Tran, 2018, p. 8). The research revealed learning gains in specific CS concepts related to algorithm, loops, and debugging, as well as increased interest in computing, and positive dispositions around perseverance.

Middle School

As noted above, only 38 percent of middle schools offer instruction in computing. Greater than 80 percent of middle school mathematics and science teachers report never integrating coding into their classes (see Table 7.1; Banilower et al, 2018).

There are promising examples, however, for integrating computing into other subjects (Basu et al., 2016; Grover, 2011; Sengupta et al., 2013; Weintrop et al., 2016). Bootstrap, a curriculum that supports learners in programming a video game of their own design, integrates programming concepts into algebra, physics, and data science instruction (Schanzer et al., 2015). With the focus on algebra, Bootstrap has been used at both the middle school and high school levels. This curriculum has goals in terms of increasing learners' interest and knowledge about CS, but also has goals that facilitate the improvement of problem-solving around algebra word problems (Schanzer et al., 2015; Schanzer, Fisler, and Krishnamurthi, 2018). Schanzer and colleagues (2015) reported that learners exhibited some evidence of transfer of learning when provided with the opportunity to take Bootstrap as compared to a control group (that had not taken Bootstrap). Similarly, Project GUTS approaches computing education through the integration of week-long curricular units on agent-based modeling in middle school science classrooms (Lee et al., 2011). Both of these middle-school oriented computing curriculum offer professional development (PD) to support teacher integration of these learning resources; however a limitation of this work is the degree to which transfer of learning can occur between computing and other content areas (Schanzer et al., 2015).

There are potentially some organizational advantages to integrating computing into other courses instead of creating a stand-alone course. For example, an integrated approach does not require making space in the schedule or hiring additional staff. Indeed, one study of Utah's middle school teachers noted that teachers have difficulty "fitting" CS into their teaching schedules and into the selection of learners' elective choices (Rich and Hu, 2019). However, these teachers also noted they felt under-prepared and under-supported to teach computing.

Computing in Elementary and Middle School Summary

In sum, less than half of schools across the country are providing robust opportunities to learn computing at the elementary and middle school levels. Integrating computing into other courses, such as mathematics and science, seems like a promising approach. However, teachers need opportunities to develop the knowledge and skill to support this integration.

Further, little is known about the nature of the learning experiences themselves in elementary and middle school. This makes it difficult to assess whether they incorporate features that the committee might consider to be either professionally or personally authentic. It does appear, however, that there may be missed opportunities to incorporate authentic experiences for computing at the elementary and middle school levels.

COMPUTING IN HIGH SCHOOL

High schools have a long history of including computing education in the curriculum, mainly as stand-alone computing or CS courses. Recent years have seen a shift from computing-related courses being offered only in advanced, enrichment spaces toward computing being offered as a core part of a well-rounded school curriculum for all learners.

Making space for CS within an already-crowded secondary school curriculum has been variable across U.S. public schools (Banilower et al., 2018; Nager and Atkinson, 2016). State and district policies diverge in their requirements and awarding of academic credit toward graduation for learners who complete high school CS courses. According to survey responses from NSSME+, in three-quarters of high schools, even when CS courses are offered, they are considered "elective" in that they are not required for graduation and only a small percentage allow CS to count toward graduation requirements in other subjects (Banilower et al., 2018). Only 1 percent of schools require 2–4 years of coursework in CS for graduation, 17 percent of schools require 1 year of coursework, and 8 percent of schools require a semester of coursework (Banilower et al., 2018). Further, some schools apply academic coursework in CS toward other disciplinary graduation requirements. The NSSME+ study notes that CS counts toward a mathematics graduation requirement in 15 percent of schools, as a science graduation requirement in 12 percent of schools, and as a foreign language requirement in 7 percent of schools.

High schools offer a variety of courses in computing or CS (see Table 6-3). These include courses for which students may receive college credit (AP, IB, and dual enrollment) as well as those that do not qualify for college credit. As noted in the overview section of the chapter, the availability of learning opportunities in computing are not proportionately distributed across high schools. Instead, these opportunities are more prevalent in schools enrolling learners from high-income communities as well as schools in which the majority are White, especially for advanced high school courses (Banilower et al., 2018).

Advanced Placement Courses in Computer Science

In general, AP courses, including CS courses, are offered by the College Board to provide advanced learning opportunities at the secondary school level. Learners who score particular grades on an end-of-course exam might have the opportunity to earn college credit, depending on the college they go on to attend. For CS there are two courses offered: Computer Science A

TABLE 6-3 High Schools Offering Computer Science and Technology Courses

Course	Percentage of Schools
Advanced Placement (AP) computer science courses	21 (1.6)
International Baccalaureate (IB) computer science courses	1 (0.4)
Concurrent college and high school credit/dual enrollment computer science courses	19 (1.9)
Computer technology courses that do not include programming	47 (2.4)
Introductory high school computer science courses that include programming but do not qualify for college credit	36 (2.4)
Specialized/elective computer science courses with programming as a prerequisite that do not qualify for college credit	21 (1.7)

SOURCE: Banilower et al. (2018).

(CSA) and Computer Science Principles (CSP). Nager and Atkinson (2016) have shown that there is a lack of women and minorities not only taking these courses, but also taking the exam.

Though these advanced courses are important in many computing education high school pathways, the distribution of AP courses across school sites is uneven, privileging large, suburban and urban, and more affluent schools. Specifically, studies have demonstrated the following inequities in course availability (Banilower et al., 2018; Scott et al., 2019):

- Large schools are more likely to have AP CS than small schools;
- Rural schools are less likely than suburban or urban schools to offer AP CS; and
- High-poverty schools are less likely than low-poverty schools to offer AP CS.

Computer Science A

CSA, first introduced in 1984, aims to give learners a comparable experience to a first-semester undergraduate CS course. The course focuses on object-oriented programming and data structures, with Java as the primary emphasis and designated programming language of the course (College Board, 2014). Though the AP CSA course has been offered for decades, until recently the number of test takers was relatively low compared to other AP mathematics and science courses, with only 15,000 learners taking the test a decade ago (College Board, 2008). Since then, participation in the AP CSA exam has surged with a student participation growth rate of between 9 percent and 26 percent each year through 2017. In 2017, 60,519 learners completed the AP CSA exam (College Board, 2017), with 5,040 schools across the United States offering the exam.

Within the AP program, of all the AP course offerings across STEM areas, CSA has historically sustained the lowest rates of participation for minoritized populations (Sax et al., 2020). Of test takers in 2017, girls represent 24 percent of participants; Native Americans 0.2 percent of participants, African Americans 4 percent of participants, Latinx learners 12 percent of participants, and Native Hawaiians and Pacific Islanders just 0.1 percent of participants (Sax et al., 2020). Lim and Lewis (2020) recently proposed three metrics for evaluating the impact of state-level initiatives aimed to broaden participation in computing at the high school level.

Enrollment in CSA in high school has been shown to better predict interest and persistence in technology and computing for college women (Weston, Dubow, and Kaminsky, 2019), compared to technology internships or participation in other computing-related activities before college. In fact, a large sample of surveyed college freshman revealed that 28 percent of learners who take AP CSA planned on majoring in computer science (Sax et al., 2020).

Computer Science Principles

In a concerted effort to broaden participation in computing, the College Board and the National Science Foundation joined together in 2008 to design, develop, and implement CSP, described as a more accessible, college-level CS course (Cuny, 2015; Sax et al., 2020). CSP aims to be equivalent to a non-CS major's introduction to computing course.

After 8 years of development and piloting, the course was launched in 2016 (Kamenetz, 2017). In 2017, the first year of the course, more than 44,000 students at 2,625 schools took the exam (College Board, 2017). In 2018, 70,000 students at 4,022 schools took the exam (College Board, 2018).

The focus of the course is on appreciating the big ideas of computer science. The CSP course includes seven core computing concepts (creativity, abstraction, data and information, algorithms, programming, the Internet, and global impact) and six computational practices (connecting computing, creating computational artifacts, abstracting, analyzing problems and artifacts, communicating, and collaborating) (College Board, 2020). In an effort to focus more on the principles and interdisciplinary nature of CS, the course and exam are programming-language agnostic (Nager and Atkinson, 2016), allowing for instructors to select the programming language they deem most appropriate for student success in their own classrooms. Also unique to CSP, in comparison to other AP courses, is a through-course, teacher-supervised, task-based performance assessment (the Create Performance Task: Application to Ideas) that is a portion of a learner's final AP score.

While preliminary evidence suggests that students who enroll in CSP are more diverse with respect to gender, race, and ethnicity (although no differences were observed for some groups) than CSA learners, students who took CSP are less inclined to indicate their intent to pursue CS majors and careers than students who complete CSA (Howard and Havard, 2019; Sax et al., 2020). Even in the specifically-designed-to-broaden-participation AP CSP course, the course has not attracted a heterogenous and representative population of learners that reflects the demographics of learners in public schools. Among the inaugural group of CSP exam-takers in 2017, girls comprised 30 percent of test takers, and only 28 percent of learners were Black, Latinx or Indigenous (College Board, 2017).

Equity in AP Computer Science Courses

Both CSA and CSP are taken predominantly by men, and the number of enrollees is lower in contrast to other AP courses in mathematics and science. In 2019, CSP test takers consisted of 32 percent women with CSA test takers consisting of 24 percent women. In contrast, AP Biology was 62.6 percent women and AP Calculus AB was 49 percent women. Table 6-4 presents the number of test takers in the CS AP exams as compared to other STEM exams, such as Biology and Calculus AB. Overall, the percentages of Black and Latinx learners completing the AP CSA exam were lower, with fairly comparable percentages observed for AP CSP as compared to AP Biology and AP Calculus AB. These patterns in test taking reinforce the known patterns of underrepresentation by race and ethnicity in STEM fields (see Chapter 2).

The Exploring Computer Science Course

The Exploring Computer Science (ECS) course, developed in 2008 with National Science Foundation support, provides a foundational approach to introducing CS to learners with no assumption of prior knowledge or experience in computing. The introductory ECS course's primary goal is to introduce CS at a level that is highly accessible for all high school learners. The goal is to promote equity by engaging a broad range of learners in an inclusive approach to CS to build foundational knowledge about CS. Currently offered in schools across 34 states and Puerto Rico, ECS enrolls about 55,000 learners each year.[2] The ECS course originated in Los Angeles and demographic data from Los Angeles suggests that the ethnic and racial representation matches that of Los Angeles learners more generally, and 43 percent of ECS learners in Los Angeles are girls.[3] These numbers, along with evidence in growth of student efficacy, increased interest in computing, and sense of belonging gains, suggest that this course may successfully engage girls and Black and Latinx learners in CS (Dettori et al., 2016; Goode and Margolis, 2011).

The course includes a complete year-long curriculum with the following possible instructional units: human computer interaction, problem-solving, web design, programming, data and analysis, robotics, electronic textiles, and artificial intelligence. Importantly, the ECS course also includes a 2-year PD program for teachers that focuses on inquiry-based teaching and anti-racist instruction (Goode, Chapman, and Margolis, 2012; Goode, Johnson, and Sundstrom, 2020), as well as a validated and open-ended assessment tool to gauge student learning.

---

[2] For more information, see http://www.exploringcs.org/about/about-ecs.

[3] Additional data and information can be found at https://www.exploringcs.org/for-researchers-policymakers/reports/ecs-enrollment-data.

TABLE 6-4 Contrasting Participation in the 2019 AP CSP and CSA Exams versus AP Biology and AP Calculus AB

	AP CSP	AP CSA	AP Biology	AP Calculus AB
Overall	94,360	64,197	253,212	285,923
Black	6,559 (6.9%)	2,521 (3.9%)	16,484 (6.5%)	14,037 (4.9%)
Latinx	18,601 (19.7%)	7,728 (12.0%)	48,512 (19.2%)	51,365 (18.0%)

NOTE: During this reporting period, 4,930,147 exams were administered. However, it is not known how many individual learners this translates to as a learner can take multiple exams. AP = Advanced Placement, CSA = Computer Science A, CSP = Computer Science Principles. SOURCE: College Board (2019). Data are available at https://secure-media.collegeboard.org/digitalServices/misc/ap/national-summary-2019.xlsx.

Learners who took ECS as their introductory computing course, as compared to more traditional programming-centric computing courses, were twice as likely to go on and take more advanced coursework (McGee et al., 2018). Learners who completed ECS before taking the AP CSA course also out-scored their peers by 1/3 point on the 5-point AP CS A exam (McGee et al., 2019).

The inclusion of e-textiles as part of the ECS curriculum has been a recent (2018) and novel addition as a supplemental unit (Unit 6: Electronic Textiles), done in an effort to incorporate makerspaces in schools, and in particular, to offer tactile approaches to learning that combine computing, circuitry, and crafting. A study that accompanied the introduction of e-textiles unit in 17 ECS classrooms in Los Angeles detailed how teachers adjusted their pedagogical practices to support creativity, connection, and culturally responsive student learning. The study mapped out how rich and equitable teaching practices in computing and making can move learners from initial engagement into more complex projects that deepened their learning experiences. As the study concludes, this approach in placing e-textiles in a project-based computing curriculum with extensive PD for teachers "addresses a piece of the puzzle that has been missing in connecting informal and formal implementations of making activities" (Fields et al., 2018, p. 16).

ECS seems to be a potential context for incorporating authentic experiences in computing that focus more on personal authenticity. The ECS course is designed around project-based learning, engaging learners in learning activities that apply conceptual knowledge and allowing learners to craft original computational creations. The course is aligned with foundational K–12 computing standards; its goal is to reach the general student population through inclusive, equity-based instruction that counters the dominant practices in professionally authentic technology settings.

Career and Technical Education Courses

Career and Technical Education (CTE) courses provide a direct connection with careers and pathways to industry. These high school courses, funded in part by federal Perkins funding, vary greatly between states and schools, yet often have an applied focus to computing curriculum. Examples of these types of courses include professional certification on specific technical competencies that transfer directly to professional work settings such as Networking, Software Engineering, or Cybersecurity. The applied courses in these programs are geared toward learners already interested in technical careers and seek to closely mirror existing workplace tools, knowledge, and skills.

The typical course composition of STEM-related CTE courses suggest they are not gender-inclusive (Lufkin et al., 2007), with girls composing 32 percent of learners nationally in the IT concentration of CTE pathways in (Perkins Data Explorer, 2020). It is worth acknowledging that there was a history of placing learners into a CTE track (Goode, Flapan, and Margolis, 2018); however, both ECS and CSP are also taught as CTE courses.[4]

High School Experiences Summary

Although computing education has had a longer history within high schools as compared to elementary and middle school spaces, primarily as stand-alone courses, CS is typically considered as an elective and not a requirement toward graduation. Moreover, despite efforts to design AP CS courses to address known inequities in learner participation, underrepresentation of women and learners of color persist. The ECS course was designed to introduce learners to computing with no assumption of prior knowledge or experience in computing. This course has shown some promise in promoting equity as findings suggest that learners who complete this course are more likely to go on and take more advanced coursework.

EQUITY AND ACCESS IN COMPUTING IN SCHOOLS

While there have been ongoing efforts to expand learning opportunities for computing in schools, there are still disparities in access and participation. There are multiple factors contributing to these trends.

In secondary schools, classroom teachers are the primary instructors of stand-alone CS classes. The characteristics of high school CS teachers are similar to those of high school science and mathematics teachers in some

---

[4]For more information, see: https://ecepalliance.org/sites/default/files/RethinkingPerkins_Paper.pdf.

areas and markedly different in others (Banilower et al., 2018). Similar to science and mathematics teachers, nearly all high school CS teachers characterize themselves as White (94%), and most are older than 40. In contrast with most K–12 teachers, the majority of CS teachers (60%) are men. The dramatically low numbers of Black, Indigenous, and Latinx teachers represent a missed opportunity in terms of providing learners exposure to role models and pedagogies informed by minoritized perspectives and experiences in computing. In particular, women teachers of color bring important commitments to computing education in terms of serving learners from minoritized communities, connecting to community knowledge, and serving as a role model to their learners (Johnson et al., 2020).

In addition to the problem of lack of diversity among teachers, structural inequalities and bias also play a role. In *Stuck in the Shallow End: Education, Race, and Computing,* Margolis et al. (2008; 2017) detail an ethnographic study examining student access and participation in computing learning across three demographically diverse high schools: an overcrowded urban high school, a math and science magnet school, and a well-funded school in an affluent neighborhood. The study revealed that systemic racism—which impacted learners' access to course offerings, qualified teachers, and school resources, accompanied by educator belief systems about which learners belong in computing classrooms—perpetuated race and gender differences in participation that were reproduced across each of the school sites. Research in this area highlights the importance of examining equity in school settings in terms of access to computing courses, necessary resources, and qualified teachers; as well as examining equity in terms of the quality of learning environments for learners that are characterized by inclusion, encouragement, effective pedagogy, and culturally relevant and responsive curriculum.

Belief systems among educators play an important part in ensuring, or constricting, opportunities for learners. Educators' biased beliefs about who belongs in CS and who might be interested in studying CS often are enacted in ways that reinforce and reify those ideas by guiding White and Asian boys toward—and Black and Latinx learners and girls away from—classroom learning experiences (Goode, Estrella, and Margolis, 2006; Margolis et al., 2017). One response, in this case aimed specifically at school counselors, comes out of the National Center for Women in Technology, which has developed a Counselors for Computing (C4C) program that provides immersive professional development and set of resources to encourage school counselors to understand and advocate for increased CS learning opportunities for learners at their schools (Hug and Krauss, 2016).

Inside high school CS classrooms, multiple features have been identified that signal and support an inclusive learning ecosystem for learners. As first noted in Chapter 2, classroom learning spaces that support collaboration and avoid "geeky" stereotypical signifiers, such as posters or exclusionary discourse patterns, are important for creating a positive learning atmosphere for girls (Goode, Estrella, and Margolis, 2006; Master, Cheryan, and Meltzoff, 2016). When teachers connect computing curriculum to the lived experiences and values of learners (a tenet of culturally responsive teaching), there is strong student engagement, particularly among learners from minoritized groups (Madkins et al., 2019; Ryoo et al., 2013; 2019).

Further, though there is only nascent research, scholars point to the visual nature of programming languages, and also to the tactile nature of creating e-textiles, in supporting the computing learning for English language learners in CS classrooms (Jacob et al., 2018); however, simply relying upon the modality of the activity (i.e., visual and/or tactile) may make these activities inaccessible to some learners (because of impairments). In their study of learners learning computing in a bilingual middle school classroom, Vogel et al. (2019) note that the development of learners' computational literacies are entwined with learners' repertoire of other linguistic and discourse literacies. Their findings suggest that educators should not treat CS education as a fixed learning progression of concepts alongside "remediation" or "differentiation" for emergent bilinguals. Rather, they encourage educators to build upon the varied literacies learners bring to the classroom with potential computational literacies, for both bilingual and monolingual learners (Vogel et al., 2019).

Professional and personal authenticity in learning experiences for computing provide other lenses for understanding the problems of equity in computing. In particular, authenticity has traditionally been considered to be discipline-driven, with experiences designed to reflect the practices of the discipline. As illustrated in Chapter 2, some learners may have stereotypes about the culture of CS—including the kind of people, the work involved, and the values of the field—and the emphasis on the professional practices may steer learners from underrepresented groups from engaging in authentic computing experiences (Cheryan, Master, and Meltzoff, 2015). However, curriculum that leverages learners' interests, identities, and backgrounds (personal authenticity) may encourage increased participation of women, learners of colors, and those with differences in perceived ability (Eglash et al., 2006; Goode, Johnson, and Sundstrom, 2020; Israel et al., 2015a; Ryoo et al., 2020).

PREPARING TEACHERS FOR K–12 COMPUTING CLASSROOMS

The previous section helped to identify spaces in K–12 education where authentic learning experiences in computing could be situated. However, a key piece of doing this successfully is providing teachers with opportunities to develop the necessary knowledge and skills. In fact, the expertise of teachers is a key limiting factor in expanding computing in K–12 more generally, regardless of whether the learning opportunities are authentic in the way the committee has described. In this section we consider the knowledge and experience of the current cadre of computing teachers and describe professional development practices for supporting teachers of computing.

Teachers' Knowledge and Experience in Computing

There are few direct measures of teachers' knowledge of computing. Instead courses taken during preservice preparation, undergraduate degree, area of certification, and previous teaching experiences are all used as proxies for knowledge. In the NSSME+ there are also measures of teachers' confidence in teaching computing.

Elementary and Middle School Teachers

In the United States, fewer than 1 in 4 elementary teachers reported having experience or just a "crash course" in computing before they began teaching computing to their learners. Not surprisingly, this lack of sufficient preparation can leave teachers apprehensive about their own knowledge and skills as they begin to teach computing to learners (Israel et al., 2015a; Rich, Yadav, and Schwarz, 2019). A study of elementary teachers demonstrated that those who participated in continuous professional development around computing and engineering had statistically significant greater confidence in computing after a year than their elementary teacher colleagues who did not have access to this preparation, highlighting the importance of professional development experiences (Rich et al., 2017).

High School Teachers

Scholarship on teacher knowledge in CS suggests that effective computing teachers are able to join together content, engaging pedagogy, knowledge of their learners' identities and backgrounds, and understanding of the school context to support learners in meaningful learning opportunities (Goode and Ryoo, 2019). Yet a recent large-scale survey of STEM teachers (Banilower et al., 2018) indicates that the current cadre of high school CS teachers have variable degrees of experience, knowledge, and capacity in these areas.

Many CS teachers might have significant experience teaching high school but are new to teaching CS. Though nearly half of CS teachers have more than 10 years of experience teaching at the K–12 level, many are novice teachers of CS, with 35 percent of teachers having 0–2 years of experience and 28 percent of teachers having 3–5 years of experience teaching the subject (Banilower et al., 2018). In addition to being new to teaching CS, CS teachers are also teaching outside of their primary areas and/or are teaching CS in addition to other subjects (CSTA, 2015; Yadav et al., 2016).

In terms of content knowledge, only 25 percent of high school computing teachers have degrees in CS. Still, most teachers have participated in CS college courses. In fact, 87 percent of high school teachers had completed at least one class in computing, and two out of three teachers reported completing two or more college courses related to CS. Additionally, 35 percent of responding high school CS teachers reported prior job experience in the field of computing before they became teachers. However, the recency of the courses or job experiences before teaching is unknown.

This experience with content-focused computing courses does not seem to translate to teachers' sense of preparation in teaching CS. In fact, less than 50 percent of high school teachers feel confident in teaching any of the topics[5] associated with high school computing courses, and compared with other STEM teachers, they generally feel less prepared to teach their subject-area content (Banilower et al., 2018).

In terms of pedagogical preparation, of the 84 percent of CS teachers who hold teaching certifications, 44 percent have a CS teacher certification, 34 percent in mathematics, 28 percent in business, 10 percent in engineering, and 9 percent in science (Banilower et al., 2018). Yet, the survey also revealed that fewer than half of high school CS teachers feel prepared to encourage learners or develop capacity in a number of ways, such as encouraging learners' interests in computing (49%), encouraging participation of all learners (45%), developing learners' awareness of STEM careers (36%), or incorporating learners' cultural backgrounds into CS instruction (16%). Given how few states award primary teaching endorsements in CS (see Box 6-2), the majority of preparatory learning opportunities for computing teachers occur in professional development settings for in-service teachers, as will be discussed in further detail below.

Professional Development in Computing for In-Service Teachers

Because most teacher education programs do not offer computing methods courses (Yadav, Stephenson, and Hong, 2014), the primary place for teachers to learn about teaching computing takes place in curriculum-specific professional development sessions. Research on teacher preparation for teaching CS courses highlights the importance of sustained, long-term professional learning experiences that support the emerging content-related and pedagogical needs of teachers (Goode, Margolis, and Chapman, 2014;

---

[5]These topics include algorithms and programming, impacts of computing, computing systems, data and analysis, and networks and the Internet.

Menekse, 2015). This research for CS teachers aligns with earlier research about necessary length and duration of effective professional learning programs for STEM teachers (Loucks-Horsley et al., 2009).

Yet for most schools, professional development opportunities for CS teachers are not plentiful, with only 19 percent of high school teachers noting that they had access to local professional development opportunities in their school or district (see Table 6-5; Banilower et al., 2018). Instead, teachers took advantage of regional or national professional development opportunities and online opportunities to learn about computing education. When computing teachers did participate in professional workshops, they reported that the most common emphases related to understanding and doing CS: deepening their CS content knowledge, including programming (70%); learning how to use programming activities that require a computer (64%); and deepening understanding of how CS is done (63%). Half of CS teachers' professional development has had a substantial focus on implementing the CS curricular materials to be used in their classroom. But only about a quarter of high school computing teachers have participated in professional learning that addresses meeting the needs of learners who are underrepresented based on gender, race, ethnicity, or perceived ability or incorporating learners' cultural backgrounds into CS instruction, despite the known diversity issues in computing education (Banilower et al., 2018). Moreover, there is a lack of professional development that specifically relates to CS pedagogical content knowledge (Yadav and Berges, 2019; Yadav et al., 2016).

In another professional learning structure, instructional coaches who work with teachers within the context of their own classrooms have been shown to be particularly effective in supporting the needs of novice CS teachers as they begin to teach new high school courses in schools (Dettori et al., 2018; Margolis, Ryoo, and Goode, 2017). In fact, in high schools that offer CS, about one in five offer instructional coaches to CS teachers (Banilower et al., 2018).

The dynamic nature of computing can also provide ongoing opportunities for more seasoned computing educators to augment their knowledge and learn to incorporate new technologies. Promising approaches have been demonstrated to recharge (as self-reported by teachers as a renewal in excitement through reflection) the teaching practices of experienced teachers in CS classrooms (Nakajima and Goode, 2019) as they learn to incorporate e-textiles in their classrooms.

In addition to individual professional development around content, pedagogy, and engaging diverse groups of learners, teachers also report deeply valuing their membership in sustained face-to-face and online CS teacher learning communities as a way of learning from peers and breaking the school-level isolation they experience at their schools as the sole com-

BOX 6-2
Teacher Certification

Few states currently offer CS teacher certification. A 2017 report from Code. org mentions only two explicitly.[a] The Home4CS report *Priming the Computer Science Teacher Pump*[b] (DeLyser et al., 2018) tells us that only 2 out of 50 states and the District of Columbia (4%) require CS certification/licensure for teachers to teach any CS course, and only 7 states (14%) require it to teach AP Computer Science.

To get a sense of trends in teacher certification in the United States, the landscape reports issued by the Expanding Computing Education Pathways (ECEP) Alliance can be useful. The ECEP Alliance is funded by the National Science Foundation (NSF) to broaden participation in computing education by supporting states in implementation efforts.[c] ECEP encourages its member states to prepare landscape reports that describe computing education in that state.

In Indiana, as in many states, CS is classified as a CTE course. A business certification allows a teacher to teach CTE classes such as CS. Indiana has a Computer Education License that requires teachers to be knowledgeable about a breadth of topics from web design and computer applications to library media and technical repair support. The definition of computing education is vague and tends to include a large number of topics. Only Indiana University-Bloomington (IU) and Ball State University (BSU) offer preservice teacher education for computing education. In both of these programs, teachers need to achieve an elementary or secondary education certification, and then they can add-on the computer educa-

---

[a] See https://code.org/files/TeacherPathwayRecommendations.pdf.
[b] See https://www.computingteacher.org.
[c] For more information, see https://ecepalliance.org.

TABLE 6-5 Computer Science-Focused PD Activities Offered in the Past 3 Years

Type of PD activity	Elementary	Middle	High
PD Workshops	35 (2.5)	28 (2.4)	19 (1.9)
Teacher Study Groups	43 (3.1)	41 (3.3)	33 (2.9)
One-on-One Computer Science-Focused Coaching	28 (2.4)	27 (2.3)	21 (2.3)

NOTE: PD = professional development.
SOURCE: Banilower et al. (2018).

tion license. These programs are fragile. Purdue University had a program until the sole faculty member supporting the program left in 2013, and the program formally closed in 2016. These programs will have to be more robust to be successful at growing computing educators systematically.

In South Carolina, researchers found even less opportunity for teachers to pursue PD or certification in CS. There is no certification or program in higher education to prepare teachers in computing education in South Carolina. Part of the challenge for South Carolina in developing such programs is the lack of statewide standards in computing education; a lack of definition makes it difficult to grow teacher programs in CS and, consequently, increase the number of CS teachers. The absence of teacher programs and the lack of clearly-defined standards have had an effect on K–12 learners.

Texas has a rigorous CS education certification process; however, relatively few teachers pursue certification. The CS certification process requires teachers to be equipped with a significant number of technical skills and involves developing a proficiency with topics such as software design and programming, loops and recursion, data structures, object-oriented programming, algorithms, Big-O notation, discrete math, digital forensics, robotics, and game and mobile app development.

CS teacher certification in Nevada is based on Praxis exams. In states that allow certification by examination, there may be less incentive to create preservice programs. While the definition of what is computing is clear when testing by exam, preparation is the responsibility of the teacher, more typically in-service.

SOURCE: Committee generated based on reports available at https://ecepalliance.org.

puting teacher (Goode, Johnson, and Sundstrom, 2020; Ni, 2011; Ryoo, Goode, and Margolis, 2015).

SUMMARY

Formal educational experiences are important settings for engaging learners in authentic computing experiences that have the potential to influence interest and competencies for computing. But, as for any context, the conditions have to be right. Schools have the opportunity to provide experiences that may allow for sustained engagement, which is important for developing learners' individual interests in computing. However, just as with out-of-school-time settings, formal educational environments may not be able to provide experiences due to lack of resources and adequate teacher preparation, or learners may find that the options are not engaging. Moreover, the opportunities in formal educational context are inequitably distributed. Not only are there more opportunities available in high school as compared to middle and elementary schools, but also large schools, low-poverty schools, and suburban/urban schools are more likely to offer AP CS courses (Banilower et al., 2018). Additionally, women and learners of color continue to be underrepresented in AP CS courses.

Overall, this chapter has considered how professionally and personally authentic experiences with computing have been offered in United States schools across K–12 settings. The review highlighted that although course offerings are variable and inequitably distributed across schools, there are also promising practices and approaches that support more foundational approaches to bring computing education to all learners.

7

Designing Authentic Experiences for Computing

Throughout this report, the committee has emphasized that learning is an active process that is social, embedded in a particular context, and enhanced by intentional support provided by knowledgeable individuals, be they peers, mentors, or teachers. These contexts can exist in formal or out-of-school-time settings, which have different affordances and constraints associated with them. Moreover, learning takes place across space and time, suggesting a need for partnerships, brokering, and connections made across settings. However, the evidence on *whether and how* authentic experiences develop interest and competencies for computing is still emerging. Based on the evidence to date, the committee offers broad guidance to program designers.

This chapter is written to serve as a guide to readers who wish to design authentic experiences for computing that attract and support diverse learners. The committee identifies important questions to ask and issues to address during the design process. As a starting point, this chapter begins with a discussion of why design matters; that is, why having a clear and intentioned set of goals and emphasis on authenticity is critical in the design of experiences. The chapter then offers a number of considerations for design that may be important for facilitating the development of interests and competencies in computing.

WHY DESIGN MATTERS

Stakeholders have a vested interest in science, technology, engineering, and mathematics (STEM) and computing for a wide variety of reasons that may or may not be explicit. However, it is important for design, in any context, to begin with a sense of "why" and "for what purpose" one is designing. That is, designers need to have a clear and intentioned set of goals in the beginning when setting up and designing the program or experience (Laporte and Zaman, 2016; Li et al., 2019; Plass, Homer, and Kinzer, 2014). Having an explicit understanding of the purpose and clearly articulated goals for design allows for better alignment between intentions and actions.

Brennan (in press) synthesized the research to uncover the *why* for computing and identified three broad categories of goals: general education (i.e., technological literacy, learning and skill development); affective (i.e., identity development, supporting creative agency); and economic/ societal (i.e., civic engagement, economic opportunities, and workforce development). The first is essential for equitable participation in society; the second is important for laying the foundation for equitable access to computing occupations; and the third is important for our economic and social well-being in the long term. It is worth noting that these categories can overlap and that the *why* of a program or experience can have multiple goals; however, many programs appear to have vague or unspecified goals.

When considering these various programmatic goals, it is important to consider how authenticity is being prioritized, as its use has been inconsistent across learning and research (Strobel et al., 2013). The two forms of authentic experiences identified by the committee—professional authenticity and personal authenticity—can play a big role in shaping the intention of design. It is critical to integrate disciplinary content with the practices and contexts of that discipline (i.e., cultivating professionally authentic experiences), and it is equally critical to connect this disciplinary content with a learner's environment and prior knowledge (i.e., cultivating personally authentic experiences). That said, providing experiences that are *both* professionally and personally authentic is difficult, as there is often a tension between professional and personal authenticity that the design of learning experiences must address. If the goal of the program or experience is meant to align with the practices of the discipline (i.e., to provide a professional authentic experience), then it is worth recognizing the ways in which these practices may be at odds with the cultural and experiential background of the learners involved (see Chapter 2).

Overall, answering *why* will vary from context to context. However, once answered, the *why* informs what it is that learners are expected to know or to be able to do. In the remainder of this chapter, we discuss design considerations that may support the creation of authentic experiences that serve to develop interests and competencies in computing.

DESIGN CONSIDERATIONS

As suggested above, the first step in design is to have a clear set of goals and expectations for the learning experience. From there, a number of different features, or characteristics of design, are important to consider. The committee approached the work through the lens of diversity, equity, and inclusion. Unfortunately, as illustrated in Chapter 2, STEM educational and professional environments have historically been profoundly inequitable and unjust spaces (Bobb, 2016; Lewis, Shah, and Falkner, 2019; Ryoo et al., 2019). Design has the potential to exacerbate those inequities and injustices, or to redress them, advancing a vision of learning and participation that is diverse, equitable, inclusive (DEI), and promotes belonging. Throughout the chapter, the committee calls attention to elements of design that serve to promote participation of learners traditionally underrepresented based on gender, race, ethnicity, or perceived ability.

The committee offers a set of seven design considerations, which include (1) Learners; (2) Community; (3) Activities; (4) Environment; (5) Duration; (6) Tools; and (7) Iteration. For each of the design considerations, there are questions to keep in mind that can have an impact on design. Table 7-1 lists some of these possible questions, which are not intended to be all-inclusive but only serve as a starting point.

Before delving into each of the different design considerations, there are a few important points to highlight. These design considerations serve as a guide and are not intended to be interpreted as a set of "boxes to check." Although the committee presents examples to illustrate how a program may have approached a particular issue, these examples are illustrative, not exhaustive, and may not reflect the realities for all environments. It is crucial to consider the local context and infrastructure in place when designing a program or experience. Additionally, the design considerations are nonlinear and interdependent (National Research Council [NRC], 2009). Decisions made for one aspect of design can have implications for one (or more) of the others. For example, if the program is designed to enhance interest and identity for a particular population of learners, this not only applies to the "learners," but also affects many of the other design considerations (e.g., the social aspects of design [community], whether the activities are meaningful for the learner [activities], and whether the physical space is conducive to support the activity [environment]).

As stated above, learning takes places across space and time. Fundamental to design is considering the ways in which partnerships and connections across settings can be established. For example, Chapter 5 noted that museums can play a role in developing curriculum materials and providing professional development opportunities. It may be advantageous to create a partnership so that the relevant expertise can be leveraged and resources

TABLE 7-1 Potential Questions RE: Designing Authentic Experiences for Computing

Design Consideration	Possible Questions
Learners	• Who are the learners, including their demographics, prior experiences, current circumstances, etc.? • How are the prior experiences of learners acknowledged and incorporated, particularly in relation to computing?
Community	• Who supports a learner in a community of learners? • How do facilitators/educators support a learner? • How is the learning of facilitators/educators supported? • How does the community of people, and the experiences they bring, influence the learning environment? • What ways of knowing are valued within the community? • What identities (racialized, gendered, socioeconomic, etc.) are being navigated within the space? • What are the facilitators' identities in relation to learners? • What are the existing power relationships with the community of learners?
Activities	• What is the basis for the planned activities? Are they grounded from the learners' perspective or the industry's practice or neither? • In what ways do activities incorporate previous experiences of learners or relate to skills and projects in the computing profession? • What goals and outcomes are expected from learners as they engage in the activity? How are those skills, competencies, and understanding made visible, and how are they valued? • How are educators facilitating the activity in a way that supports intellectual growth, such as increased skills and competencies in computing, while simultaneously recognizing learners' abilities, contributions, and cultures?
Environment	• How far away is the physical learning location from the learner's home and/or school? • How accessible is the physical environment, i.e., compliant with ADA and other regulatory frameworks? • If the location is home, how equitably equipped is the locale for the learning experiences? • What characteristics of the environment are unique and support learning in distinct ways? What aspects of the environments can be further designed to better support learning?
Duration	• How are the total time and frequency of the learning experiences related to desired learning outcomes? • What duration-related constraints are presented by the learning setting for personal and/or professional authenticity in computing?

TABLE 7-1 Continued

Design Consideration	Possible Questions
Tools	• What assumptions are made about the accessibility and affordability of tools? • How do the tools reflect commitments to personal authenticity and/or professional authenticity in computing?
Iteration	• How does the design incorporate learning from each design iteration?

shared, so that capacity within the ecosystem can be developed (Allen, Lewis-Warner, and Noam, 2020; Traill, Traphagen, and Devaney, 2015; Vance et al., 2016). The STEM Learning Ecosystems Community of Practice framework includes "cultivating dynamic, diverse partnerships; experimenting with creative means of partnering across sectors; and increasing the quantity and quality of active, inquiry-based formal and informal STEM learning opportunities for all, including young people historically underrepresented in STEM" (Allen, Lewis-Warner, and Noam, 2020, p. 31).

Finally, important for this report, these types of experiences can be designed across a range of settings to include in-school and out-of-school activities (e.g., clubs, libraries, museums, other youth-oriented organizations, and households) (NRC, 2009). Although there are a number of differences across the various settings (highlighted in the preceding chapters), the design considerations are intended to have broad applicability. What follows is the evidence for each design consideration and example programs that are suggestive of showing promise.

Learners

As is true for almost all designed experiences, it is important to consider the individuals who will participate in (or engage with) the experience. Researchers have been examining how having a deeper understanding of the learners involved, beyond simple numbers or basic demographics, can enable the development of a more robust, personally meaningful authentic experience (Calabrese Barton and Tan, 2019; Cornelius-White, 2007; Eccles and Wigfield, 2002; Farrington et al., 2012; Guzdial, 2015; Immordino-Yang and Damasio, 2007; Pintrich, 2003; Roorda et al., 2011; Weinberg, Basile, and Albright, 2011). In particular, as called out in Table 7-1, it is worth considering both "who are the learners" and "how are learners' prior experiences acknowledged and incorporated into the design."

Who Are the Learners?

There are a number of basic and key demographics that can have differential impacts on the design of authentic experiences for computing. These demographics include (but may not be limited to) age/grade, gender, sexual orientation, race, ethnicity, income, language ability, prior knowledge, learning ability and disability status, and geographical location. Such categories may be fluid at any given time, may change over time, and may overlap or inform one another (Ashcraft, Eger, Scott, 2017; Rodriguez and Lehman, 2018; Thomas et al., 2018). Each of these categories (and the way they may intersect with and interact upon one another) can have implications for the ways in which an experience can be structured.

A first step may be determining whether the materials are suitable or developmentally appropriate, which is crucial, given the progression of learning that takes place across age or grade levels. Previous research shows that learners as young as age 4 can learn simple programming concepts (Bers, 2007; 2012); however, most tools target learners ages 7–8 and older (Flannery et al., 2013). Younger learners may have trouble with the technical aspects of reading (that may be associated with strict syntax of text-based computer languages) as well as may lack the dexterity needed to use a mouse or touchpad to move elements around on the screen (Bers, 2018). ScratchJr and KIBO (a tangible robotics kit) have been developed for learners in early childhood spaces. These programs are built on the premise that these young learners *can* learn and apply programming concepts and problem-solving (Bers, 2018; Flannery et al., 2013; Portelance, Strawhacker, and Bers, 2016).

The strict syntactic demands of programming languages may be an obstacle to English Learners (ELs); linguistic scaffolding and culturally responsive pedagogies (discussed in the next section) can be supportive and effective (Jacob et al., 2018). The use of everyday language, as opposed to content-specific vocabulary, may help ELs learn and master disciplinary concepts as well as develop English proficiency (Jacob et al., 2018; National Academies of Sciences, Engineering, and Medicine [NASEM], 2018c). Inquiry-based practices have also been suggested to be promising when working with ELs in STEM (Estrella et al., 2018). Jacob et al. (2020) found that a more structured inquiry approach—use of modeling techniques, simulating algorithmic processes, physically enacting computational concepts, and incrementally increasing levels of complexity (p. 7)—led to the development of interest and competencies (more sophisticated computational artifacts) for computing.

For learners who may vary in their learning ability and needs, including those with physical disabilities, explicit focus on the principles of Universal Design for Learning is needed (Israel, 2019; Israel et al., 2015a,b;

King-Sears et al., 2014; Ok et al., 2017; Ralabate, 2016; Van Merriënboer and Sweller, 2005). Moreover, computing can be used to facilitate learning. Peppler and Warschauer (2011) details a case example of "Brandy," a 9-year-old girl with cognitive disabilities and little reading or writing ability, and her use of Scratch. During the 2.5-year observation period, Brandy not only developed literacy skills, but also immersed herself in computer programming and created a number of Scratch projects. These findings point to the potential of using digital media, especially in early literacy development, as a way to create more opportunities. Integrating computing into the curriculum, while having affordances, requires teachers to consider their instructional practices. Box 7-1 illustrates the perspectives and strategies classroom teachers used when creating classroom environments that integrate computational thinking into elementary instruction.

Another dimension is the intersection between the perception of computing and the learners' ongoing self-fashioning of identity—as an individual, in relation to various groups, and in terms of various abstract categories. With respect to perception, learners may have different ideas for what counts as a programming language, which in turn affects their perceived confidence to use those tools (Lewis et al., 2014). Alternatively, girls and more novice programmers may be drawn to using other tools, like Storytelling Alice, which is a program that enables users to program

---

BOX 7-1
Computational Thinking in Elementary Classrooms

Israel et al. (2015a) conducted a cross-case analysis study to understand how computational thinking was integrated in elementary instruction; in particular, they examined the impacts on learners from diverse backgrounds including learners with disabilities and those living in poverty. This study focused explicitly on teacher implementation of computing rather than specific learner outcomes. However, through observation and interview data, it was found that teachers spent a great deal of time and effort making computing accessible. That is, the teachers viewed learners as able to thrive within computing environments "but needed additional scaffolds to help them fully engage" (p. 277). This was accomplished through the creation of learning experiences that "were flexible, included modeling, and scaffolded computing instruction and independent work through both guided practice and collaborative problem solving" (p. 276). In some classrooms, differentiated instruction with multiple options for expressing understanding allowed struggling learners to find success and share that with their peers, which served to position them in leadership roles.

SOURCE: Committee generated with information from Israel et al. (2015a).

animated stories. The storytelling component has been theorized to be more appealing to girls, while the visual programming aspects have been theorized to be more appealing to novices, because of the lack of syntax errors (Kelleher and Pausch, 2007). Thus, this program has been suggested as a means to reach middle school learners, particularly girls. For some learners, their perceptions of computing may call into question the authenticity of the tool—if they perceive themselves as "good at programming" but do not perceive the tool as professionally authentic, then they might perceive the tool as being less personally authentic. However, for others, a more personally authentic tool may serve as an entry point into developing interest and competency.

Furthermore, learners' motivations for engaging with computing and their perceptions of computing have been shown to intersect with learner's race/ethnicity. For example, DiSalvo and Bruckman (2010) examined the relationship between gaming practices and race and gender. This study was based upon the findings that (1) young Black and Hispanic men play video games more hours per day than White men and (2) gaming practices in computer science majors consisted of a desire to make games, understand the underlying mathematics, or hack/modify games. To understand the gaming practices in Black men, DiSalvo and Bruckman surveyed 13 learners. They found that although they play video games frequently, their motivation for playing was primarily social—to connect with family and friends and to practice for future social situations. This finding suggests that it may be important to build social components into design.

How Are Learners' Background and Experience(s) Acknowledged?

As described above, learners vary with respect to their demographics and by extension with respect to their backgrounds and experiences. One dimension in which learners may differ is their experience with computing (e.g., whether learners prefer to engage in video game playing,[1] taking classes, watching videos online to learn more about specific computing concepts). Chapter 2 provides illustrative examples of learners and how their particular experiences shaped their interest and skills with respect to computing. This variability can even extend to whether or not the learner has caregivers or other siblings that are interested in computing; when learners have familial experiences, this can create a sense of confidence or belonging with the content (Margolis and Fisher, 2002). Knowing how

---

[1] Playing video games have been suggested to "inspire and wonder," and self-reports with computer scientists have indicated that video game playing sparked their interest in computing (DiSalvo and Bruckman, 2010, p. 56).

much and what type of exposure learners have when engaging in computing activities is key to ensuring appropriate design.

Moreover, all learners are shaped by the communities that they grow up in, which have their own cultural practices that have developed historically and are shaped in ongoing ways to achieve the goals and values of the communities (Moll, 2015; Nasir et al., 2006). Each community has particular ways of conceptualizing, representing, evaluating, and engaging with the world (Gutiérrez and Rogoff, 2003; NASEM, 2018b). A number of efforts, such as culturally-relevant and culturally-sustaining pedagogies, have been used to increase representation and combat cultural and systemic barriers to participation (see Chapter 2 for discussion). However, it is important to recognize that potential implicit biases may be built into the design of experiences; evaluating activities to determine whether they promote stereotypical representations is essential.

In the past two decades, a growing number of schools and other youth-serving organizations have either been founded (or, if pre-existing institutions, refocused) to create and deploy culturally-responsive, inclusive programming for particular minoritized communities within STEM and computer science. For instance, long-time national groups such as Girls Inc., The Hispanic Heritage Foundation, and the Girl Scouts of America have invested heavily in STEM and computing for their constituencies, sometimes partnering with other groups such as *FIRST*® Robotics. The lack of culturally-relevant curricula, educator/mentor professional development, and program delivery models likewise spurred the launch of numerous new programs: Techbridge Girls (established 2000); Technovation Girls (2006); CompuGIRLS (2007); Black Girls Code (2011); RePublic Charter Schools, in Nashville, Tennessee and Jackson, Mississippi (2011); Girls Who Code (2012); All Star Code (2013); Bulldog Bytes at Mississippi State University (2013); America on Tech (2014); The Knowledge House (2014); Digital Pioneers Academy in Washington, DC (2018), to name just a few. Box 7-2 provides a discussion of how CompuGirls navigates the intertwined social processes. Acknowledging the cultural backgrounds and experiences of learners by taking the time to ask about and understand their conceptualizations of STEM and computing is essential, as this can allow for diversity in perspectives and broaden the range of personally meaningful experiences for design (Calabrese Barton et al., 2013; Krivet and Krajcik, 2008).

Designing an optimally effective STEM and/or computing curriculum thus entails gaining an understanding of the individual and collective identities in question, an iterative process whereby the learning goals, lesson plans, activities, etc. may in turn influence the learner's sense of identity (Carlone and Johnson, 2007; Holmegaard, Madsen, and Ulriksen, 2014; Polman and Miller, 2010; Sfard and Prusak, 2005).

BOX 7-2
CompuGirls

Created in 2007, CompuGirls was developed as a culturally-relevant technology program specifically designed to challenge deficit narratives of girls of color in STEM (Scott, Aist, and Hood, 2009). The program is designed from girls in grades 8–12 from school districts characterized as under-resourced in Arizona, Colorado, New Jersey, and Wisconsin. Learners meet during the summer and after-school during the school year (4 hours a week) in small groups to learn the latest technologies. These learners have access to a college campus and necessary resources to complete projects of interest. Survey data suggest that the program serves as that meaningful experience that enables the learner to see themselves within "the dominant culture, its practice of power, and potential to make change using multimedia projects" (Scott and White, 2013, p. 675).

Designed and administered through Arizona State Center for Gender Equity in Science and Technology, central to the program's goal is the transformation of girls' perceptions of themselves as innovators and producers of technology. The program defines techno-social change agents as "individuals who can challenge dominant narratives and construct more liberating identities and social relations as they create new technologies" (Ashcraft, Eger, and Scott, 2017, p. 234). Throughout the program, girls are encouraged to analyze their own identities through technology and better understand how their individual experiences fit within the context of STEM disciplines. In this example, we can see the importance of developing an understanding of the power dynamics within a STEM community as well as the strategic framing of the types of knowledge and people that are valued within it.

SOURCE: Based in part on information available at https://cgest.asu.edu/compugirls.

Community

Learning is a social process, supported in formal and informal ways by the people that a learner encounters over the course of various learning experiences. As introduced in Chapter 3, a growing body of literature suggests that learning is a matter of participation, engagement, and membership in a community of practice (Nasir and Cook, 2009; Wenger, 1998). Given these social processes at work, designers of authentic experiences for computing must understand not only who the actors are within an environment, but also the dynamics that influence the ways in which learning occurs (or does not occur) with others within a community. What follows is a discussion centered on how people in a community of learners support a learner: the role of *facilitators/educators* in supporting learning and the role of *others* within a community in supporting learning.

Facilitators/Educators and Their Roles

Social supports for learning as provided by facilitators are ubiquitous, occur in a variety of settings, and are present in all cultures (NRC, 2009). There are a number of different possible facilitators, including educators (e.g., teachers, librarians, museum professionals), mentors, caregivers, experts (e.g., scientists or engineers), hobbyists, other professionals (i.e., in industry or other settings), peers, and even oneself. Further, an experience can be primarily guided by the learner, there can be one facilitator/educator, or there can be many playing different roles within the environment. Regardless of how the facilitation is situated, key ingredients for effective learning are the availability of appropriate support to help learners engage in an activity in a meaningful way, the gradual withdrawal of these supports as the learners' competence increases, and instruction and guidance in the use of tools that support learning (NRC, 2000).

Generally, facilitators and educators help orient learners to new learning experiences and prompt them to ask new questions and pursue new types of learning (Clegg and Kolodner, 2014; NRC, 2009, 2011b, 2012), enabling learners to more fully explore their curiosities and develop new and deepened interests. As learners become more comfortable and active in driving their own learning, facilitators/educators may also find themselves becoming learners, working together with the learners to co-create the learning experience (Clegg and Kolodner, 2014; NRC, 2009, 2011b, 2012). In this role, facilitators engage learners in conversations about their own interests, motivations, and day-to-day life experiences. Through these interactions, facilitators not only build personal rapport, but also help guide learners through the learning (Clegg and Kolodner, 2014; NRC, 2009, 2011b, 2012).

Whether in or out of school, facilitators must continuously seek specific ways to promote equity in their learning community and focus on repeatedly positioning learners in their contexts to take on engaged roles. Promoting equity involves, in part, paying attention to the culture of the environment in which learning is taking place. It also involves continuously watching out for patterns that favor one group over another (Barron et al., 2014). For example, in the Digital Youth Network, Barron et al. (2014) observed that more boys were engaging in STEM opportunities than girls. They continuously monitored for differential engagement and introduced new ways to engage girls in STEM activities. They observe that monitoring for engagement is not something that is just done once but that must be continuously observed and addressed throughout the life of a program (Barron et al., 2014). Promoting equity also requires welcoming non-traditional participation (as might be observed in video game play), specifically offering a variety of ways learners can contribute to the learning community (Gee, 2007).

Facilitation, whether in school or out of school, is a complex activity that depends centrally on a facilitator's knowledge, skill, and judgment. Facilitators will flourish when they have opportunities to develop that knowledge, skill, and judgment—and to refine that expertise over time. Box 7-3 describes one model for supporting the evolving expertise of and community of support for PK–12 computer science teachers: the Computer Science Teachers Association.

Supporting Participants and their Role(s)

Facilitators need not be the "expert" or "adult" in the room. Other supporting participants, such as peers (including same-aged or older peers) and families, can play active roles in helping to facilitate the learning experience. A number of different programs have been developed to explicitly consider families and family learning as a central thread in their design. PowerMyLearning[2] and Technovation[3] are two examples of programs that have family learning at the core of their approach. Engaging families can help to increase family members' confidence in support of the learners' learning.

At all levels, a learner's understanding and skills can be improved when peers work together on challenging tasks, especially when the interaction is cooperative (Gauvain, 2001; Light and Littleton, 1999). These interactions may include tutoring, discussion, or joint problem-solving, with the latter offering different opportunities for learning because peers can define and structure a problem in a way that is mutually accessible (Ellis and Gauvain, 1992). Many youth-development programs that involve computing have some variant of peer facilitation (Kafai, Peppler, and Chapman, 2009; Martin, 2017; Schusler and Krasny, 2010).

Activities

This section turns from a discussion of who the learner and the other individuals involved in the learning are to focus on what the learner is doing, in what we have chosen to call Activities. That is, what are learners learning? And how are they learning? The process of learning—what learners are learning and how that learning is supported by educators, environment, tools, and community—is inextricably linked to the design of

---

[2] For more information about PowerMyLearning's approach and outcomes associated with families, see https://powermylearning.org.

[3] Technovation is a "global tech education non-profit that inspires girls and families to be leaders and problem solvers in their lives and their community" (https://www.technovation. org/). Its family program is built around the use of AI tools as a family to solve problems of personal relevance.

BOX 7-3
Computer Science Teachers Association

PK–12 teaching can be isolated, solitary work, and that isolation can be even greater for computer science teachers, who sometimes are the only content-expert in their school or even their district (Yadav et al., 2016). Established in 2004, the Computer Science Teachers Association (CSTA) is a teacher-led organization intended to support computer science teachers' professional learning and teaching. CSTA provides support to teachers to establish local chapters, which are geographically-organized gatherings for discussing challenges and opportunities teachers are experiencing, and disseminates a monthly newsletter. CSTA organizes an annual conference, where teachers have opportunities to share practices with each other. For example, sessions from CSTA 2020 included "Critical Race Theory in Computer Science Education," "Making Computer Science Accessible to Diverse Learners," "Computational Thinking and Social Emotional Learning," and "Incorporating Culturally Authentic PBL Practices in CS." CSTA also serves as an advocacy and policy group, with an explicitly named commitment to supporting equity in computer science. Among its policy efforts, CSTA developed a widely-referenced set of K–12 computer science standards.

SOURCES: Committee generated based on information from https://www.csteachers.org/ and https://hopin.to/events/csta-2020-virtual-conference#schedule.

---

an activity, as it determines how learners may engage, whether the content will stick, and what skills, competencies, and interest may develop from the activity or sequence of activities.

This section divides its discussion of learning and activities into two substantial topics—(1) content and pedagogy and (2) outcomes and assessment—and considers both topics in relation to authenticity, computing, and equity. Just as in other sections of this chapter, while the focus is on the design of activities and the ideas correlate with the guiding questions around activities, listed in Table 7-1, there is influence on and overlap with community, environment, and other design considerations.

Content and Pedagogy

The emphasis throughout this section is on what the learner will learn and do: the content of the activity—what it is that learners will be learning—is central to the design of the experience. But content does not exist in a vacuum. And thus, while it is certainly fundamentally important that the learning activity clearly addresses the subject matter or disciplinary content (or the integration of content areas, see Box 7-4), this content is inflected by other elements in the learning environment and design. One of these is the

BOX 7-4
Integrating STEM with Arts and Humanities

The intersection of engineering and humanities may enhance and reinforce learning in the individual disciplines, and the intentional integration of art, storytelling, music, dance, composition, and other activities has gained traction in the past decade in many K–12 environments emerging as STEAM (science, technology, engineering, arts, and mathematics) (Leonard et al., 2020; Peppler, 2013). This movement has been motivated by the desire to broaden pathways to STEM fields for diverse groups of learners (Cavallo et al., 2004), the need to engage learners in real-world transdisciplinary problem-solving, and the belief that arts-based creativity is associated with innovation (Liao, 2019). In addition, as digital media arts has emerged as another discipline of art within education (Peppler, 2010), the tools inherent to this discipline support the development of skills, competencies, and dispositions relevant to STEM subjects as well (Halverson and Sheridan, 2014).

DreamYard, located and serving the Bronx, NY, is a community arts organization that leverages the arts, digital tools, and social justice to support learning and community building in numerous settings across school and out-of-school-time spaces. In addition to running DreamYard Preparatory High School, it offers a number of programs and integrates digital learning into its offerings in ways that "activate STEAM learning and spark interest in design, coding, digital art, and more by supporting youth as they experiment in hands-on, real-world situations."

SOURCE: Committee generated with information from https://www.dreamyard.com/about.

intention that drives activity design. As discussed in the beginning sections of this chapter, articulating the *why* is a crucial step in designing effective programs. The *why* that guides design of the activity and pedagogical approach in authentic experiences for computing may apply not only to the subject matter, but also to social, educational, and affective aspects.

Activities are designed in alignment with one or multiple pedagogical frameworks or learning approaches. Even in instances when there may not be an active educator supporting the learner and activity, pedagogy is still taken into consideration.

Constructionism (Papert, 1980) is a theory of learning and an approach to learning design that encourages learning through personalizing, making, sharing, and reflecting (Brennan, 2015; Resnick, 2017). It centers learner agency and "powerful ideas"—an early commitment to advancing both personally authentic and professionally authentic (in terms of disciplinary authenticity) experiences, which have been linked to developing interest and competences (Bevan, 2017; Kafai and Burke, 2015). The history of K–12 computing education can be traced back to LOGO and this movement in constructionism. LOGO, for example, was not about computing as an end, but rather computing as a means; LOGO was designed to support learners' explorations with mathematics, creative expression, and learning itself. In designing constructionist activities, the designer needs to consider ways that they can make the activities personally meaningful to their learners, and ways that the community plays an integral role in facilitating sharing of artifacts with peers. There is a significant amount of recent work looking at how to do this effectively with everything from e-textiles (Kafai and Fields, 2018) to physical computing (Blikstein, 2013b) to games (Kafai and Burke, 2015) and other forms of computing (Brennan, 2013; Papavlasopoulou, Giannakos, and Jaccheri, 2019).

Previous research has suggested that there may be benefits to engaging in project-based learning (Bevan, 2017; Erdogan et al., 2016; NASEM, 2018b). However, there are differences in how project-based learning is operationalized. Learners in programs such as CompuGirls (Box 7-2), DreamYard (Box 7-5), Digital Youth Divas (Box 7-5), the Clubhouse Network (Box 7-6), *FIRST*®, and Providence Public Library's Rhode Coders 2.0 (Box 4-5) are frequently engaged in learning activities and environments that mirror a project-based approach. Exploring Computer Science (ECS), a year-long introductory high school computer science course, readily integrates projects and inquiry into its curriculum units. Project Lead the Way (PLTW), which provides programs, curriculum, and professional development for classrooms across K–12, including PLTW Computer Science, centers its instruction on projects and problems. Beam Camp brings together more than 90 older elementary, middle, and high school campers to create one massive art project installed in the middle of the New Hampshire woods every summer, utilizing skills related to architecture, physical computing, ceramics, and welding, to name a few.

Throughout this report, the role of personal authenticity has been amplified. As suggested above (see Learners and Community), it is important that the facilitator of the activity takes time to understand learners' perspectives and what knowledge, skills, and other ways of knowing they bring; that learners have agency over their own learning; and that there exist opportunities to apply and connect relevant everyday experiences (Gutiérrez and Rogoff, 2003; Nasir et al., 2006; Vossoughi, Hooper, and Escudé, 2016). Inclusive and culturally-relevant pedagogies offer insights into the approaches that can be successful in engaging learners from a wide range of diverse backgrounds and abilities (Gay, 2010; Ladson-Billings, 1995; Paris, 2012). In particular, these pedagogies speak to the importance of activities being personally authentic to the learner and bring to the surface the need for learners from marginalized and non-dominant communities to be seen as contributors and actors (Ladson-Billings, 2014).

BOX 7-5
Digital Youth Divas

Digital Youth Divas puts a critical focus on activities, community, and environment, all in an effort to support middle school girls from underrepresented communities to engage in computing and, specifically, in computational making. Alongside the components addressing community and environment, the work and research aims to develops understanding around the multiple issues of equity in computational learning and computing education (i.e., increasing access, diversifying how computing is represented, and deepening participation and knowledge) (Fields et al., 2018).

Pinkard, Martin, and Erete (2020) note the five components of the program:

(1) self-paced, project-based computational learning activities; (2) a face-to-face community of learners including adult mentors and collaborative peers; (3) an online social learning platform where girls access project instructions and other learning resources, develop a portfolio of submitted work, and interact with others around projects; (4) alternative instructional resources including narrative stories that launch project work; and (5) resources and workshops to establish a network of parents and caring adults. (p. 3)

While these components must all work in concert with one another, activity design—components 1 and 4—is significant in its connectedness, involving content, pedagogy, and goals, as well as the crucial links to peers, community, and home that make it authentic to the individuals involved.

There are two open-ended projects that the learner-participants engage with: an engineering project based in fashion and a programming project based in dance. Learners are supported by resources, instruction, peers, and mentors, and they work on the project at their own pace and can continue efforts in their home settings. The disciplinary content and cognitive and non-cognitive goals are embedded within arts-related contexts that may be more familiar, comfortable, and accessible to middle school girls. Simultaneously, participants collaborate with one another and are supported to persist, prototype, and imagine and create their own artifacts over a period of multiple weeks.

Inextricably linked to activity design are the considerations of the learners and their identities, the environments and communities that they are a part of, and the tools and resources used. Research studies on Digital Youth Divas have also highlighted the importance of narratives and stories (Erete et al., 2016; Pinkard et al., 2017); involvement of family and mentors (Martin et al., 2017); and careful consideration of language in program design and recruitment strategies (Martin, Erete, and Pinkard, 2015).

SOURCES: Based on Martin, Erete, and Pinkard (2015) and Pinkard et al. (2017).

BOX 7-6
Time at the Clubhouse Network

The Clubhouse Network is an international network of out-of-school learning experiences for young people to learn about technology. The Clubhouse Network celebrated its 25th anniversary in 2018, with more than 100 groups in 20 countries. In his 2017 book, *Lifelong Kindergarten*, Mitch Resnick (one of the co-founders of the Computer Clubhouse) describes the Clubhouse learning environment. It is a space where young people are encouraged to develop familiarity and fluency with technology through project-based learning: defining and pursuing work that is personally and/or socially relevant, finding support from adult mentors, and connecting with peers. Deep engagement with projects over time is encouraged at the Clubhouse. Resnick describes the engagement as grounded in a variety of interests—personal hobbies, important events, meaningful relationships—and providing fuel for sustained work over time. He writes, "Clubhouse members often worked long hours on these projects, coming back to the Clubhouse day after day." For some Clubhouse members, that time at the Clubhouse developing projects that were personally authentic led to opportunities for professionally authentic learning experiences, as well as returning to the Clubhouse to support the personally authentic learning of others through intergenerational learning. Resnick interviews Jaleesa, who had become the coordinator of the Clubhouse of which she had been a member. In the interview, Jaleesa attributes her time at the Clubhouse to shaping her choice of college major; she had long envisioned herself as a hairstylist, but through experiences with Microsoft at the Clubhouse, decided to pursue human-centered design and engineering in college.

SOURCE: Based in part on The Clubhouse Network website at https://theclubhousenetwork.org.

Fostering personal authenticity also involves recognizing cultural and everyday practices as legitimate practices, whether related to mathematics, literature, or science (Nasir et al., 2006). Eglash et al. (2013) describe possible approaches of culturally responsive computing education, including ways to showcase, pay respect to, and link to the creativity, problem-solving, and computational thinking inherent (but rarely recognized in such ways) in practices such as Native American beadwork, Black cornrow hairstyles, and Latinx rhythms. By understanding and leveraging how members of diverse communities conceptualize and apply these concepts in their own ways—and by adopting pedagogical approaches to content that promote personally authentic experiences—the computing field can become more relevant and approachable for all communities and particularly those typically underrepresented (see Boxes 7-2 and 7-5).

Outcomes and Assessment

Aligned closely with the purposes and motivations of a design are the goals and outcomes we can expect from its implementation. The activity can be designed to develop skills associated with computing, or the design may emphasize the individual goals (e.g., development of interest and identity) or collective goals (e.g., equity and community health). Other constructs may also be highly relevant, and these need not be mutually exclusive. As stated above, goals of authentic experiences for computing may include outcomes that are societal, educational, and affective in nature (Brennan, in press), and all are relevant. Many of the examples shared in this report touch upon all three, often overlapping and interwoven.

That being said, it is essential to design ways in which educators and learners, or others in the learning environment and community, can obtain accurate and relevant measures of these goals. Previous reports (NRC, 2000) suggested that the design of learning environments be learner-, knowledge-, community-, and assessment-centered. Assessment offers opportunities for learners to iterate (i.e., evaluate whether they are learning intended content and skills and adjust their learning strategies as appropriate), for educators to provide feedback, and for both learners and educators to converse and share in growing and deepening understandings. Key to assessment is the need to be "congruent with one's learning goals" (NRC, 2000, p. 140). In the design of a computing activity—and the associated design of the assessment—it is worthwhile to address questions about the claims and outcomes desired (NRC, 2001), and how might we collect evidence to support those claims.

Formative and summative assessments are commonly used across learning environments, but their use is inconsistent, and the focus is often on memorization, not understanding (NRC, 2000). When evaluating activities and learning environments that are collaborative, open-ended, occurring across different physical spaces and online platforms, and long in duration, which describe many of the pedagogies and examples used in authentic learning for computing, conventional assessment techniques can be harder to apply (Murai et al., 2019). Almost two decades ago it was recommended that more research be done into effective ways to conduct formative assessment, offering opportunities for feedback, self-assessment, and integration of technology (NRC, 2000). Today, resources, tools, and capacity for assessing learning remain widely variable.

Environment

The environment in which an authentic experience for computing takes place can facilitate or hinder many aspects of the intended design (as described below), including equitable access, perceived authenticity, and learning outcomes. Environments may be wholly physical, wholly digital, or (as is increasingly the case) a blend or hybrid of the two—with the relationship between "space" and "place" and the connections across various environments important for the ways in which authentic and equitable interactions are designed and experienced. (The COVID-19 crisis, with its sudden, wholesale move to remote learning, has sharply foregrounded these elements). The physical environment might be a school, an after-school venue, a library, a museum, a botanical garden, a workplace, or a home. The digital environment might be a wholly online community (e.g., a learning management system used in a formal setting or an immersive game in an informal setting [of course the participant is logging on from some physical environment]) or it might be interwoven (via screen, joystick, headset, DJ mixer, robot, circuitry, e-textile, microcontroller, etc.) with the face-to-face interactions within the physical environment.

Design for environment(s) means attention to how control (of access, of resources, of standards) and agency are manifested: who creates the blueprints, who decides whether there shall be gates and locks (and, if so, who controls the keys?), who in effect owns the space and holds title to the place? Design for environment(s) also includes the intent for duration: is the environment meant to be fixed, sustained and continuous (e.g., a 10th-grade computer science classroom, a wet lab) or to be flexible, ephemeral and/or sporadic (e.g., a pop-up locale hosting a hackathon, a game jam, a robotics competition, a stitchfest or similar DIY maker event)? Is the environment intended as a stand-alone or as a connected part of a systemic whole? Is the environment purpose-built, or is it a space repurposed/retro-fitted to meet new design intentions?

Physical Spaces

Researchers from many disciplines[4] have examined the ways in which the configuration and conceptualization of physical spaces work to invite, hinder, or facilitate interaction (Lupton, 2014; Nussbaumer, 2018). Substantial, if inconclusive, research exists specifically for the impact of the physical environment on formal K–12 and postsecondary education (Barrett et al., 2015; Cleveland and Fisher, 2014; Davies et al., 2013; O'Neil, 2010; Rands and Gensemer-Topf, 2017; Strong-Wilson and Ellis, 2007). Higgins et al. (2005) summarize that "[i]t is extremely difficult to come to firm conclusions about the impact of learning environments because of the multi-faceted nature of environments and the subsequent

---

[4]These disciplines include architecture, engineering, design, ergonomics, psychology, ethnography, and learning sciences.

diverse and disconnected nature of the research literature" (p. 6). The lack of definitive findings is even more pronounced with respect to informal environments, both because informal environments are much more varied and because there is far less research done on them compared to the formal environments. Having said that, the maker movement and various informal STEM and computer science initiatives have propelled much experimentation (Bennett and Monahan, 2013; Brahms and Werner, 2013; Dooley and Witthoft, 2012; Martinez and Stager, 2019; NRC, 2015; Peppler, Halverson, and Kafai, 2016; Stornaiulo and Nichols, 2018).

Effective designs of physical spaces also consider the needs and goals of the learning community members. Lighting, color schemes, acoustics, airflow, temperature, furniture and device design and configuration, hallway orientation, and the location and nature of common areas and storage space can foster planned collaboration and spontaneous informal learning among learners in the program or experience (Amedeo and Dyck, 2003; Yang, Becerik-Gerber, and Mino, 2013).

In recent decades, researchers have focused particularly on space/place-related issues relating to STEM and to computer science (Dasgupta, Magana, and Vieira, 2019; Denson et al., 2015) and even more recently on issues of access, inclusion, and equity (Beers and Summers, 2018; Holeton, 2020; Israel, 2019; Ladner and Israel, 2016; Mader and Lynch, 2020; Santo, Vogel, and Ching, 2019; Wilson and Randall, 2010). The equitable distribution of space and amenities, the age of facilities, equitable access to physical space and place (including consideration of regulations, such as the Americans with Disabilities Act, and popularized guidelines, such as Universal Design for Learning), and equitable access to required hardware and software, including physical network connectivity, bandwidth, download speeds and data storage capacities, all need to be considered. Adaptations to the environment may be needed if a learner has a physical disability so that they can continue to meaningfully engage with the content. For example, if the learner uses a wheelchair, then it may be necessary to adjust not only the table height, but also white boards around the room used for collaborative engagement (Center for Applied Special Technology, 2020).

Schools or Campus-Style Learning Environments

Inspired by heightened interest in STEM and computer science, and deliberately designing for equity, some schools and youth development programs have created holistic, large-scale, sometimes campus-style learning environments. These spaces are often co-created/funded by a consortium of public-sector, corporate, and non-profit actors, typically situated within the community being served and simultaneously adapting some tech workplace practices to suit community-determined norms.[5] Some examples include High Tech High in San Diego (launched 2000); The School of the Future in Philadelphia (2006); Digital Harbor Foundation in Baltimore (2011); Pathways In Technology Early College High School in Brooklyn (2011); Harlem Children's Zone Promise Academy Charter School (2012); Digital NEST in Watsonville and Salinas, California (2014); The Knowledge House in the Bronx (2014); and the Brooklyn STEAM Center (2019). Some of these models were designed for replication and have begun to be replicated. Relatively little research is yet available on the efficacy of these various models in terms of their environmental design features.

Online Communities

Learners may engage with computing through gaming and online communities, which are individuals who come together and share "feelings of camaraderie, empathy and support" around a common interest (Preece and Maloney-Krichmar, 2005). It is important to distinguish between voluntary or open-call online communities (e.g., individuals playing Fortnite or creating and commenting on TikTok videos) and mandated or circumscribed communities (e.g., an online math class required to pass the ninth grade). Design considerations may differ for the two scenarios, and research on how best to design online environments for involuntary participants is not yet available—though a surge in such research is expected on remote learning triggered by the COVID-19 crisis.

Several environmental design dimensions are associated with the success of online communities. The first of these is, collectively, the purpose, rules, rhetoric, and graphic representations for the community (and who controls these), that is, the means by which the community creates the boundaries for its sense of "ambient belonging" (Cheryan et al., 2009) and the sense of "rightful presence" for its participants (Calabrese Barton and Tan, 2019). Just as in physical environments, participants may be attracted or repelled by elements of an online environment, with enormous implications for learning outcomes, authenticity, and equity (Ito et al., 2018).[6] Flowing from and supporting the above are other elements, including whether or not the community is completely virtual or has a physical

---

[5]Their antecedents include the original Dewey-influenced Gary Plan schools launched in 1907, the "Schools of Tomorrow" movement in the 1960s, and the work of the Coalition of Essential Schools in the 1990s; they also overlap with the community schools approach more generally.

[6]It should be recognized that widespread male harassment of women game creators and reviewers, in what became known as "GamerGate," is a harsh and blatant example of the stakes involved (Barnes, 2018; Todd, 2015).

presence; the software environments that support the community (e.g., listservs, chat, blogs, wikis, apps and app creation, game design, authoring tools and play protocols, virtual reality design, video creation and use), including whether that environment is via traditional fixed computer or via a mobile device, or via some form of ubiquitous "Internet of Things" network; and the size and longevity of the community (Barbour, 2013; Bers, 2012; Corry and Stella, 2012; Gee, 2007; Harris-Packer and Ségol, 2015; Martinez-Garza, 2013; Pasnik, 2019; Preece and Maloney-Krichmar, 2005; Sobel, 2019; Statti and Villegas, 2020). As is true of all physical environments, the social experience in an online community is fundamental and dynamic, changing with who is present, the number of individuals present, and the nature of the interaction. And central to the continuation of such communities is knowing who the intended audience is.

Duration

How long a young person is engaged within an individual learning experience—and across an ecosystem of learning experiences—is another consideration of design. Duration includes the time in which a learner is engaged in a particular activity, as well as the frequency with which the learner engages in a particular learning experience. Both of these duration factors (i.e., total time and frequency) are important to consider in relation to the goals underlying the learning experience. For example, if the goal is to spark interest in a particular activity, a single, brief encounter may be sufficiently catalytic for a learner, inspiring them to continue with similar experiences or to identify resources to support further exploration (Barron, 2006; Chao et al., 2016). By contrast, if a program is designed to develop deep knowledge or greater fluency, more time and more frequent time within an experience and across an ecosystem of experiences may be needed (Barron, 2006).

Research suggests a relationship between time engaged in an activity and performance (Crowley et al., 2015; NRC, 2009; 2015); however, that does not mean that simply providing more time will lead to increased learning. The amount of time devoted to an activity needs to be developmentally and contextually appropriate. It is worth considering whether the appropriate frequency is a one-time event, weekly (or multiple times per week), or over a more extended time period, such as multiple classes; this will, of course, depend on the goal(s) of learning (e.g., to develop deeper expertise). Whether a learning experience is in the service of personal authenticity or professional authenticity, authenticity in learning necessitates time. Inquiry processes take time (Edelson, Gordin, and Pea, 1999; Kapur and Bielaczyc, 2012); likewise, personally-meaningful creative activities take time (Sternberg and Lubart, 1991).

But total time and frequency present challenges when designing both within and beyond the school setting. Highly structured learning environments such as K–12 classrooms typically enjoy the benefit of participants who are required to be present; classroom teachers, unlike museum educators or librarians, do not have to worry about learners opting out of a learning experience. That said, computing experiences are typically not included as part of core curricular experiences, and so finding time for them presents a challenge as K–12 classroom teachers navigate numerous demands on instructional time and manage competing interests within an already-crowded curriculum. Another challenge in the school context is the compartmentalization of the school day. Many K–12 teachers in the United States operate within fixed and relatively brief class periods. These encounters make it difficult to engage in deep work; authentic learning for computing, whether personally or professionally authentic, does not flourish in settings where thinking and creating are continually disrupted and restarted (Mehta and Fine, 2019).

Out-of-school learning experiences are not immune to duration-related challenges (see Box 7-6). Unlike the requisite participation of the school setting, out-of-school experiences typically rely on voluntary participation from learners. But the lack of expectation of commitment can result in attrition, either completely or partially, leading to discontinuity in the learning experience and undermining the time required to foster learning in authentic experiences. As discussed in Chapter 5, it is important to note, also, that there are inherent inequities in access to out-of-school learning opportunities, due to cost, accessibility of locations, or varying personal or family responsibilities.

Tools

Authentic experiences for computing often call on learners to engage in activities that involve the use of tools or manipulation of objects (physical or digital). In particular, authentic experiences that cultivate interest and competencies in *computing* are unsurprisingly dependent on interactions with the tools of computing. Tools are not neutral as they are designed with explicit and implicit intent (Costanza-Chock, 2020; DiGiano, Goldman, and Chorost, 2008; Svihla and Reeve, 2016); but they are both used in intended and unanticipated ways (de Certeau, 1984). This section will outline several key considerations related to tools and platforms for computing—factors that influence the design of tools with which young people are learning computing and worth considering by designers when selecting tools to support learners.

Learning how to program is a common entry point into computing. Although there are numerous programming languages and platforms explicitly designed for professional use, starting novices with professionally-authentic tools has been shown to be discouraging and alienating to young people having their first experiences with computing (Kelleher and Pausch, 2005). Several decades of design research have focused on how to design programming languages and computing environments that are developmentally appropriate and appealing to young, novice learners.

One framework (du Boulay, O'Shea, and Monk, 1981) for thinking about how to make programming more accessible to novices introduces the ideas of "simplicity and visibility" as central principles for design. Simplicity means a small number of commands, and visibility means providing insights into how the machine works. Others have commented on this framework to note it still needs to be "easy to use" (Mendelsohn, Green, and Brna, 1990), which has led to the development of "easy to use" graphical programming languages, from the early days of Boxer (diSessa and Abelson, 1986) and AgentSheets (Repenning, 1991), to data flow languages like Prograph (Cox, Giles, and Pietrzykowski, 1989).

Resnick and Silverman (2005) describe the kind of intended environment as one with "low floors, high ceilings, and wide walls." The image of low floors represents a commitment to simplicity, visibility, and ease of use—qualities that are especially important when designing tools for novices. High ceilings represent the ability to create programs that are programmatically sophisticated or complex. The image of wide walls captures the importance of being able to create many different types of things, complexity notwithstanding; a language or tool enables a learner to produce different types of programs, not just a narrow focus on one genre of creative product. Box 7-7 describes Scratch, a programming environment for novices whose designers explicitly engaged the aspirations of low floors, high ceilings, and wide walls.

Some tool designers may encounter constraints that cause them to choose to sacrifice wide walls (despite how they might support the vision); this may be true for particular genres of creations or particular disciplinary commitments. As an example of constraining genres of projects, the Scratch programming environment opted to support programming 2D worlds, while the Alice programming environment opted to support programming 3D worlds. Both Scratch and Alice have been designed to make programming accessible to learners and teachers with little to no programming experience (i.e., the "low floor") and computationally sophisticated programs can be created (i.e., the "high ceiling"), but they have each intentionally constrained what is easy to create (i.e., a learner who is passionate about 3D virtual worlds would ideally select a tool that supports that type of work).

Computing tools need not be constrained to a computer, and there is a long history of how tangible interfaces can be used to support introduction

---

BOX 7-7
Scratch

The Scratch programming environment is one of the most widely-used tools for novice programmers. Building on the aspirations for novice programmers established by LOGO in the 1980s, the developers of Scratch similarly pursued a commitment to low floors, high ceilings, and wide walls (Resnick et al., 2009). The developers identified three design principles to guide their support of that commitment. First, Scratch was designed to be tinkerable through, among other properties, its blocks-based graphical interface, which reduces syntax errors. Second, Scratch was designed to support personally meaningful project creation by not restricting the genres of projects that can be created. Since its launch in 2007, millions of young people have created enormously diverse projects, from stories, to games, to animations, to simulations. Finally, Scratch was designed to support social interactions, by being not only a programming language, but also an online community where learners can share, discuss, and build on their own and others' creations.

SOURCE: Based on Resnick et al. (2009).

---

to computing education (Bers, 2017; Horn and Bers, 2019; Kafai, Fields, and Searle, 2014; Resnick and Rosenbaum, 2013). Tangible interfaces, such as robotics kits (e.g., Mindstorms), interactive blocks (e.g., KIBO), and e-textiles (e.g., LilyPad Arduino; see Box 7-8), offer access to computing without the traditional computer (Buechley and Eisenberg, 2008; Buechley et al., 2008). Tangible interfaces have been used to both lower the floor and widen the walls of participation. For example, instead of snapping virtual programming blocks together, young children snap together physical programming blocks with the KIBO programming environment, a developmentally easier entry point for small children. E-textiles expand the range of creative production, widening (or maybe moving) the walls of creative participation, inviting young people and women who perhaps did not see the expressiveness of code until it was paired with more traditional crafting activities. An equity-related concern regarding tangible interfaces is their cost; robotics kits and tangible programming interfaces can be hundreds of dollars; even lower-cost e-textiles become cost-prohibitive when trying to serve large numbers of learners.

The intent and expressive capacity of a tool are important factors to consider when selecting a tool to include in the broader design of a learning experience. No one tool will be ideal for all learners or for every type of learning experience, so thinking about the vast array of tools as part of a larger ecosystem of learning is key. Transfer between different

---

BOX 7-8
LilyPad Arduino

The LilyPad Arduino, developed by Leah Buechley, is a small computer that is sewable; it is a tool that is often at the center of electronic textile ("e-textile") projects. As described on the LilyPad Arduino project page, the LilyPad can support both input, such as measuring pressure or temperature, and output, such as flashing lights or playing sounds. One early example of an e-textile project made with the LilyPad Arduino was a light-up jacket for cyclists. By pressure-sensitive controls placed in the ends of the jacket sleeves, the cyclist sporting the jacket was able to signal left and right turns through lights stitched into the back panel of the garment.

SOURCES: Based in part on Leah Buechley, see http://leahbuechley.com/?p=81, and Arduino's site at https://www.arduino.cc/en/Main/ArduinoBoardLilyPad.

---

tools for novices and then later from tools for novices to tools for professionals is possible. Researchers have studied transfer between languages through additional scaffolding (Shrestha, Barik, and Parnin, 2018), including moving from visual languages to textual languages (Weintrop and Wilensky, 2015).

Iteration

As stated in the opening section of this chapter, developing a clear and intentioned set of goals is an important early step in the process of program or experience design. To create alignment among the intended goals, reflection provides opportunities for designers to evaluate the alignment of the experience so that they can iterate until alignment is achieved. Moreover, understanding why previous efforts have faltered can greatly benefit the process of creating and implementing programs. There are countless initiatives to improve STEM learning and engagement, including computing. Many of these have met with some success and contributed greatly to the field. Others provide fodder for a number of important areas for consideration when designing programs around a specific intended goal. Table 7-2 highlights some particular goals of iteration and strategies to consider as part of reflection and the continuous improvement process.

Ultimately, the design of authentic experiences for computing yields the strongest results when it is conducted as an iterative, rather than linear, process. The design of a learning experience is not about the application of relevant principles and hoping they lead to the desired outcomes. Rather it

TABLE 7-2 Program Goals and Strategies for Iteration

If the goal of iteration is to . . .	Possible strategies to consider . . .
Design for Authenticity	Professional Authenticity • Ensure practices modeled align with professional practices and communicate alignment • Examine activities and resources • Determine whether the duration is sufficient to develop skills associated with profession Personal Authenticity • Consult with audience to understand whether personal authenticity is being achieved • Determine what adjustments are needed to activities
Attract Learners	• Consider original objectives of design in relation to intended audience • Examine marketing strategies and messaging • Use data to inform initial iterations
Measure Learning Objectives	• Work backwards from learning objectives to activities to ensure alignment • Ensure learning objectives are clearly defined • Assess what matters • Ensure relevant data are produced
Measure Interest	• Document whether interest is changing • Collect and include feedback on interest impact from learners • Identify and modify breaking points that may lead learners to disengage
Evaluate Program Drift	• Determine whether program still has intended focus • Restructure, reframe, or change activities to align with goals • Bring in additional expertise as needed
Take Programs to Scale	• Ensure program grounded in clearly articulated and specific principles • Connect outcomes to a logic model • Build capacity to support the program or partner with organizations that have capacity • Begin testing hypotheses at small scales and supplement program with materials as needed • Generate evidence to determine program effectiveness • Continuously test and refine program, as needed

is about using feedback to adjust course as things unfold, making changes to better achieve the activity's goals. While designers hope for success, there are many ways that well-intentioned initiatives can fail. But it is really only failure if we do not learn anything from that experience. If instead, designers learn from each iteration of their implementation and adjust key components of the experience, either in small or large ways, there is continuous improvement.

SUMMARY

There are a number of important considerations to the design of any authentic experience for computing. The goal of this chapter was to provide guidance with respect to the design of authentic experiences for computing based on the available evidence. To that end, the chapter identified a number of important questions to ask and issues to consider during the design process. Having a clear and intentioned set of goals and attending to authenticity is critical in the design of authentic experiences for computing. Important considerations for design include attending to the social elements of the experience, such as who the intended learners are and the prior experiences they bring as well as who supports the learners and what experiences educators and facilitators need. Central to any authentic experience for computing is the activity—or what the learner is doing—as well as the ways in which the environment and duration of the activity can sufficiently engage learners. There is also a need for intentional consideration of the content and pedagogy, and of how best to assess the intended outcomes. Additional considerations include the connections in and out of the program to other learning opportunities. Just as important to the design is evaluating the program/experience to ensure alignment with the goals; as such, reflection is key.

8

Conclusions, Recommendations, and Research Agenda

The committee was tasked with exploring the role of authentic learning experiences in computing and their potential to cultivate interest and competencies necessary for pursuing careers in computing. To address this, the committee examined the evidence on learning and teaching using authentic experiences for computing in both formal and informal settings in children and youth ages 5–18, with particular attention to engaging learners who have been typically underrepresented in computing fields based on gender, race, ethnicity, or perceived ability.

The committee recognized that the term "authenticity" has taken on multiple meanings. It is often used to refer to a broad range of learning experiences in science, technology, engineering, and mathematics (STEM) that incorporate open-ended, hands-on pedagogical approaches grounded in real-world contexts. It is also used to refer to learning experiences that are designed to closely resemble professional practice in a STEM discipline. Authenticity can also refer to how meaningful or relevant a learning experience seems from the learner's perspective. Given the complexity of the term, the committee identified two key facets of authenticity: "professional authenticity"—that is, aligned with professional STEM practices and culture—and "personal authenticity"—that is, personally or culturally meaningful to the learner.

In reviewing the relevant research, the committee began by using the broadest definition of authenticity—open-ended, problem or project based, and making—to examine the evidence for whether these kinds of approaches in general hold promise for supporting the development of interest, identity, and competence in computing. The studies reviewed did not distinguish between professional and personal authenticity in the way the committee describes. However, research on learning more generally and in the context of other STEM disciplines suggests that attention to personal authenticity—that is considering what might make the experience meaningful for the learner—may be especially important for engaging learners who have been under-represented in computing due to gender, race, ethnicity, or perceived ability.

The committee recognizes that computing is more than just coding or computer science. Computing is now a part of nearly every occupation, not only those in the technology industry. As a result, competencies for comput-ing are needed for a wide range of jobs and careers—computer scientist, database manager, software developer for media in the arts and music industries, spreadsheet developers—across multiple industries. Developing competence in computing requires computing-specific foundational knowl-edge and skills, as well as skills and knowledge that are applicable and use-ful in contexts beyond computing, such as critical thinking and creativity. This broad framing means that the outcomes go beyond a narrow focus on coding to include a larger set of foundational knowledge and competencies.

Finally, the committee considered the range of settings in which authen-tic learning experiences in computing occur, including schools, informal set-tings, home, and online communities. The committee focused particularly on learning experiences that are designed and facilitated by educators or other professionals (National Research Council, 2009). In examining pro-grams across these settings, the committee identified promising elements of design that can guide development of more effective authentic learning experiences in computing.

This final chapter presents the committee's conclusions and recom-mendations for policy, practice, and research and data collection drawing on the evidence discussed across the chapters. These are followed by a research agenda that identifies gaps in current knowledge with respect to the ways that authentic learning experiences in computing can lead to the development of interest and competencies for computing, especially among learners who have been historically underrepresented in computing because of gender, race, ethnicity, or perceived ability.

CONCLUSIONS

In reviewing the available information on authentic learning experiences for developing interest and competencies for computing, the committee reached the following conclusions, which inform the recommendations that follow.

CONCLUSION 1: Women, Black, Latinx, and Indigenous people are under-represented in computing-related careers and in the educational pathways

into them when compared to their representation in the population of the United States. This underrepresentation is due, in part, to historic inequities, systemic biases, and stereotypes about who can succeed in computing as well as to lack of access to learning opportunities.

The substantial impact of computing on society, personally and professionally, over the past 20 years has prompted more urgent calls to engage all learners in computing. There has been particular attention to providing learning opportunities that engage individuals from groups that are currently underrepresented in computing-related careers. The intent is to broaden participation in computing careers by increasing the diversity of the individuals who enter the pathways into the profession. Authentic learning experiences in computing are often thought to be more appealing to and engaging for a broader range of learners (Chapter 2).

CONCLUSION 2: Authentic learning experiences in computing that are designed to closely mirror professional practice—professional authenticity—may engage some learners. However, historical inequities in computing, biases, and stereotypes may also make these kinds of experiences unattractive to learners from communities that have typically been underrepresented in computing.

Authentic experiences in computing are often designed with the goal of providing learners with an opportunity to gain a sense of what a career in computing might entail. This focus on professional practice can unintentionally bring with it some of the problematic elements of professional practice that perpetuate exclusion of people from particular demographic groups. In addition, due to stereotypes about who is most likely to succeed in computing, learners themselves understand that these experiences are not designed for them (Chapter 2).

CONCLUSION 3: Research on learning more generally, and in the context of other STEM disciplines, indicates that interest, motivation, perception of the discipline, and self-efficacy play important roles in learning and can shape later choices and identity development. They are likely to play similar roles in learning in computing and in shaping choices and identity development related to computing.

CONCLUSION 4: Learning experiences in computing that are designed with attention to learners' interests, identities, and backgrounds—personal authenticity—may attract and retain more learners who are underrepresented in computing because of their gender, race, ethnicity, or perceived ability than learning experiences that focus solely on professional practice.

CONCLUSION 5: STEM experiences can be both professionally and personally authentic at the same time. These facets of authenticity do not need to be in opposition and ideally experiences can be designed to incorporate both.

The above set of conclusions builds upon the evidence presented in Chapter 3. Research from the broader field of STEM learning suggests that motivation to learn and learning outcomes are associated with learners' personal interest in a topic or discipline, their perception of value and use of what they are learning, and their sense of competence in engaging in the practices and community of the discipline. When a STEM learning experience is connected to cultural referents, places, and social relationships that learners find personally meaningful, it can foster a sense of disciplinary learning that is relevant to the learner. In view of this research, authentic experiences in computing that reflect professional practice and also connect learners to problems that they care about are one possible approach for reaching a broader range of learners.

CONCLUSION 6: For most individuals, a single authentic STEM experience may not be sufficient to sustain interest and develop a suite of competencies in computing. Multiple experiences over time and across settings and contexts may help facilitate the development of enduring interest and competencies.

Developing knowledge and skills in computing takes time, as does developing an identity as someone who can succeed in computing. As described in Chapter 3, research on learning in other STEM disciplines suggests that multiple, connected experiences in different settings across time can be a powerful way to develop competencies and identity in STEM disciplines. Some researchers have pointed to the importance of considering the "ecosystem" of learning opportunities a learner may have open to them and how a learner's experience may unfold and connect across different settings. Access to and participation in computing activities across multiple settings can help shape whether emerging interests and competencies develop further and eventually result in long-term participation in computing (see Chapter 3). Consistently positive experiences may facilitate continued growth and confidence, while negative or conflicting experiences may undermine learning and engagement. This is consistent with retrospective accounts in the field, including the personal trajectories presented in Chapter 2.

CONCLUSION 7: Research on authentic learning experiences in computing is in the early stages with few studies that employ causal designs and uneven attention to different cognitive, behavioral, and affective outcomes. The evidence that is currently available shows mixed results. However, research on authentic learning experiences in other STEM subjects suggests that such experiences can increase interest and competencies for those disciplines.

Although the research in other STEM disciplines points to ways in which participation in authentic experiences can increase interest and competencies in STEM (see Chapter 3), the research on computing is emergent (Chapter 4). There is an increasing number of studies examining the relationship between authentic learning experiences in computing and specific affective, cognitive, and behavioral outcomes. In some cases, the results are positive and promising, whereas in other cases the findings are either inconclusive or are not significant.

Settings for Authentic Experiences in Computing

Authentic learning experiences in computing come in a variety of forms. They may include recreational pursuits such as participating in online games and creative communities to more structured activities in classrooms, after-school programs, or camps. They also include experiences in school settings.

CONCLUSION 8: Authentic learning experiences in computing can occur in a wide range of settings, including classrooms, community organizations, homes as well as online. Each setting brings constraints as well as affordances with respect to the potential to provide experiences that combine both personal and professional authenticity.

CONCLUSION 9: Programs in out-of-school settings often have the flexibility to design learning experiences in computing that reflect the interests and identities of the learners and communities they serve. This flexibility may provide an opportunity to incorporate greater attention to personal authenticity. At the same time, wide variations in the nature of settings themselves, funding mechanisms, organizational capacity, and program design can make it difficult to arrive at broad generalizations about the outcomes of these programs.

Program designers in out-of-school settings have the opportunity to tailor learning experiences that are reflective of the culture, interests, and assets of the learners and communities they serve. However, the evidence suggests that the distribution and quality of out-of-school opportunities are tied to various factors, such as time, cost, transportation constraints, as well as reliable access to physical spaces, knowledgeable facilitators, and materials that are conducive to such activities and learning experiences. Although experiences may be designed to be more personally authentic to the learner, they may not be promoted broadly enough to reach learners from underrepresented communities (Chapter 5).

CONCLUSION 10: Participation in learning experiences for computing in K–12 schools is uneven. There are fewer opportunities, either as stand-alone courses or integrated into other school subjects, at the elementary and middle school grades, and relatively more opportunities in high school. In high school, there have been recent efforts to design courses to engage learners who have been traditionally underrepresented in computing based on gender, race, ethnicity, or perceived ability. However, at all grade levels there is little information about the nature of the learning experiences themselves and the degree to which they might reflect professional and personal authenticity.

Providing learning experiences in computing in K–12 schools has the potential to reach learners who otherwise would not have sought them out. However, as described in Chapter 6, factors within schools such as time in the curriculum, access to technology and the expertise of teachers make it difficult to provide learning opportunities that address both personal and professional authenticity. In addition, inequities in access to computing experiences both within and across schools mean that Black, Latinx, and Indigenous students and students from rural and low-income communities have fewer opportunities to engage in any kind of learning experiences in computing. At the high school level, there have been efforts to design courses that can attract students from groups who have historically not been represented in computing courses (Chapter 6).

CONCLUSION 11: In both formal and out-of-school settings, educators and program facilitators who have strong backgrounds in computing and are proficient in pedagogical approaches that engage learners are key to implementing professionally and personally authentic learning experiences in computing. Educators and facilitators benefit from professional preparation that equips them with the necessary skills, resources, and experiences to adequately implement authentic STEM experiences for learners.

With the press to expand the numbers of programs that provide learning experiences in computing, there is increased demand for educators and facilitators who have the knowledge and skills to lead them. There are recent efforts to more systematically understand the types of professional learning experiences that are beneficial for facilitators in out-of-school settings as they work to develop and refine their knowledge and skills (see

Chapter 5). In school settings, elementary and middle school teachers typically do not have formal training in computing (Chapter 6).

Designing Authentic Learning Experiences in Computing

CONCLUSION 12: Principles for good program design for STEM learning, which incorporate attention to both professional and personal authenticity, suggest that careful attention to the following factors is essential:

- programmatic goals, including specification of desired outcomes;
- characteristics of the learners to be served;
- learners' interests, identities, and backgrounds;
- involvement of supportive caregivers, peers, educators, facilitators, and mentors;
- preparation of the individuals who will support the experience;
- ensuring participants have access to necessary materials and resources; and
- the organizational contexts within which the learning will occur.

Design, in any context, should begin with a sense of "why" and "for what purpose" one is designing. Having an explicit understanding of the purpose and clearly articulated goals allows for better alignment between intentions and actions such that it will be easier for program designers to specify what it is that they want participants to know or be able to do, and as a result what should be taught, to whom, and how. Chapter 7 elevates a number of key design considerations (i.e., learners, community, activities, environment, duration, tools, and iteration) that can guide development of programs that are tailored to the characteristics of a particular setting and community.

CONCLUSION 13: In order to build competencies for and sustained interest and identity in computing, learners need to engage in multiple learning experiences over time. To ensure that learners are aware of, guided through, and have access to opportunities to engage in authentic STEM experiences for computing, it may be ideal to leverage the contrasting strengths of out-of-school and formal settings by building and brokering stronger connections and pathways between them, as well as with home, community contexts, and youth-driven online communities.

Learners' experiences in out-of-school and in-school contexts often happen with little connection to each other. Yet, evidence from other STEM subjects (Chapter 3) suggests there is power in developing connections between learners' experiences across different settings and designing opportunities with these connections in mind. Partnerships between settings can enhance these connections, for example, museums partnering with schools to develop curriculum and provide professional development opportunities (Chapters 5 and 7). Furthermore, research suggests that relevance and personal authenticity may be supported by connections to place and culture and reinforced when supported and connected across settings (see Chapter 3).

RECOMMENDATIONS

In light of the evidence discussed throughout the report and the conclusions above, the committee recommends the following actions to ensure that a broader, more representative set of learners have access to authentic STEM experiences that can spark and cultivate interest and competencies for computing. The committee recognizes that while there is a strong call to expand the number of opportunities to learn computing, the evidence exploring how these experiences relate to developing interest and competences for computing is still emerging. Despite the limitations in the research, the committee offers a set of recommendations that focus on how research, design, and professional preparation and continued learning can support these changes while also emphasizing a systemic view of the changes needed to make progress toward more widespread, equitable access to authentic STEM experiences for computing.

RECOMMENDATION 1: Program designers should be intentional in the design and implementation of programs offering *authentic* learning experiences that build interest and competencies for computing. This includes:

- having clear and explicit programmatic goals and continuous refinement of the program to ensure alignment to those goals;
- designing for personal authenticity that builds on learners' interests, identities, and backgrounds while also designing for professional authenticity;
- ensuring that the participants include people who are underrepresented in computing because of their gender, race, ethnicity, or perceived ability;
- considering inclusion of families and community members as well as learners in opportunities to co-create activities;
- ensuring educators and facilitators have adequate preparation and access to necessary materials and resources; and
- reflecting on whether the communication, outreach, and operation of the program are inviting for learners who are underrepresented in computing because of their gender, race, ethnicity, or perceived ability.

RECOMMENDATION 2: Practicing teachers in schools and facilitators in out-of-school time settings should seek out opportunities and materials on how to incorporate effective practices for creating authentic learning experiences in computing within an existing program that includes utilizing problem-/project-based learning strategies, allowing learner choice among activities, and considering learners' contexts outside of school time.

RECOMMENDATION 3: Preservice and in-service teacher educators and trainers of out-of-school time facilitators should ensure that educators and facilitators are equipped to engage learners in personally authentic learning experiences in computing. This includes providing ongoing opportunities for educators to learn and practice using inclusive pedagogical approaches, as well as having access to materials and resources that build on learners' interests, identities, and backgrounds.

RECOMMENDATION 4: School leaders should consider a variety of ways to provide access to authentic learning experiences for computing. These include (1) addressing challenges (e.g., lack of instructional time and teacher expertise) associated with integrating authentic computing experiences into instruction in a variety of subjects, (2) increasing access to stand-alone computing courses, and (3) ensuring schools have adequate resources such as equipment, reliable broadband Internet, and time.

RECOMMENDATION 5: Program providers in out-of-school settings should increase efforts to expand access to authentic learning experiences for computing through growth of opportunities and active program promotion within underserved communities and in rural areas. This includes considering ways to reduce barriers to participation such as time, cost, and transportation. It also includes offering programs multiple times or during the evening and weekends, reducing program costs or offering financial assistance, and subsidizing transportation.

RECOMMENDATION 6: Program evaluators should develop and apply robust models of evaluation that take into account the distinctive features of authentic learning experiences in computing. More specifically, this includes attending to personal and professional authenticity, considering connections across settings, and to the extent possible, disaggregating findings and examining differences between and within groups (e.g., gender, race, ethnicity, socio-economic status) for computing outcomes as a central part of model building and evaluation.

RECOMMENDATION 7: There should be a broad-based effort to cultivate a network of opportunities, as well as supports for learners to navigate between them both in and out of school to increase access and opportunities for sustained engagement with computing. To achieve this:

- funders should support initiatives that make connections across settings—both formal and out-of-school settings including home and online—and between industry and educational efforts for authentic learning experiences in computing;
- designers and educators across formal and out-of-school settings should consider tailoring to the community context, learners' backgrounds and experiences, and attending to cultural relevance;
- local STEM institutions, schools, and out-of-school providers should develop partnerships that allow them to develop complementary programs that fill gaps and connect learners to other opportunities within the network; and
- stakeholders in the network should be sure that they are providing opportunities in communities of underrepresented learners.

RESEARCH AGENDA

During the course of the committee's review of the existing literature, numerous opportunities for research were identified that could help provide a deeper understanding of the ways in which authentic learning experiences can develop and cultivate interest and competencies for computing. Research on learning experiences in computing specifically is relatively sparse; however, findings from other STEM disciplines offer some guidance. The pressure to expand access to computing and the proliferation of programs for computing creates urgency for the research community to better understand how these experiences can best support learners.

The major gaps in the evidence base related to learning experiences in computing include a lack of knowledge about the access and participation in authentic learning experiences in computing, particularly those that occur outside of the formal school setting; a lack of evidence about the specific design features and pedagogies that facilitate high-quality authentic learning experiences in computing; and a lack of evidence about the effectiveness and outcomes of programs that provide authentic learning experiences in computing.

What was clear from the review of the literature is that in published studies of particular educational programs authors need to provide more detail including better descriptions of the program design, length, participants, role/approach of teacher/facilitator, data collection techniques, analysis, and findings. The field may also benefit from development and use of standardized measures of outcomes.

Future research needs to explore and identify the varied images and narratives of diverse students' trajectories in computing. This type of research would also include a need for longitudinal studies to establish relationships between authentic STEM opportunities and outcomes in computing careers and majors.

This report has also highlighted the lack of and need for research on learning experiences in computing that take place in home and family contexts and online. The COVID-19 pandemic has highlighted the importance of this line of research. Descriptive research could illuminate the landscape of such opportunities and provide insights into the quality and type of experiences available; it could also show the extent to which students of different backgrounds have access to and participate in such opportunities. For example, the field would benefit from an understanding more about the affordances of virtual experiences, and what goals can be achieved virtually versus those in real-life settings.

This section identifies priorities for research and discusses multiple methodological approaches needed to answer questions about access to, participation in, and outcomes related to computing that vary for students of different backgrounds and geographic contexts. That is, more research is needed to identify specific practices and designs for effective inclusive programming. It is worth noting that this research is challenging due to the heterogeneity of learners as well as type and quality of authentic STEM experiences. The possible areas for study below are an invitation for continued dialogue and a guide for funders or researchers seeking to understand the role of authentic learning experiences in developing interest, foundational knowledge, and competencies in computing.

Equity and Inclusion

Possible research areas that center equity and inclusion include studies that

- examine programs with proven success for students from minoritized communities as well as those in rural settings in computing-related activities;
- focus on effectiveness of specific instructional practice supporting inquiry-based and project-based learning and making-oriented activities (e.g., e-textiles) in computing, particularly for historically underrepresented populations;
- investigate under what circumstances and how ethnocomputing, and other culturally responsive and culturally sustaining pedagogical

approaches, can improve students' knowledge, sense of belonging, and aspirations in computing; and

- examine how the racial/ethnic, gender, and sexual orientation identity of educators or facilitators shapes students' perceptions of computing and their own sense of belonging.

Policy

Research needs in the area of policy include studies that

- examine how particular educational policies support the availability and quality of authentic computing experiences for students, particularly for historically underrepresented groups of students;
- explore effective recruitment of diverse (particularly Black, Latinx, and Indigenous) educators and facilitators;
- examine the role of the private sector and commercial products and platforms in supporting and inhibiting access to authentic learning experiences in computing; and
- analyze the nature and impact of schools, districts, or states adding computing education in K–5, middle, and high school settings (e.g., integrated within STEM subjects and/or standalone courses, duration of experiences).

Supporting Learning

How to best support authentic learning experiences in computing might be explored through studies that

- outline effective professional preparation and professional development programs, including pedagogy and content knowledge, for teachers and facilitators;
- probe how in-school and out-of-school, home, online, and youth-driven learning experiences can mutually support students' ongoing participation and aspirations in computing;
- examine how accumulated learning experiences about computing, over time, support students' efficacy, interests, and knowledge growth toward pursuing computing;
- detail the impact of peer and adult encouragement for supporting students' interest in pursuing computing; and
- identify the skills, interest, and competencies in computing that are developed in home-based settings or outside of structured (in-school or out-of-school) learning environments, such as hobbies, crafting, gaming, and entrepreneurship.

Personal and Professional Authenticity

Research areas that center personal and/or professional authenticity in learning experiences for computing includes studies that

- investigate how specific computing learning experiences can support a combination of both professionally and personally authentic computing learning experiences;
- seek to understand the trade-offs for different groups of learners of the relative emphasis given to personal or professional authenticity;
- explore personally authentic experiences for underrepresented learners, and how they align or differ from those that are professionally authentic and personally authentic experiences for groups dominant in STEM fields; and
- explore the effective practices for creating more inclusive professionally authentic settings, including college computing departments and the technology industry, for students who participate in computing education experiences.

FINAL REFLECTIONS

As articulated throughout this chapter and report, the profound impact of computing has substantially shaped our everyday lives. Engaging learners in opportunities that enable them to develop computational literacy and skills is imperative. However, as this final chapter suggests, there is much more that can and should be learned about the outcomes, nature, and design and implementation of authentic learning experiences for computing. This should not discourage those designing, implementing, or studying such experiences. On the contrary, our conclusions, recommendations, and research agenda strongly suggest the potential for authentic learning experiences to cultivate the interest and competencies for computing.

In order to realize this potential, the energy, creativity, and resources of researchers, practitioners, and concerned funders must now be directed at generating more thoughtful, high-quality, and evidence-based work. Given the inherent complexities, it will not be a surprise to find that designing, implementing, and documenting effective authentic learning experiences for computing is both time consuming and expensive. Despite these very real challenges, the possibility of ensuring learners have access to authentic experiences that will allow for the development of interest and competencies for computing is enticing in its potential for developing both a knowledgeable and creative citizenry and a robust and diverse computing workforce.

References

Afterschool Alliance. (2014). *America After 3PM and the African-American Community.* Available: http://www.afterschoolalliance.org/documents/AA3PM-2014/African. American-AA3PM-2014-Fact-Sheet.pdf.

Afterschool Alliance. (2016). *Growing Computer Science Education in Afterschool: Opportunities and Challenges.* Available: http://afterschoolalliance.org/documents/Growing_Computer_Science_Education_2016.pdf.

Ahn, J., Subramaniam, M., Bonsignore, E., Pellicone, A., Waugh, A., and Yip, J. (2014). *I Want to Be a Game Designer or Scientist: Connected Learning and Developing Identities with Urban, African-American Youth.* Boulder, CO: International Society of the Learning Sciences.

Aivaloglou, E., and Hermans, F. (2019). Early programming education and career orientation: the effects of gender, self-efficacy, motivation and stereotypes. In *Proceedings of the 50th ACM Technical Symposium on Computer Science Education* (pp. 679–685).

Allen, A., Michalchik, V., Van Horne, M., Harris, M., Chang-Order, J., and Wortman, A. (2020). *Full STEAM Ahead at Los Angeles Public Library.* Connected Learning Alliance. Available: https://clalliance.org/wp-content/uploads/2020/03/Full-Steam-Ahead-LA-Public-Library.pdf.

Allen, C.D., and Eisenhart, M. (2017). Fighting for desired versions of a future self: How young women negotiated STEM-related identities in the discursive landscape of educational opportunity. *Journal of the Learning Sciences, 26*(3), 407–436.

Allen, P.J., Lewis-Warner, K., and Noam, G.G. (2020). *Partnerships to Transform STEM Learning: A Case Study of a STEM Learning Ecosystem.* Available: https://files.eric.ed.gov/fulltext/EJ1249559.pdf.

Allison, C.J., and Cossette, I. (2007). Theory and practice in recruiting women for STEM careers. In *Proceedings of the 2007 WEPAN National Conference, Women in Engineering ProActive Network.* Available: https://journals.psu.edu/wepan/article/view/58487/58175.

Allsop, Y. (2019). Assessing computational thinking process using a multiple evaluation approach. *International Journal of Child-Computer Interaction, 19*, 30–55.

Amadei, B., and Sandekian, R. (2010). Model of integrating humanitarian development into engineering education. *Journal of Professional Issues in Engineering Education and Practice, 132*(2), 84–92.

Amedeo, D., and Dyck, J.A. (2003). Activity-enhancing arenas of designs: A case study of the classroom layout. *Journal of Architectural and Planning Research, 20*(4), 323–343.

Amelink, C.T., and Creamer, E.G. (2010). Gender differences in elements of the undergraduate experience that influence satisfaction with the engineering major and the intent to pursue engineering as a career. *Journal of Engineering Education, 99*(1), 81–92.

American Alliance of Museums. (2018). *Facing Change: Insights from AAM's Diversity, Equity, Accessibility, and Inclusion Working Group.* Available: https://www.aam-us.org/wp-content/uploads/2018/04/AAM-DEAI-Working-Group-Full-Report-2018.pdf.

American Library Association. (2019). *The State of America's Libraries 2019: A Report from the American Library Association.* Available: http://www.ala.org/news/state-americas-libraries-report-2019.

Americans with Disabilities Act. (1990). Available: https://adata.org/factsheet/ADA-overview.

Amo, L.C., Liao, R., Frank, E., Rao, R., and Upadhyaya, S. (2019). Cybersecurity interventions for teens: Two time-based approaches. *IEEE Transactions on Education, 62*(2), 134–140.

Arya, A., Gold, S., Farber, M., and Miklasz, K. (2019). GGJ-Next: The global game jam for youth. In *ICGJ 2019: Proceedings of the International Conference on Game Jams, Hackathons and Game Creation Events* (pp. 1–4).

Asgari, S., Dasgupta, N., and Stout, J.G. (2012). When do counterstereotypic ingroup members inspire versus deflate? The effect of successful professional women on young women's leadership self-concept. *Personality and Social Psychology Bulletin, 38*(3), 370–383.

Ashcraft, C., Eger, E.K., and Scott, K.A. (2017). Becoming technosocial change agents: Intersectionality and culturally responsive pedagogies as vital resources for increasing girls' participation in computing. *Anthropology & Education Quarterly, 48*(3), 233–251.

Ashford, S.N., Wilson, J.A., King, N.S., and Nyachae, T.M. (2017). STEM SISTA spaces: Creating counterspaces for black girls and women. In T. S. Ransaw and R. Majors (Eds.), *Emerging Issues and Trends in Education* (pp. 3–38). East Lansing, MI: Michigan State University Press.

Association for Library Services for Children. (2015). *Competencies for Librarians Serving Children in Public Libraries.* Available: http://www.ala.org/alsc/edcareers/alsccorecomps.

Association of Science Technology Centers. (2020). *Out-of-School Time Programs: Advice and Lessons Learned.* Available: https://www.astc.org/astc-dimensions/out-of-school-time-programs-advice-and-lessons-learned.

Athman, J., and Monroe, M. (2004). The effects of environment-based education on students' achievement motivation. *Journal of Interpretation Research, 9*(1), 9–25.

Azevedo, F.S. (2011). Lines of practice: A practice-centered theory of interest relationships. *Cognition and Instruction, 29*(2), 147–184.

Azevedo, F.S. (2013). The tailored practice of hobbies and its implication for the design of interest-driven learning environments. *Journal of the Learning Sciences, 22*(3), 462–510.

Azevedo, F.S. (2018). An inquiry into the structure of situational interests. *Science Education, 102*(1), 108–127.

Azevedo, F.S., diSessa, A.A., and Sherin, B.L. (2012). An evolving framework for describing student engagement in classroom activities. *The Journal of Mathematical Behavior, 31*(2), 270–289.

Ball, M., Mock, L., Garcia, D., Barnes, T., Hill, M., Milliken, A., Paley, J., Lopez, E., and Bohrer, J. (2020). The Beauty and Joy of Computing Curriculum and Teacher Professional Development. In *Proceedings of the 51st ACM Technical Symposium on Computer Science Education* (pp. 1398-1398).

Bandura, A. (1997). *Self-Efficacy: The Exercise of Control.* New York, NY: W.H. Freeman.

Bang, M., Warren, B., Rosebery, A.S., and Medin, D. (2013). Desettling expectations in science education. *Human Development, 55*(5–6), 302–318.

Banilower, E.R., Smith, P.S., Malzahn, K.A., Plumley, C.L., Gordon, E.M., and Hayes, M.L. (2018). *Report of the 2018 NSSME+.* Chapel Hill, NC: Horizon Research, Inc.

Barbour M. (2013). The landscape of K–12 online learning. In M.G. Moore (Ed.), *Handbook of Distance Education* (3rd ed.). London, UK and New York, NY: Routledge.

Barker, B.S., Nugent, G., Grandgenett, N., Keshwani, J., Nelson, C.A., and Leduc-Mills, B. (2018). Developing an elementary engineering education program through problem-based wearable technologies activities. In *K–12 STEM Education: Breakthroughs in Research and Practice* (pp. 29–55). Hershey, PA: IGI Global.

Barker, L.J., McDowell, C., and Kalahar, K. (2009). Exploring factors that influence computer science introductory course students to persist in the major. *ACM SIGCSE Bulletin, 41*(1), 153–157.

Barnes, R. (2018). *Uncovering Online Commenting Culture: Trolls, Fanboys, and Lurkers.* London, UK: Palgrave Macmillan.

Barratt, R., and Hacking, E.B. (2011). Place-based education and practice: Observations from the field. *Children Youth and Environments, 21*(1), 1–13.

Barrett, P., Davies, F., Zhang, Y., and Barrett, L. (2015). The impact of classroom design on pupils' learning: Final results of a holistic, multi-level analysis. *Building and Environment, 89*, 118–133.

Barron, B. (2006). Interest and self-sustained learning as catalysts of development: A learning ecology perspective. *Human Development, 49*(4), 193–224.

Barron, B., Gomez, K., Pinkard, N., and Martin, C.K. (2014). *The Digital Youth Network: Cultivating New Media Citizenship in Urban Communities.* Cambridge, MA: MIT Press.

Basu, S., Biswas, G., Sengupta, P., Dickes, A., Kinnebrew, J.S., and Clark, D. (2016). Identifying middle school students' challenges in computational thinking-based science learning. *Research and Practice in Technology Enhanced Learning, 11*(1), 13.

Bathgate, M., and Schunn, C. (2017). The psychological characteristics of experiences that influence science motivation and content knowledge. *International Journal of Science Education, 39*(17), 2402–2432.

Baumeister, R.F., and Leary, M.R. (1995). The need to belong: Desire for interpersonal attachments as a fundamental human motivation. *Psychological Bulletin, 117*(3), 497.

Beasley, M.A., and Fischer, M.J. (2012). Why they leave: The impact of stereotype threat on the attrition of women and minorities from science, math and engineering majors. *Social Psychology of Education, 15*(4), 427–448.

Beers, M., and Summers T. (2018, May 7). Educational equity and the classroom: Designing learning-ready spaces for all students. *Educause Review, 54*–55.

Bell, P., Bricker, L.A., Tzou, C., Lee, T., and Van Horne, K. (2012). Engaging learners in scientific practices related to obtaining, evaluating, and communicating information. *The Science Teacher, 79*(8), 31–36.

Ben-Eliyahu, A., Rhodes, J.E., and Scales, P. (2014). The interest-driven pursuits of 15 year olds: "Sparks" and their association with caring relationships and developmental outcomes. *Applied Developmental Science, 18*(2), 76–89.

Bennett, D., and Monahan, P. (2013). NYSCI design lab: No bored kids! In M. Honey and D. Kanter (Eds.), *Design, Make, Play: Growing the Next Generation of STEM Innovators* (pp. 151–168). London, UK and New York, NY: Routledge.

Bequette, M., Causey, L., Schreiber, R., Pennington, R., Braafladt, K., and Svarovsky, G.N. (2018). *Summaries of the Making Connections Project and Play Tinker Make Activities.* Science Museum of Minnesota. Available: https://www.informalscience.org/sites/default/files/Making%20Connections%20Practitioner%20Guide.pdf.

Berland, M. (2016). Making, tinkering, and computational literacy. *Makeology: Makers as Learners, 2*, 196–205.

Bers, M.U. (2007). Project InterActions: A multigenerational robotic learning environment. *Journal of Science and Technology Education, 16*(6), 537–552.

Bers, M.U. (2012). *Designing Digital Experiences for Positive Youth Development: From Playpen to Playground.* Oxford, UK: Oxford University Press.

Bers, M.U. (2017). *Coding as a Playground: Programming and Computational Thinking in the Early Childhood Classroom.* London, UK and New York, NY: Routledge.

Bers, M.U. (2018). Coding, playgrounds and literacy in early childhood education: The development of KIBO robotics and ScratchJr. In *2018 IEEE Global Engineering Education Conference (EDUCON)* (pp. 2100–2108).

Bertot, J.C., Sarin, L.C., and Percell, J. (2015). *Re-Envisioning the MLS: Findings, Issues, and Considerations.* University of Maryland. Available: http://mls.umd.edu/wp-content/uploads/2015/08/ReEnvisioningFinalReport.pdf.

Bevan, B. (2017). The promise and the promises of Making in science education. *Studies in Science Education, 53*(1), 75–103.

Bevan, B., and Xanthoudaki, M. (2008). Professional development for museum educators: Unpinning the underpinnings. *Journal of Museum Education, 33*(2), 107–119.

Bevan, B., Dillon, J., Hein, G.E., Macdonald, M., Michalchik, V., Miller, D., Root, D., Rudder, L., Xanthoudaki, M., and Yoon, S. (2010). *Making Science Matter: Collaborations Between Informal Science Education Organizations and Schools. A CAISE Inquiry Group Report.* Washington, DC: Center for Advancement of Informal Science Education.

Beyer, S. (2014). Why are women underrepresented in computer science? Gender differences in stereotypes, self-efficacy, values, and interests and predictors of future CS course-taking and grades. *Computer Science Education, 24*(2–3), 153–192.

Beyer, S., and Haller, S. (2006). Gender differences and intragender differences in computer science students: Are female CS majors more similar to male CS majors or female non-majors? *Journal of Women and Minorities in Science and Engineering, 12*(4), 337–365.

Beyer, S., Rynes, K., Perrault, J., Hay, K., and Haller, S. (2003). Gender differences in computer science students. *SIGCSE Bulletin, 35*, 49–53.

Bicer, A., Nite, S.B., Capraro, R.M., Barroso, L.R., Capraro, M.M., and Lee, Y. (2017). Moving from STEM to STEAM: The effects of informal STEM learning on students' creativity and problem-solving skills with 3D printing. In *2017 IEEE Frontiers in Education Conference (FIE)* (pp. 1–6).

Billig, S. (2000). Research on K–12 school-based service-learning: The evidence builds. *Phi Delta Kappan, 81*(9), 658–664.

Björkman, C. (2005). *Crossing Boundaries, Focusing Foundations, Trying Translations: Feminist Technoscience Strategies in Computer Science.* Doctoral dissertation, Blekinge Institute of Technology, Sweden. (Unpublished).

Blickenstaff, J.C. (2005). Women and science careers: leaky pipeline or gender filter?. *Gender and Education, 17*(4), 369–386.

Blikstein, P. (2013a). Digital fabrication and "making" in education: The democratization of invention. In J. Water-Herrmann and C. Büching (Eds.), *FabLabs: Of Machines, Makers and Inventors* (pp. 203–221). Bielefeld, Germany: transcript Verlag.

Blikstein, P. (2013b). Gears of our childhood: Constructionist toolkits, robotics, and physical computing, past and future. In *Proceedings of the 12th International Conference on Interaction Design and Children (IDC '13)* (pp. 173–182).

Blikstein, P. (2018). Maker movement in education: History and prospects. In M. de Vries (Ed.), *Handbook of Technology Education* (pp. 419–437). New York, NY: Springer International Publishing.

Boaler, J., William, D., and Zevenbergen, R. (2000). *The Construction of Identity in Secondary Mathematics Education.* Paper presented at the International Mathematics Education and Society Conference, Montechoro, Portugal. Available: https://files.eric.ed.gov/fulltext/ED482654.pdf.

Bobb, K. (2016). Broadening participation in computing: A critical perspective. *ACM Inroads,* 7(4), 49–51.

Bortz, W., Gautam, A., Tatar, D., and Lipscomb, K. (2020). Missing in measurement: Why identifying learning in integrated domains is so hard. *Journal of Science Education and Technology, 29,* 121–136.

Bouffard, S., and Little, P. (2004). *Promoting Quality through Professional Development: A Framework for Evaluation. Issues and Opportunities in Out-of-School Time Evaluation, No. 8.* Harvard Family Research Project. Available: https://files.eric.ed.gov/fulltext/ED484816.pdf.

Bowie, L., and Bronte-Tinkew, J. (2006). The importance of professional development for youth workers. *Child Trends.* Available: https://www.cyfar.org/sites/default/files/Bowie%202006.pdf.

Brahms, L. (2014). *Making as a Learning Process: Identifying and Supporting Family Learning in Informal Settings.* Doctoral Dissertation, University of Pittsburgh. (Unpublished).

Brahms, L., and Crowley, K. (2016). Learning to make in the museum: The role of maker educators. In K. Peppler, E. Halverson and Y. Kafai (Eds.), *Makeology: Makerspaces as Learning Environments* (Vol. 1). London, UK: Taylor & Francis. Available: http://upclose.pitt.edu/articles/Brahms_Crowley_Maker_Educator2016.pdf.

Brahms, L., and Werner, J. (2013). Designing makerspaces for family learning in museums and science centers. In M. Honey and D. Kanter (Eds.), *Design, Make, Play: Growing the Next Generation of STEM Innovators* (pp. 71–94). London, UK: Routledge.

Bransford, J.D., Barron, B., Pea, R.D., Meltzoff, A., Kuhl, P., Bell, P., Stevens, R., Schwartz, D.V., Vye, N., Reeves, B., Roschelle, R., and Sabelli, N. (2005). Foundations and opportunities for an interdisciplinary science of learning. In R.K. Sawyer (Ed.), *The Cambridge Handbook of the Learning Sciences* (pp. 19–34). Cambridge, UK: Cambridge University Press.

Braun, L., and Visser, M. (2017). *Ready to Code: Connecting Youth to CS Opportunities Through Libraries.* Washington, DC: The American Library Association's Office for Information Technology Policy. Available: http://www.ala.org/advocacy/sites/ala.org.advocacy/files/content/pp/Ready_To_Code_Report_FINAL.pdf.

Braun, L.W., Hartman, M.L., Hughes-Hassell, S., and Kumasi, K. (2014). *The Future of Library Services for and with Teens: A Call to Action* [White paper]. Chicago, IL: Young Adult Library Services Association (YALSA). Available: http://www.ala.org/yaforum/sites/ala.org.yaforum/files/content/YALSA_nationalforum_Final_web_0.pdf.

Brennan, K. (2013). Learning computing through creating and connecting. *Computer, 46*(9), 52–59.

Brennan, K. (2015). Beyond technocentrism: Supporting constructionism in the classroom. *Constructivist Foundations, 10*(3), 289–296.

Brennan, K. (in press). A case for why: Society, school, self. In S.-C. Kong and H. Abelson (Eds.), *Computational Thinking Education in K–12.* Cambridge, MA: MIT Press.

Brickhouse, N.W., Lowery, P., and Schultz, K. (2000). What kind of a girl does science? The construction of school science identities. *Journal of Research in Science Teaching: The Official Journal of the National Association for Research in Science Teaching, 37*(5), 441–458.

Brooks, E., and Sjöberg, J. (2019). Evolving playful and creative activities when school children develop game-based designs. In *Interactivity, Game Creation, Design Learning, and Innovation* (pp. 485–495). Cham, Switzerland: Springer.

Brough, M. (2016). *Game On! Connected Learning and Parental Support in the CyberPatriot Program*. Irvine, CA; Digital Media Learning and Research Hub. Available: https://dmlhub.net/publications/game-on-connected-learning-parental-support-cyberpatriot-program/index.html.

Brown, J.S., Collins, A., and Duguid, P. (1989). Situated cognition and the culture of learning. *Educational Researcher, 18*(1), 32–42.

Brown, P.L., Concannon, J.P., Marx, D., Donaldson, C.W., and Black, A. (2016). An examination of middle school students' STEM self-efficacy with relation to interest and perceptions of STEM. *Journal of STEM Education, 17*(3), 27–38.

Buckingham, D. (2007). Media education goes digital: An introduction. *Learning, Media and Technology, 32*(2), 111–119.

Buckingham, D. (2013). *Media Education: Literacy, Learning and Contemporary Culture*. Hoboken, NJ: John Wiley & Sons.

Buechley, L., and Eisenberg, M. (2008). The LilyPad Arduino: Toward wearable engineering for everyone. *IEEE Pervasive Computing, 7*(2), 12–15.

Buechley, L., Eisenberg, M., Catchen, J., and Crockett, A. (2008). The LilyPad Arduino: Using Computational Textiles to Investigate Engagement, Aesthetics, and Diversity in Computer Science Education. In *Proceedings of the SIGCHI Conference on Human Factors in Computing Systems* (pp. 423–432).

Bugallo, M.F., and Kelly, A.M. (2014). A pre-college recruitment strategy for electrical and computer engineering study. In *2014 IEEE Integrated STEM Education Conference* (pp. 1–4).

Bugallo, M.F., Kelly, A.M., and Ha, M. (2015). Impact of a university-based electrical and computer engineering summer program for high school students. *International Journal of Engineering Education, 31*(5), 1419–1427.

Buitrago Flórez, F., Casallas, R., Hernández, M., Reyes, A., Restrepo, S., and Danies, G. (2017). Changing a generation's way of thinking: Teaching computational thinking through programming. *Review of Educational Research, 87*(4), 834–860.

Bureau of Labor Statistics. (2020). *Occupational Outlook Handbook*. Available: http://www.bls.gov/ooh/computer-and-information-technology/home.

Byrne, D., and Louw, M. (2020). Tools with histories: Exploring NFC-tagging to support hybrid documentation practices and knowledge discovery in makerspaces. In *International Conference on Human-Computer Interaction* (pp. 51–67).

Calabrese Barton, A., and Tan, E. (2018). *STEM-Rich Maker Learning: Designing for Equity with Youth of Color*. New York, NY: Teachers College Press.

Calabrese Barton, A., and Tan, E. (2019). Designing for rightful presence in STEM: Community ethnography as pedagogy as an equity-oriented design approach. *Journal of the Learning Sciences, 28*(4–5), 616–658.

Calabrese Barton, A., Tan, E., and Greenberg, D. (2017). The Makerspace movement: Sites of possibilities for equitable opportunities to engage underrepresented youth in STEM. *Teachers College Record, 119*.

Calabrese Barton, A., Tan, E., and Rivet, A. (2008). Creating hybrid spaces for engaging school science among urban middle school girls. *American Educational Research Journal, 45*(1), 68–103.

Calabrese Barton, A., Kang, H., Tan, E., O'Neill, T.B., Bautista-Guerra, J., and Brecklin, C. (2013). Crafting a future in science: Tracing middle school girls' identity work over time and space. *American Educational Research Journal, 50*(1), 37–75.

Callahan, J., Ito, M., Campbell Rea, S., and Wortman, A. (2019). *Influences on Occupational Identity in Adolescence: A Review of Research and Programs*. Irvine, CA: Connected Learning Alliance.

Capraro, R.M., and Slough, S.W. (2013). Why PBL? Why STEM? Why now? An introduction to STEM project-based learning: An integrated science, technology, engineering, and mathematics (STEM) approach. In R.M. Capraro, M.M. Capraro, and J.R. Morgan (Eds.), *STEM Project-Based Learning*. Leiden, The Netherlands: Brill I Sense.

Carlone, H.B., and Johnson, A. (2007). Understanding the science experiences of successful women of color: Science identity as an analytic lens. *Journal of Research in Science Teaching: The Official Journal of the National Association for Research in Science Teaching*, 44(8), 1187–1218.

Carlone, H.B., Scott, C.M., and Lowder, C. (2014). Becoming (less) scientific: A longitudinal study of students' identity work from elementary to middle school science. *Journal of Research in Science Teaching*, 51(7), 836–869.

Carter-Black, J. (2008). A Black woman's journey into a predominately White academic world. *Affilia*, 23(2), 112–122.

Cavallo, D., Basu, A., Bryant, S., and Sipitakiat, A. (2004). *Opening Pathways to Higher Education Through Engineering Projects*. Paper presented at the ASEE Annual Conference and Exposition, Salt Lake City, UT.

Center for Applied Special Technology. (2020). *Key Questions to Consider When Planning Lessons*. Wakefield, MA: Author.

Center for the Future of Museums. (2014). *Building the Future of Education: Museums and the Learning Ecosystem*. American Alliance of Museums. Available: https://www.aam-us.org/wp-content/uploads/2017/12/Building-the-Future-of-Education.pdf.

Chao, T., Chen, J., Star, J.R., and Dede, C. (2016). Using digital resources for motivation and engagement in learning mathematics: Reflections from teachers and students. *Digital Experiences in Mathematics Education*, 2, 253–277.

Charleston, L.J., George, P.L., Jackson, J.F.L., Berhanu, J., and Amechi, M.H. (2014). Navigating underrepresented STEM spaces: Experiences of Black women in U.S. computing science higher education programs who actualize success. *Journal of Diversity in Higher Education*, 7(3), 166–176.

Charlton, P., and Poslad, S. (2016). A sharable wearable maker community IoT application. In *2016 12th International Conference on Intelligent Environments (IE)* (pp. 16–23).

Cheryan, S., Master, A., and Meltzoff, A.N. (2015). Cultural stereotypes as gatekeepers: Increasing girls' interest in computer science and engineering by diversifying stereotypes. *Frontiers in Psychology*, 6, Article 49.

Cheryan, S., Plaut, V.C., Davies, P.G., and Steele, C.M. (2009). Ambient belonging: How stereotypical cues impact gender participation in computer science. *Journal of Personality and Social Psychology*, 97(6), 1045–1060.

Cheryan, S., Plaut, V.C., Handron, C., and Hudson, L. (2013). The stereotypical computer scientist: Gendered media representations as a barrier to inclusion for women. *Sex Roles*, 69(1–2), 58–71.

Cheryan, S., Ziegler, S.A., Montoya, A. K., and Jiang, L. (2016). Why are some STEM fields more gender balanced than others? *Psychological Bulletin*, 143, 1–35.

Cheryan, S., Siy, J.O., Vichayapai, M., Drury, B.J., and Kim, S. (2011). Do female and male role models who embody STEM stereotypes hinder women's anticipated success in STEM? *Social Psychological and Personality Science*, 2(6), 656–664.

Chi, B., Dorph, R., and Reisman, L. (2015). *Evidence & Impact: Museum-Managed STEM Programs in Out-of-School Settings*. National Research Council Committee on Out-of-School Time STEM. Washington, DC: The National Academies Press.

Chinn, C.A., and Malhotra, B.A. (2002). Epistemologically authentic inquiry in schools: A theoretical framework for evaluating inquiry tasks. *Science Education*, 86(2), 175–218.

Choudhury, V., Lopes, A.B., and Arthur, D. (2010). IT careers camp: An early intervention strategy to increase IS enrollments. *Information Systems Research*, 21(1), 1–14.

Clapp, E.P., Ross, J., Ryan, J.O., and Tishman, S. (2017). *Maker-Centered Learning: Empowering Young People to Shape Their Worlds*. San Francisco, CA: Jossey-Bass.

Clarke-Midura, J., Poole, F., Pantic, K., Hamilton, M., Sun, C., and Allan, V. (2018). How near peer mentoring affects middle school mentees. In *Proceedings of the 49th ACM Technical Symposium on Computer Science Education* (pp. 664–669).

Clegg, T., and Kolodner, J. (2014). Scientizing and cooking: Helping middle-school learners develop scientific dispositions. *Science Education, 98*(1), 36–63.

Clegg, T., and Subramaniam, M. (2018). Redefining mentorship in facilitating interest-driven learning in libraries. In V.R. Lee and A.L. Phillips (Eds.), *Reconceptualizing Libraries: Perspectives from the Information and Learning Sciences* (pp. 140–157). London, UK and New York, NY: Routledge.

Cleveland, B., and Fisher, K. (2014). The evaluation of physical learning environments: A critical review of the literature. *Learning Environments Research* 17, 1–28.

Code.org, Computer Science Teachers Association, and Expanding Computing Education Pathways. (2019). *2019 State of Computer Science Education*. New York, NY: Authors. Available: https://advocacy.code.org/2019_state_of_cs.pdf.

Cohoon, J.M. (2002). Recruiting and retaining women in undergraduate computing majors. *ACM SIGCSE Bulletin, 34*(2), 48–52.

Cole, E.R. (2009). Intersectionality and research in psychology. *American Psychologies, 64*, 170–180.

College Board. (2008). *AP Program Participation and Performance Statistics*. New York, NY: Author. Available: https://research.collegeboard.org/programs/ap/data/archived/2008.

——. (2014). *AP Computer Science A Course Description*. New York, NY: Author. Available: https://apcentral.collegeboard.org/pdf/ap-computer-science-a-course-and-exam-description.pdf?course=ap-computer-science-a.

——. (2017). *AP National Report 2017*. New York, NY: Author. Available: https://research.collegeboard.org/programs/ap/data/archived/ap-2017.

——. (2018). *AP National Report 2018*. New York, NY: Author. Available: https://research.collegeboard.org/programs/ap/data/archived/ap-2018.

——. (2019). *AP National Report 2019*. New York, NY: Author. Available: https://secure-media.collegeboard.org/digitalServices/misc/ap/national-summary-2019.xlsx.

——. (2020). *AP Computer Science Principles: The Course*. New York, NY: Author. Available: https://apcentral.collegeboard.org/courses/ap-computer-science-principles/course.

Computer Science Teachers Association, and International Society for Technology in Education. (2011). *Computational Thinking: Leadership Toolkit*. Available: http://www.iste.org/docs/ct-documents/ct-leadershipt-toolkit.pdf.

Concannon, J.P., and Barrow, L.H. (2010). Men's and women's intentions to persist in undergraduate engineering degree programs. *Journal of Science Education and Technology, 19*(2), 133–145.

Cornelius-White, J. (2007). Learner-centered teacher-student relationships are effective: A meta-analysis. *Review of Educational Research, 77*(1), 113–143.

Corry, M., and Stella, J. (2012). Developing a framework for research in online K–12 distance education. *The Quarterly Review of Distance Education, 13*(3), 133–151.

Costanza-Chock, S. (2020). *Design Justice: Community-Led Practices to Build the Worlds We Need*. Cambridge, MA: MIT Press.

Costley, J. (1998). *Building a Professional Development System That Works for the Field of Out-of-School Time*. Wellesley, MA: National Institute on Out-of-School Time, Center for Research on Women, Wellesley College.

Cox, P.T., Giles, F.R., and Pietrzykowski, T. (1989). Prograph: A step towards liberating programming from textual conditioning. In *1989 IEEE Workshop on Visual languages* (pp. 150–151).

Coyle, E.J., Jamieson, L.H., and Oakes, W.C. (2006). Integrating engineering education and community service: Themes for the future of engineering education. *Journal of Engineering Education, 95*(1), 7–11.

Crawford, M. (2012). *Engineering Still Needs More Women.* American Society of Mechanical Engineers. Available: https://www.asme.org/topics-resources/content/engineering-still-needs-more-women.

Crenshaw, K.W. (1994). Mapping the Margins: Intersectionality, Identity Politics, and Violence Against Women of Color. In M.A. Fineman and R. Mykitiuk (Eds.), *The public nature of private violence* (pp. 93–118). New York, NY: Routledge.

Crowley, K., Pierroux, P., and Knutson, K. (2014). Informal learning in museums. In R.K. Sawyer (Ed.), *The Cambridge Handbook of the Learning Sciences* (pp. 461–478). Cambridge, UK: Cambridge University Press.

Crowley, K., Barron, B.J., Knutson, K., and Martin, C.K. (2015). Interest and the development of pathways to science. In K.A. Renninger, M. Nieswandt, and S. Hidi (Eds.), *Interest in Mathematics and Science Learning* (pp. 297–313). Washington, DC: AERA.

CSTA. (2015). *National Secondary School Computer Science Survey.* Available: https://www.csteachers.org/documents/en-us/02c2735f-f0cb-4425-930b-fa71c2acc2d4/1.

Cun, A., Abramovich, S., and Smith, J. (2019). An assessment matrix for library makerspaces. *Library & Information Science Research, 41*(1), 39–47.

Cundiff, J.L., Vescio, T.K., Loken, E., and Lo, L. (2013). Do gender–science stereotypes predict science identification and science career aspirations among undergraduate science majors? *Social Psychology of Education, 16*(4), 541–554.

Cuny, J. (2015). Transforming K–12 computing education: An update and a call to action. *ACM Inroads, 6*(3), 54–57.

Danticat, E. (2013). *Making Art in Cities of Exile* [Lecture]. Florida International University, University Videos. Available: https://digitalcommons.fiu.edu/fiu_video/109.

Dasgupta, C., Magana, A.M., and Vieira, C. (2019). Investigating the affordances of a CAD enabled learning environment for promoting integrated STEM learning. *Computers & Education, 129*, 122–142.

Davies, D., Jindal-Snape, D., Collier, C., Digby, R., Hay, P., and Howe, A. (2013). Creative learning environments in education—A systematic literature review. *Thinking Skills and Creativity, 8*, 80–91.

Davis, K., Subramaniam, M., Hoffman, K.M., and Romeijn-Stout, M. (2018). Technology use in rural and urban public libraries: Implication for connected learning in youth programming. In *Proceedings of the 2018 Connected Learning Summit* (pp. 47–56).

de Certeau, M. (1984). *The Practice of Everyday Life.* Berkeley, CA: University of California Press.

de Paula, B.H., Burn, A., Noss, R., and Valente, J.A. (2018). Playing Beowulf: Bridging computational thinking, arts and literature through game-making. *International Journal of Child-Computer Interaction, 16*, 39–46.

Debusschere, B. (2018). How do we create more equitable, diverse, and inclusive organizations, and why does it matter? A white male's perspective. *Computing in Science & Engineering, 20*(1), 79–83.

Dee, T., and Gershenson, S. (2017). *Unconscious Bias in the Classroom: Evidence and Opportunities.* Stanford Center for Education Policy Analysis. Available: https://files.eric.ed.gov/fulltext/ED579284.pdf.

Delyser, L.A., Goode, J., Guzdial, M., Kafai, Y., and Yadav, A. (2018). *Priming the Computer Science Teacher Pump: Integrating Computer Science Education into Schools of Education.* New York, NY: CSforAll.

Dempsey, J., Snodgrass, R.T., Kishi, I., and Titcomb, A. (2015). The emerging role of self perception in student intentions. In *Proceedings of the 46th ACM Technical Symposium on Computer Science Education* (pp. 108–113). New York, NY: ACM.

Denault, A., Kienzle, J., and Vybihal, J. (2008). Be a computer scientist for a week the McGill "game programming guru" Summer Camp. In *2008 38th Annual Frontiers in Education Conference* (pp. T3D–1).

Denner, J., Werner, L., Martinez, J., and Bean, S. (2012). Computing goals, values, and expectations: Results from an after-school program for girls. *Journal of Women and Minorities in Science and Engineering, 18*(3).

Denner, J., Werner, L., Campe, S., and Ortiz, E. (2014). Pair programming: Under what conditions is it advantageous for middle school students? *Journal of Research on Technology in Education, 46*(3), 277–296.

Denson, C., Austin, C., Hailey, C., and Householder, D. (2015). Benefits of informal learning environments: A focused examination of STEM-based program environments. *Journal of STEM Education, 16(*1).

Dettori, L., Greenberg, R.I., McGee, S., and Reed, D. (2016). The impact of the exploring computer science instructional model in Chicago Public Schools. *Computing in Science & Engineering, 18*(2), 10.

Dettori, L., Greenberg, R.I., McGee, S., Reed, D., Wilkerson, B., and Yanek, D. (2018). CS as a graduation requirement: Catalyst for systemic change. In *Proceedings of the 49th ACM Technical Symposium on Computer Science Education* (pp. 406–407).

Dezuanni, M., O'Mara, J., and Beavis, C. (2015). "Redstone is like electricity": Children's performative representations in and around *Minecraft*. *E-Learning and Digital Media, 12*(2), 147–163.

DiGiano, C., Goldman, S., and Chorost, M. (2008). *Educating Learning Technology Designers: Guiding and Inspiring Creators of Innovative Educational Tools*. London, UK and New York, NY: Routledge.

Dillenbourg, P. (1999). What do you mean by collaborative learning? In P. Dillenbourg (Ed.), *Collaborative-Learning: Cognitive and Computational Approaches* (pp. 1–19). Oxford, UK: Elsevier.

DiSalvo, B., and Bruckman, A. (2010). Race and gender in play practices: Young African American males. In *Proceedings of the Fifth International Conference on the Foundations of Digital Games* (pp. 56–63).

Dischino, M., DeLaura, J.A., Donnelly, J., Massa, N.M., and Hanes, F. (2011). Increasing the STEM pipeline through problem-based learning. *Proceedings of the 2011 IAJC-ASEE International Conference*. Available: https://www.pblprojects.org/wp-content/uploads/2019/02/Increasing-the-STEM-Pipeline.pdf.

diSessa, A.A. (2000). *Changing Minds: Computers, Learning, and Literacy*. Cambridge, MA: MIT Press.

diSessa, A.A., and Abelson, H. (1986). Boxer: A reconstructible computational medium. *Communications of the ACM, 29*(9), 859–868.

Doerschuk, P., Juarez, V., Liu, J., Vincent, D., Doss, K., and Mann, J. (2013). Introducing programming concepts through video game creation. In *2013 IEEE Frontiers in Education Conference (FIE)* (pp. 523–529).

Dooley, S., and Witthoft, S. (2012). *Make Space: How to Set the Stage for Creative Collaboration*. Hoboken, NJ: John Wiley and Sons.

Donovan, R.A. (2011). Tough or tender: (Dis)similarities in White college students' perceptions of Black and White women. *Psychology of Women Quarterly, 35*(3), 458–468.

Dou, R., and Gibbs, K.D. (2013). Engaging all students in the pursuit of STEM careers. *School Science Review, 95*(351), 106–112.

Druin, A. (1999). Cooperative inquiry: Developing new technologies for children with children. In *Proceedings of the SIGCHI conference on Human Factors in Computing Systems* (pp. 592–599).

du Boulay, B., O'Shea, T., and Monk, J. (1981). The black box inside the glass box: Presenting computing concepts to novices. *International Journal of Man-Machine Studies, 14*(3), 237–249.

Duffin, M., Powers, A., and Tremblay, G. (2004). *Place-Based Education Evaluation Collaborative (PEEC): Report on Cross-Program Research and Other Program Evaluation Activities 2003–2004.* PEER Associates. Available: http://www.seer.org/pages/research/PEEC%202004.pdf.

Duncan, G.J., and Murnane, R.J. (Eds.). (2011). *Whither Opportunity?: Rising Inequality, Schools, and Children's Life Chances.* New York, NY: Russell Sage Foundation.

Dunn, T.J., and Kennedy, M. (2019). Technology enhanced learning in higher education: Motivations, engagement and academic achievement. *Computers & Education, 137,* 104–113.

Earle, J., Maynard, R., Neild, R.C., Easton, J.Q., Ferrini-Mundy, J., Albro, E., and Winter, S. (2013). *Common Guidelines for Education Research and Development.* Washington, DC: IES, U.S. Department of Education, and National Science Foundation.

Eccles, J.S., and Wigfield, A. (2002). Motivational beliefs, values, and goals. *Annual Review of Psychology, 53*(1), 109–132.

Eccles, J.S., Jacobs, J.E., and Harold, R.D. (1990). Gender role stereotypes, expectancy effects, and parents' socialization of gender differences. *Journal of Social Issues, 46,* 183–201.

Eckert, P., and McConnell-Ginet, S. (1995). Constructing meaning, constructing selves. In K. Hall and M. Buchholtz (Eds.), *Gender Articulated: Language and the Socially Constructed Self* (pp. 469–507). London, UK and New York, NY: Routledge.

Edelson, D.C. (1998). Realising authentic science learning through the adaptation of scientific practice. In K. Tobin and B. Fraser (Eds.), *International Handbook of Science Education 1,* 317–331. Dordrecht, Netherlands: Kluwer.

Edelson, D.C., and Reiser, B.J. (2006). Making authentic practices accessible to learners: Design challenges and strategies. In R.K. Sawyer (Ed.), *The Cambridge Handbook of the Learning Sciences* (pp. 335–354). Cambridge, UK: Cambridge University Press.

Edelson, D.C., Gordin, D.N., and Pea, R.D. (1999). Addressing the challenges of inquiry-based learning through technology and curriculum design. *Journal of the Learning Sciences, 8*(3–4), 391–450.

Eglash, R., Gilbert, J.E., Taylor, V., and Geier, S.R. (2013). Culturally responsive computing in urban, after-school contexts: Two approaches. *Urban Education, 48*(5), 629–656.

Eglash, R., Bennett, A., O'Donnell, C., Jennings, S., and Cintorino, M. (2006). Culturally situated design tools: Ethnocomputing from field site to classroom. *American Anthropologist, 108*(2), 347–362.

Ellis, S.A., and Gauvain, M. (1992). Social and cultural influences on children's collaborative interactions. In L.T. Winegar and J. Valsiner (Eds.), *Children's Development Within Social Context: Research and Methodology* (Vol. 2, pp. 155–180). Hillsdale, NJ: Erlbaum.

Erdogan, N., Navruz, B., Younes, R., and Capraro, R.M. (2016). Viewing how STEM project-based learning influences students' science achievement through the implementation lens: A latent growth modeling. *Eurasia Journal of Mathematics, Science and Technology Education, 12*(8), 2139–2154.

Erete, S., Martin, C.K., and Pinkard, N. (2017). Digital Youth Divas: A program model for increasing knowledge, confidence, and perceptions of fit in STEM amongst black and brown middle school girls. In *Moving Students of Color from Consumers to Producers of Technology* (pp. 152–173). Hershey, PA: IGI Global.

Erete, S., Pinkard, N., Martin, C.K., and Sandherr, J. (2016). Exploring the use of interactive narratives to engage inner-city girls in computational activities. In *2016 Research on Equity and Sustained Participation in Engineering, Computing, and Technology (RESPECT)* (pp. 1–4). doi: 10.1109/RESPECT.2016.7836168.

Erikson, E.H. (1968). *Identity, Youth and Crisis.* New York, NY: W.W. Norton & Company.

Estrella, G., Au, J., Jaeggi, S.M., and Collins, P. (2018). Is inquiry science instruction effective for English language learners? A meta-analytic review. *AERA Open, 4.*

Evans, P.M., and Schares, E.J. (2017). *Board# 31: Work in Progress: FLEx—University X's Mobile Technology Classroom.* Paper presented at the ASEE Annual Conference and Exposition, Columbus, OH.

Falco, E.H. (2004). *Environment-Based Education: Improving Attitudes and Academics for Adolescents.* Columbia, SC: South Carolina Department of Education.

Falk, J.H., and Dierking, L.D. (2018). *Learning from Museums.* Lanham, MD: Rowman & Littlefield Publishers.

Falk, J.H., and Needham, M. (2011). Measuring the impact of a science center on its community. *Journal of Research in Science Teaching, 48*(1), 1–12.

Falk, J.H., Staus, N., Dierking, L.D., Wyld, J., Bailey, D., and Penuel, W. (2015). The SYNERGIES project: Preliminary results and insights from two years of longitudinal survey research. *Museology Quarterly, 29*(1), 15–21.

Fancsali, C., Mirakhur, Z., Klevan, S., and Rivera-Cash, E. (2019). "Making" science relevant for the 21st century: Early lessons from a research-practice partnership. In *Proceedings of FabLearn 2019* (pp. 136–139). https://doi.org/10.1145/3311890.3311910.

Farrington, C.A., Roderick, M., Allensworth, E.A., Nagaoka, J., Johnson, D.W., Keyes, T.S., and Beechum, N. (2012). *Teaching Adolescents to Become Learners: The Role of Non-cognitive Factors in Academic Performance—A Critical Literature Review.* Chicago, IL: University of Chicago Consortium on Chicago School Research.

Faulkner, W. (2001). The technology question in feminism: A view from feminist technology studies. *Women's Studies International Forum, 24*(1), 79–95.

Federal Communications Commission. (2015). *2015 Broadband Progress Report.* Available: https://www.fcc.gov/reports-research/reports/broadband-progress-reports/2015-broadband-progress-report.

Fields, D.A., and Lee, V.R. (2016). The maker movement and learning. In K. Peppler, E. Rosenfeld Halverson, and Y.B. Kafai (Eds.), *Makeology: Makerspaces as Learning Environments* (Vol. 1, pp. 285–294). London, UK and New York, NY: Routledge.

Fields, D.A., Kafai, Y., Nakajima, T., Goode, J., and Margolis, J. (2018). Putting making into high school computer science classrooms: Promoting equity in teaching and learning with electronic textiles in exploring computer science. *Equity & Excellence in Education, 51*(1), 21–35.

Flanagan, C., and Gallay, E. (2014). Adolescents' theories of the commons. In J.B. Benson (Ed.), *Advances in Child Development and Behavior* (Vol. 46, pp. 33–55). Cambridge, MA: Elsevier Academic Press.

Flannery, L.P., Kazakoff, E.R., Bontá, P., Silverman, B., Bers, M.U., and Resnick, M. (2013). Designing ScratchJr: Support for early childhood learning through computer programming. In *Proceedings of the 12th International Conference on Interaction Design and Children* (pp. 1–10).

Fleming, N. (2012). Training of out-of-school staff debated. *EdWeek.* Available: https://www.edweek.org/ew/articles/2012/04/04/27oststaff.h31.html.

Folk, R., Lee, G., Michalenko, A., Peel, A., and Pontelli, E. (2015). GK-12 DISSECT: Incorporating computational thinking with K-12 science without computer access. In *2015 IEEE Frontiers in Education Conference (FIE)* (pp. 1–8).

Fowler, A., Pirker, J., Pollock, I., de Paula, B.C., Echeveste, M.E., and Gómez, M.J. (2016). Understanding the benefits of game jams: Exploring the potential for engaging young learners in STEM. In *Proceedings of the 2016 ITiCSE Working Group Reports* (pp. 119–135). https://doi.org/10.1145/3024906.3024913.

Fredricks, J.A., and Eccles, J.S. (2006). Extracurricular involvement and adolescent adjustment: Impact of duration, number of activities, and breadth of participation. *Applied Developmental Science, 10*(3), 132–146.

Freina, L., Bottino, R., and Ferlino, L. (2019). Fostering computational thinking skills in the last years of primary school. *International Journal of Serious Games, 6*(3), 101–115.

Freudenthal, E., Duval, A., Hug, S., Ogrey, A., Lim, K., Tabor, C., Gonzalez, R.Q., and Siegel, A. (2011). Planting the seeds of computational thinking: An introduction to programming suitable for inclusion in STEM curricula. In *Proceedings of the 118th American Society for Engineering Education Annual Conference & Exposition*. Available: http://citeseerx.ist.psu.edu/viewdoc/download?doi=10.1.1.993.9627&rep=rep1&type=pdf.

Fronza, I., El Ioini, N., and Corral, L. (2015). Students want to create apps: Leveraging computational thinking to teach mobile software development. In *Proceedings of the 16th Annual Conference on Information Technology Education* (pp. 21–26). https://dl.acm.org/doi/proceedings/10.1145/2808006.

Funk, C., and Parker, K. (2018). *Women and Men in STEM Often at Odds Over Workplace Equity.* Pew Research Center. Available: https://vtechworks.lib.vt.edu/bitstream/handle/10919/92671/WomenSTEEMWorkplace.pdf?sequence=1.

Gallay, E., Marckini-Polk, L., Schroeder, B., and Flanagan, C. (2016). Place-based stewardship education: Nurturing aspirations to protect the rural commons. *Peabody Journal of Education, 91*(2), 155–175.

Gardeli, A., and Vosinakis, S. (2019). ARQuest: A tangible augmented reality approach to developing computational thinking skills. In *2019 11th International Conference on Virtual Worlds and Games for Serious Applications (VS-Games)* (pp. 1–8).

Gardner-McCune, C., McCune, D.B.D., Edwards, C.M., and Stallworth, C. (2013). I-3 Experience: Expanding research and design opportunities for under-represented high school students. In *2013 ASEE Annual Conference & Exposition* (paper ID 7985).

Garmer, A.K. (2014). *Rising to the Challenge: Re-Envisioning Public Libraries.* Aspen Institute. Available: https://csreports.aspeninstitute.org/documents/Aspen-LibrariesReport-2017-FINAL.pdf.

Garneli, V., Giannakos, M.N., Chorianopoulos, K., and Jaccheri, L. (2015). Serious game development as a creative learning experience: Lessons learnt. In *2015 IEEE/ACM 4th International Workshop on Games and Software Engineering* (pp. 36–42). DOI: 10.1109/GAS.2015.14.

Gauvain, M. (2001). *The Social Context of Cognitive Development.* London, UK and New York, NY: Guilford Press.

Gay, G. (2010). *Culturally Responsive Teaching: Theory, Research, and Practice* (2nd ed.). New York, NY: Teachers College Press.

Gee, J.P. (2007). *What Video Games Have to Teach Us About Learning and Literacy* (2nd ed.). New York, NY: St. Martin's Press.

Gibson, A.N., Chancellor, R.L., Cooke, N.A., Park Dahlen, S., Lee, S.A., and Shorish, Y.L. (2017). Libraries on the frontlines: Neutrality and social justice. *Equality, Diversity and Inclusion: An International Journal, 36*, 751–766.

Gibson, A.N., Chancellor, R., Cooke, N., Park Dahlen, S., Patin, B., and Shorish, Y. (2020). Struggling to breathe: COVID-19, protest, and the LIS response. *Equity, Diversity, and Inclusion: An International Journal.* Carolina Digital Repository. Available: https://doi.org/10.17615/yhe2-8w37.

Gick, M.L., and Holyoak, K.J. (1980). Analogical problem solving. *Cognitive Psychology*, 12, 306–355.

Glaze-Crampes, A.L. (2020). Leveraging communities of practice as professional learning communities in science, technology, engineering, math (STEM) education. *Education Sciences, 10*, 190.

Glenn, J. (2001). *Using Environment-Based Education to Advance Learning Skills and Character Development*. The North American Association for Environmental Education and the National Environmental Education & Training Foundation. Available: https://promiseofplace.org/sites/default/files/2018-05/EnviroEdReport.pdf.

Goode, J., and Margolis, J. (2011). Exploring computer science: A case study of school reform. *ACM Transactions on Computing Education (TOCE), 11*(2), 12.

Goode, J., and Ryoo, J. (2019). Teacher knowledge for inclusive computing learning. In S. Fincher and A. Robins (Eds.), *The Cambridge Handbook of Computing Education Research* (pp. 709–726). Cambridge, UK: Cambridge University Press.

Goode, J., Chapman, G., and Margolis, J. (2012). Beyond curriculum: The exploring computer science program. *ACM Inroads, 3*(2), 47–53.

Goode, J., Estrella, R., and Margolis, J. (2006). Lost in translation: Gender and high school computer science. In J.M. Cohoon and W. Aspray (Eds.), *Women and Information Technology: Research on Underrepresentation* (pp. 89–114). Cambridge, MA: MIT Press.

Goode, J., Flapan, J., and Margolis, J. (2018). Computer science for all: A school reform framework for broadening participation in computer science. In W. Tierney, Z. Corwin, and A. Ochsner (Eds.), *Diversifying Digital Learning: Online Literacy and Educational Opportunity* (pp. 45–65). Baltimore, MD: Johns Hopkins Press.

Goode, J., Johnson, S.R., and Sundstrom, K. (2020). Disrupting colorblind teacher education in computer science. *Professional Development in Education, 46*(2), 354–367.

Goode, J., Margolis, J., and Chapman, G. (2014). Curriculum is not enough: The educational theory and research foundation of the exploring computer science professional development model. In *Proceedings of the 45th ACM Technical Symposium on Computer Science Education* (pp. 493–498).

Gorski, P.C. (2002). Dismantling the digital divide: A multicultural education framework. *Multicultural Education, 10*(1), 28–30.

Gorski, P. (2005). Education equity and the digital divide. *AACE Journal, 13*(1), 3–45.

Grover, S. (2011). *Robotics and Engineering for Middle and High School Students to Develop Computational Thinking*. Paper presented at the annual meeting of the American Educational Research Association, New Orleans, LA.

Grover, S., and Pea, R. (2013). Computational thinking in K–12: A review of the state of the field. *Educational Researcher, 42*(1), 38–43.

Gruenewald, D.A. (2003). The best of both worlds: A critical pedagogy of place. *Educational Researcher, 32*(4), 3–12.

Gutiérrez, K.D., and Rogoff, B. (2003). Cultural ways of learning: Individual traits or repertoires of practice. *Educational Researcher, 32*(5), 19–25.

Guzdial, M. (2015). *Learner-Centered Design of Computing Education: Research on Computing for Everyone*. San Rafael, CA: Morgan and Claypool.

Guzdial, M., Ericson, B.J., McKlin, T., and Engelman, S. (2012). A statewide survey on computing education pathways and influences: Factors in broadening participation in computing. In *Proceedings of the Ninth Annual International Conference on International Computing Education Research* (pp. 143–150).

Haaken, J. (1996). Field dependence research: A historical analysis of a psychological construct. In B. Laslett, S.G. Kohlstedt, H. Longino, and E. Hammonds (Eds.), *Gender and Scientific Authority* (pp. 282–301). Chicago, IL: University of Chicago Press.

Halverson, E.R., and Sheridan, K. (2014). The maker movement in education. *Harvard Educational Review, 84*(4), 495–504.

Hansen, A.K., Dwyer, H.A., Iveland, A., Talesfore, M., Wright, L., Harlow, D.B., and Franklin, D. (2017). Assessing children's understanding of the work of computer scientists: The draw-a-computer-scientist test. In *Proceedings of the 2017 ACM SIGCSE Technical Symposium on Computer Science Education* (pp. 279–284). New York, NY: ACM.

Harriger, A., Magana, A.J., and Lovan, R. (2012). Identifying the impact of the SPIRIT program in student knowledge, attitudes, and perceptions toward computing careers. In *2012 Frontiers in Education Conference Proceedings* (pp. 1–6).

Harris-Packer, J.D., and Ségol, G. (2015). An empirical evaluation of distance learning's effectiveness in the K–12 setting. *American Journal of Distance Education, 29*(1), 4–17.

Harrison, S. (2011). "Up at the Shieling": Place-based action research. *Children Youth and Environments, 21*(1), 79–100.

Hartman, S.L., Hines-Bergmeier, J., and Klein, R. (2017). Informal STEM learning: The state of research, access and equity in rural early childhood settings. *Science Education and Civic Engagement, 9*(2), 32–39.

Hassinger-Das, B., Palti, I., Golinkoff, R.M., and Hirsh-Pasek, K. (2020). Urban thinkscape: Infusing public spaces with STEM conversation and interaction opportunities. *Journal of Cognition and Development, 21*(1), 125–147.

Hecht, M., Knutson, K., and Crowley, K. (2019). Becoming a naturalist: Interest development across the learning ecology. *Science Education, 103*(3), 691–713.

Hendricks, C.C., Alemdar, M., and Ogletree, T.W. (2012). *The Impact of Participation in VEX Robotics Competition on Middle and High School Students' Interest in Pursuing STEM Studies and STEM-related Careers.* Paper presented at the ASEE Annual Conference and Exposition, San Antonio, TX.

Hidi, S., and Renninger, K.A. (2006). The four-phase model of interest development. *Educational Psychologist, 41*(2), 111–127.

Higgins, S., Hall, E., Wall, K., Woolner, P., and McCaughey, C. (2005). *The Impact of School Environment: A Literature Review.* University of Newcastle Centre for Teaching & Learning. Available: https://citeseerx.ist.psu.edu/viewdoc/download?doi=10.1.1.231.7213&rep=rep1&type=pdf.

Hoffman, K., Subramaniam, M., Kawas, S., Scaff, L., and Davis, K. (2016). *Connected Libraries: Surveying the Current Landscape and Charting a Path to the Future.* The ConnectedLib Project. Available: https://papers.ssrn.com/sol3/papers.cfm?abstract_id=2982532.

Holeton, R. (2020, February 28). Toward inclusive learning spaces: Physiological, cognitive, and cultural inclusion and the learning space rating system. *Educause Review.*

Holmegaard, H., Madsen, L.M., and Ulriksen, L. (2014). To choose or not to choose science: Constructions of desirable identities among young people considering a STEM higher education programme. *International Journal of Science Education, 36*(2), 186–215.

Honey, M., and Kanter, D.E. (Eds.). (2013). *Design, Make, Play: Growing the Next Generation of STEM Innovators.* London, UK and New York, NY: Routledge.

Hooper-Greenhill, E. (2013). *Museums and Their Visitors.* London, UK: Taylor & Francis.

Horn, M., and Bers, M. (2019). Tangible computing. In S. Fincher and A. Robins (Eds.), *The Cambridge Handbook of Computing Education Research* (pp. 663–678). Cambridge, UK: Cambridge University Press.

Howard, K.E., and Havard, D.D. (2019). Advanced Placement (AP) computer science principles: Searching for equity in a two-tiered solution to underrepresentation. *Journal of Computer Science Integration, 2*(1), 1–15.

Huang, D., and Dietel, R. (2011). *Making Afterschool Programs Better. (CRESST Policy Brief).* Los Angeles, CA: University of California.

Hug, S., and Krauss, J. (2016, March). Engaging school counselors, creating computing allies. Poster presented at 47th ACM *Technical Symposium on Computing Science Education*, Kansas City, MO.

Ihrig, L.M., Lane, E., Mahatmya, D., and Assouline, S.G. (2018). STEM excellence and leadership program: Increasing the level of STEM challenge and engagement for high-achieving students in economically disadvantages rural communities. *Journal for the Education of the Gifted, 41*(1), 24–42.

Immordino-Yang, M.H., and Damasio, A. (2007). We feel, therefore we learn: The relevance of affective and social neuroscience to education. *Mind, Brain, and Education, 1*(1), 3–10.

Institute of Museum and Library Services (IMLS). (2008). *Youth in Museums and Libraries: A Practitioner's Guide.* Available: https://www.imls.gov/assets/1/workflow_staging/News/750.pdf.

——. (2019). *Public Libraries in the United States Fiscal Year 2016.* Washington, DC: Author.

Israel, M. (2019). Using assistive and instructional technologies. In J. McLuskey, L, Maheady, B. Billingsley, M. Brownell, and T. Lewis (Eds.), *High Leverage Practices for Inclusive Classrooms* (pp. 264–278). London, UK and New York, NY: Routledge

Israel, M., Pearson, J.N., Tapia, T., Wherfel, Q.M., and Reese, G. (2015a). Supporting all learners in school-wide computational thinking: A cross-case qualitative analysis. *Computers & Education, 82*, 263–279.

Israel, M., Wherfel, Q.M., Pearson, J., Shehab, S., and Tapia, T. (2015b). Empowering K–12 students with disabilities to learn computational thinking and computer programming. *TEACHING Exceptional Children, 48*(1), 45–53.

Ito, M. (2009). *Engineering Play: A Cultural History of Children's Software.* Cambridge, MA: MIT Press.

Ito, M., Martin, C., Pfister, R.C., Rafalow, M.H., Salen, K., and Wortman, A. (2018). *Affinity Online: How Connection and Shared Interest Fuel Learning* (Vol. 2). New York, NY: NYU Press.

Ito, M., Gutiérrez, K., Livingstone, S., Penuel, B., Rhodes, J., Salen, K., Schor, J., Sefton-Green, J., and Watkins, S.C. (2013). *Connected Learning: An Agenda for Research and Design* [White paper]. Digital Media and Learning Research Hub. Available: https://dmlhub.net/wp-content/uploads/files/Connected_Learning_report.pdf.

Ito, M., Baumer, S., Bittanti, M., Boyd, D., Cody, R., Herr Stephenson, B., Horts, H.A., Lange, P.G., Mahendran, D., Martinez, K.Z., Pascoe, C.J., Perkel, D., Robinson, L., Sims, C., and Tripp, L. (2019). *Hanging Out, Messing Around, and Geeking Out, Tenth Anniversary Edition.* Cambridge, MA: MIT Press.

Ito, M., Arum, R., Conley, D., Gutiérrez, K., Kirshner, B., Livingstone, S., Michalchik, V., Penuel, W., Peppler, K., Pinkard, N., Rhodes, J., Tekinbas, K.S., Schor, J., Sefton-Green, J., and Watkins, S.C. (2020). *The Connected Learning Research Network: Reflections on a Decade of Engaged Scholarship.* Connected Learning Alliance. Available: https://clalliance.org/wp-content/uploads/2020/02/CLRN_Report.pdf.

Jackson, P.B., Thoits, P.A., and Taylor, H.F. (1995). Composition of the workplace and psychological well-being: The effects of tokenism on America's Black elite. *Social Forces, 74*(2), 543–557.

Jacobs, J. (2019). New York knows its arts organizations have a diversity problem. Now what? *New York Times.* July 29. Available: https://www.nytimes.com/2019/07/29/arts/design/diversity-new-york-culture.html.

Jacobs, J.E., Davis-Kean, P., Bleeker, M., Eccles, J.S., and Malanchuk, O. (2005). "I can, but I don't want to": The impact of parents, interests, and activities on gender differences in mathematics. In A. Gallagher and J. Kaufman (Eds.), *Gender Differences in Mathematics* (pp. 246–263). Cambridge, UK: Cambridge University.

Jacob, S., Nguyen, H., Tofel-Grehl, C., Richardson, D., and Warschauer, M. (2018). Teaching computational thinking to English learners. *NYS TESOL Journal, 5*(2) 12–24.

Jacob, S., Nguyen, H., Garcia, L., Richardson, D., and Warschauer, M. (2020). Teaching computational thinking to multilingual students through inquiry-based learning. In *Proceedings of the Research on Equity & Sustained Participation in Engineering, Computing, & Technology (RESPECT) Conference*.

Jagiela, A., Laleman, J., Huschka, P., Besser, D., and Thomas, A. (2018). Developing and assessing a music technology and coding workshop for young women. In *ASEE Annual Conference and Exposition, Conference Proceedings*. Available: https://peer.asee.org/developing-and-assessing-a-music-technology-and-coding-workshop-for-young-women.pdf.

Jenson, J., Black, K., and de Castell, S. (2018). Digital game-design: Effects of single sex groups on student success. In *ECGBL 2018 12th European Conference on Game-Based Learning* (p. 258).

Jin, G., Tu, M., Kim, T.H., Heffron, J., and White, J. (2018). Game based cybersecurity training for high school students. In *Proceedings of the 49th ACM Technical Symposium on Computer Science Education* (pp. 68–73).

Johnson, D.W., and Johnson, R.T. (2009). An educational psychology success story: Social interdependence theory and cooperative learning. *Educational Researcher, 38*(5), 365–379.

Johnson, S.R., Ivey, A., Snyder, J., Skorodinsky, M., and Goode, J. (2020). Intersectional perspectives on teaching: Women of color, equity, and computer science. In *2020 Research on Equity and Sustained Participation in Engineering, Computing, and Technology (RESPECT)* (pp. 1–4).

Jones, B.D., Ruff, C., and Paretti, M.C. (2013). The impact of engineering identification and stereotypes on undergraduate women's achievement and persistence in engineering. *Social Psychology of Education, 16*(3), 471–493.

Kafai, Y.B., and Burke, Q. (2015) Constructionist gaming: Understanding the benefits of making games for learning. *Educational Psychologist, 50*(4), 313–334.

Kafai, Y.B., and Fields, D. (2018). Some reflections on designing constructionist activities for classrooms. In *Constructionism 2018: Constructionism, Computational Thinking and Educational Innovation: Conference Proceedings* (pp. 601–608).

Kafai, Y.B., Fields, D., and Searle, K. (2014). Electronic textiles as disruptive designs: Supporting and challenging maker activities in schools. *Harvard Educational Review, 84*(4), 532–556.

Kafai, Y.B., Fields, D.A., and Searle, K.A. (2019). Understanding media literacy and DIY creativity in youth digital productions. In *The International Encyclopedia of Media Literacy* (pp. 1–10). Hoboken, NJ: John Wiley and Sons.

Kafai, Y.B., Peppler, K.A., and Chapman, R.N. (Eds.). (2009). *The Computer Clubhouse: Constructionism and Creativity in Youth Communities*. New York, NY: Teachers College Press.

Kahle, J., and Meece, J. (1994). Research on girls in science lessons and applications. In D.L. Gabel (Ed.), *Handbook of Research in Science Teaching and Learning* (pp. 542–556). New York, NY: Macmillan.

Kamenetz, A. (2017). *Tens of Thousands of Minorities Are Taking Computer Science*. National Public Radio. Available: https://www.npr.org/sections/ed/2017/07/31/539853090/tens-of-thousands-more-women-and-minorities-are-taking-computer-science.

Kang, H., Barton, A.C., Tan, E., Simpkins, S.D., Rhee, H., and Turner, C. (2019). How do middle school girls of color develop STEM identities? Middle school girls' participation in science activities and identification with STEM careers. *Science Education, 103*(2), 418–439.

Kanter, R. (1977). *Men and Women of the Corporation*. New York, NY: Basic Books.

Kapon, S., Laherto, A., and Levrini, O. (2018). Disciplinary authenticity and personal relevance in school science. *Science Education, 102*, 1077–1106.

Kapur, M., and Bielaczyc, K. (2012). Designing for productive failure. *Journal of the Learning Sciences, 21*(1), 45–83.

Kazakoff, E., and Bers, M. (2012). Programming in a robotics context in the kindergarten classroom: The impact on sequencing skills. *Journal of Educational Multimedia and Hypermedia, 21*(4), 371–391.

Kelleher, C., and Paush, R. (2005). Lowering the barriers to programming: A taxonomy of programming environments and languages for novice programmers. *ACM Computing Surveys (CSUR), 37*(2), 83–137.

Kelleher, C., and Paush, R. (2007). Using storytelling to motivate programming. *Communications of the ACM, 50*(7), 59–64.

Kim, A.Y., Sinatra, G.M., and Seyranian, V. (2018). Developing a STEM identity among young women: A social identity perspective. *Review of Educational Research, 88*(4), 589–625.

King-Sears, M.E., Brawand, A.E., Jenkins, M.C., and Preston-Smith, S. (2014). Co-teaching perspectives from secondary science co-teachers and their students with disabilities. *Journal of Science Teacher Education, 25*(6), 651–680.

Klein, L. (2013). Meleon: A casual mobile game supporting immersion and reflection in learning. In *European Conference on Games Based Learning* (p. 305). Available: https://issuu.com/acpil/docs/ecgbl2013-issuu_vol_1.

Klopfer, E., Yoon, S., and Rivas, L. (2004). Comparative analysis of Palm and wearable computers for Participatory Simulations. *Journal of Computer Assisted Learning, 20*(5), 347–359.

Kochanek, J., Matthews, A., Wright, E., DiSanti, J., Neff, M., and Erickson, K. (2019). Competitive readiness: Developmental considerations to promote positive youth development in competitive activities. *Journal of Youth Development, 14*(1), 48–69.

Kolodner, J.L., Camp, P.J., Crismond, D., Fasse, B., Gray, J., Holbrook, J., Puntambekar, S., and Ryan, M. (2003). Problem-based learning meets case-based reasoning in the middle-school science classroom: Putting learning by design (tm) into practice. *The Journal of the Learning Sciences, 12*(4), 495–547.

Koshy, S. (2017). *SMASH Impact Report 2017.* SMASH. Available: https://mk0kaporcenter5ld71a.kinstacdn.com/wp-content/uploads/2018/08/FINAL-2017-SMASH-Report-Sonia-Koshy.pdf.

Kow, Y.M., and Nardi, B. (2010). Who owns the mods? *First Monday, 15*(5). Available: https://firstmonday.org/ojs/index.php/fm/article/download/2971/2529.

Kow, Y.M., Young, T., and Takinbas, K.S. (2014). *Crafting the Metagame: Connected Learning in the Starcraft II Community.* Digital Media and Learning Research Hub. Available: https://dmlhub.net/publications/crafting-metagame-connected-learning-starcraft-ii-community/index.html.

Krayem, Z.N., Kelly, A.M., McCauley, J.R., and Bugallo, M.F. (2019). Engineering exposure for pre-college women: A university-based workshop model. In *2019 IEEE Integrated STEM Education Conference (ISEC)* (pp. 156–159).

Krishnamurthi, A., Ballard, M., and Noam, G. (2014). *Examining the Impact of Afterschool STEM Programs.* Afterschool Alliance. Available: http://www.afterschoolalliance.org/ExaminingtheImpactofAfterschoolSTEMPrograms.pdf.

Krishnamurthi, A., Bevan, B., Rinehart, J., and Coulon, V.R. (2013). What afterschool STEM does best: How stakeholders describe youth learning outcomes. *Afterschool Matters, 18*, 42–49.

Krivet, A., and Krajcik, J. (2008). Contextualizing instruction: Leveraging students' prior knowledge and experiences to foster understanding of middle school science. *Journal of Research in Science Teaching, 45*(1), 79–100.

Ladeji-Osias, J.O., Partlow, L.E., and Dillon, E.C. (2018). Using mobile application development and 3-D modeling to encourage minority male interest in computing and engineering. *IEEE Transactions on Education*, 61(4), 274–280.

Ladner, R., and Israel, M. (2016). "For All" in "Computer Science For All." *Communications of the ACM*, 59(9), 26–28.

Ladson-Billings, G. (1995). Toward a theory of culturally relevant pedagogy. *American Educational Research Journal*, 32(3), 465–491.

Ladson-Billings, G. (2014). Culturally relevant pedagogy 2.0: Aka the remix. *Harvard Educational Review*, 84(1), 74–84.

LaForce, M., Noble, E., and Blackwell, C. (2017). Problem-based learning (PBL) and student interest in STEM careers: The roles of motivation and ability beliefs. *Education Sciences*, 7(4), 92.

Lange, P.G. (2014). *Kids on YouTube: Technical Identities and Digital Literacies*. Walnut Creek, CA: Left Coast Press.

Laporte, L., and Zaman, B. (2016). Informing content-driven design of computer programming games: A problems analysis and a game review. In *NordiCHI '16: Proceedings of the 9th Nordic Conference on Human-Computer Interaction* (pp. 1–10).

Lara, M., Lockwood, K., and Tao, E. (2015). Peer-Led Hackathon: An intense learning experience. In *Proceedings from the Annual Meeting of the Association for the Educational Communications and Technology* (pp. 255–259).

Larson, K., Ito, M., Brown, E., Hawkins, M., Pinkard, N., and Sebring, P. (2013). *Safe Space and Shared Interests: YOUmedia Chicago as a Laboratory for Connected Learning*. Connected Learning Lab. Available: https://dmlhub.net/publications/safe-space-and-shared-interests-youmedia-chicago-laboratory-connected-learning/index.html.

Lau, W.W., Ngai, G., Chan, S.C., and Cheung, J.C. (2009). Learning programming through fashion and design: A pilot summer course in wearable computing for middle school students. In *Proceedings of the 40th ACM Technical Symposium on Computer Science Education* (pp. 504–508).

Lauer, P., Akiba, M., Wilkerson, S.B., Apthorp, H.S., Snow, D., and Martin-Glenn, M.L (2006). Out-of-school-time programs: A meta-analysis of effects for at-risk students. *Review of Educational Research*, 76(2), 275–313.

Lave, J. (1988). *Cognition in Practice: Mind, Mathematics and Culture in Everyday Life*. Cambridge, UK: Cambridge University Press.

Lave, J., and Wenger, E. (1991). *Situated Learning: Legitimate Peripheral Participation*. Cambridge, UK: Cambridge University Press.

Lave, J., and Wenger, E. (2002). Legitimate peripheral participation in communities of practice. In F. Reeve, R. Harrison, J. Clarke, and A. Hanson (Eds.) *Supporting Lifelong Learning: Perspectives on Learning* (pp. 111–126). London, UK and New York, NY: Routledge.

Layland, E.K., Stone, G.A., Mueller, J.T., and Hodge, C.J. (2018). Injustice in mobile leisure: A conceptual exploration of Pokémon Go. *Learning Sciences*, 40(4), 288–306.

Lee, C.H., and Soep, E. (2016). None but ourselves can free our minds: Critical computational literacy as a pedagogy of resistance. *Equity & Excellence in Education*, 49(4), 480–492.

Lee, I., Martin, F., Denner, J., Coulter, B., Allan, W., Erickson, J., Malyn-Smith, J., and Werner, L. (2011). Computational thinking for youth in practice. *ACM Inroads*, 2(1), 32–37.

Lee, J., Husman, J., Scott, K.A., and Eggum-Wilkens, N.D. (2015). COMPUGIRLS: Stepping stone to future computer-based technology pathways. *Journal of Educational Computing Research*, 52(2), 199–223.

Lee, V.R., and Recker, M. (2018). Paper circuits: A tangible, low threshold, low cost entry to computational thinking. *TechTrends*, 62(2), 197–203.

Lee, V.R., Fischback, L., and Cain, R. (2019). A wearables-based approach to detect and identify momentary engagement in afterschool Makerspace programs. *Contemporary Educational Psychology*, *59*, 101789.

Leonard, A.E., Daily, S.B., Babu, S., and Jörg, S. (2020). Coding moves: Design and research on teaching computational thinking through dance choreography and virtual interactions. *Journal of Research on Technology Education*. doi: 10.1080/15391523.2020.1760754.

Lewis, C.M., Anderson, R.E., and Yasuhara, K. (2016). I don't code all day: Fitting in computer science when the stereotypes don't fit. In *Proceedings of the 2016 ACM Conference on International Computing Education Research* (pp. 23–32).

Lewis, C., Shah, N., and Falkner, K. (2019). Equity and diversity. In S. Fincher and A. Robins (Eds.), *The Cambridge Handbook of Computing Education Research* (pp. 481–510). Cambridge, UK: Cambridge University Press.

Lewis, C., Esper, S., Bhattacharyya, V., Fa-Kaji, N., Dominguez, N., and Schlesinger, A. (2014). Children's perceptions of what counts as a programming language. *Journal of Computing Sciences in Colleges*, *29*(4), 123–133.

Lewis, C.M., Yasuhara, K., and Anderson, R.E. (2011). Deciding to major in computer science: A grounded theory of students' self-assessment of ability. In *Proceedings of the Seventh International Workshop on Computing Education Research* (pp. 3–10).

Li, Y., Schoenfeld, A.H., diSessa, A.A., Graesser, A.C., Benson, L.C., English, L.D., and Duschl, R.A. (2019). Design and design thinking in STEM education. *Journal for STEM Education Research*, *2*, 93–104.

Liao, C. (2019). Creating a STEAM map: A content analysis of visual art practices in STEAM education. In M.S. Khine and S. Areepattamannil (Eds.), *STEAM Education* (pp. 37–55). Cham, Switzerland: Springer.

Light, P., and Littleton, K. (1999). *Social Processes in Children's Learning* (Vol. 4). Cambridge, UK: Cambridge University Press.

Lim, K., and Lewis, C.M. (2020, February). Three Metrics of Success for High School CSforAll Initiatives: Demographic Patterns from 2003 to 2019 on Advanced Placement Computer Science Exams. In *Proceedings of the 51st ACM Technical Symposium on Computer Science Education* (pp. 598-604).

Lim, M., and Calabrese Barton, A. (2006). Science learning and a sense of place in an urban middle school. *Cultural Studies of Science Education*, *1*(1), 107–142.

Litchfield, K., and Javernick-Will, A. (2014). Investigating gains from EWB-USA involvement. *Journal of Professional Issues in Engineering Education and Practice*, *140*(1), 04013008.

Little, P.M.D., Wimer, C., and Weiss, H.B. (2008). *After School Programs in the 21st Century: Their Potential and What It Takes to Achieve It. Issues and Opportunities in Out-of-School Time Evaluation, No. 10.* Harvard Family Research Project. Available: https://archive.globalfrp.org/evaluation/publications-resources/after-school-programs-in-the-21st-century-their-potential-and-what-it-takes-to-achieve-it.

Lockwood, P., and Kunda, Z. (1997). Superstars and me: Predicting the impact of role models on the self. *Journal of Personality and Social Psychology*, *73*(1), 91.

Lockwood, P., Marshall, T.C., and Sadler, P. (2005). Promoting success or preventing failure: Cultural differences in motivation by positive and negative role models. *Personality and Social Psychology Bulletin*, *31*(3), 379–392.

Loksa, D., Ko, A.J., Jernigan, W., Oleson, A., Mendez, C.J., and Burnett, M.M. (2016). Programming, problem solving, and self-awareness: Effects of explicit guidance. In *Proceedings of the 2016 CHI Conference on Human Factors in Computing Systems* (pp. 1449–1461).

Lopez, M.E., Caspe, M., and McWilliams, L. (2016). *Public Libraries: A Vital Space for Family Engagement.* Harvard Family Research Project. Available: http://www.ala.org/pla/sites/ala.org.pla/files/content/initiatives/familyengagement/Public-Libraries-A-Vital-Space-for-Family-Engagement_HFRP-PLA_August-2-2016.pdf.

Loucks-Horsley, S., Stiles, K.E., Mundry, S., Love, N., and Hewson, P.W. (2009). *Designing Professional Development for Teachers of Science and Mathematics.* Thousand Oaks, CA: Corwin Press.

Lufkin, M.E., Wiberg, M.M., Jenkins, C.R., Berardi, S.L.L., Boyer, T., Eardley, E., and Huss, J. (2007). Gender equity in career and technical education. *Handbook for Achieving Gender Equity through Education* (2nd ed., pp. 420–442).

Lupton, E. (2014). *Beautiful Users: Designing for People.* Princeton, NJ: Princeton Architectural Press.

Mabey, M.J., Lande, M., and Jordan, S. (2016). Young makers compare science fairs and maker faires. In *2016 ASEE Annual Conference and Exposition.* American Society for Engineering Education. Available: https://peer.asee.org/young-makers-compare-science-fairs-and-maker-faires.pdf.

Mader, N., and Lynch, T. (2020). *Learning Equitably, Digitally, and Well.* The New School/Center for New York City Affairs. Available: https://static1.squarespace.com/static/53ee4f0be4b015b9c3690d84/t/5ef3935d1db6393dc49cddd7/1593021280562/CNYCA_Learning+Equitably%2C+Digitally%2C+and+Well.pdf.

Madkins, T.C., Martin, A., Ryoo, J., Scott, K.A., Goode, J., Scott, A., and McAlear, F. (2019). Culturally relevant computer science pedagogy: From theory to practice. In *2019 Research on Equity and Sustained Participation in Engineering, Computing, and Technology (RESPECT)* (pp. 1–4).

Maltese, A.V., Simpson, A., and Anderson, A. (2018). Failing to learn: The impact of failures during making activities. *Thinking Skills and Creativity, 30,* 116–124.

Margolis, J., and Fisher, A. (2002). *Unlocking the Clubhouse: Women in Computing.* Cambridge, MA: MIT press.

Margolis, J., Estrella, R., Goode, J., Jellison-Holme, J., and Nao, K. (2008). *Stuck in the Shallow End: Education, Race, and Computing.* Cambridge, MA: MIT Press.

Margolis, J., Estrella, E., Goode, G., Holme, J.J., and Nao, K. (2017). *Stuck in the Shallow End: Education, Race, and Computing* (Revised ed.). Cambridge, MA: MIT Press.

Margolis, J., Ryoo, J., and Goode, J. (2017). Seeing myself through someone else's eyes: The value of in-classroom coaching for computer science teaching and learning. *Transactions on Computing Education, 17*(2), 1–18.

Martin, C. (2017). Libraries as facilitators of coding for all. *Knowledge Quest, 45*(3), 46–53.

Martin, C.D. (2004). Draw a computer scientist. *ACM SIGCSE Bulletin, 36*(4), 11–12.

Martin, C.K., Erete, S., and Pinkard, N. (2015). Developing focused recruitment strategies to engage youth in informal opportunities. In *2015 Research in Equity and Sustained Participation in Engineering, Computing, and Technology (RESPECT)* (pp. 1–1).

Martin, C.K., Pinkard, N., Erete, S., and Sandherr, J. (2017). Connections at the family level: Supporting parents and caring adults to engage youth in learning about computers and technology. In Y. Rankin and J. Thomas (Eds.), *Moving Students of Color from Consumers to Producers of Technology* (pp. 220–244). Hershey, PA: IGI Global.

Martin, C.K., Reyes, E., Ramirez, E., Brahms, L., McNamara, A., and Wardrip, P. (2019). *Supporting Educator Reflection and Agency through the Co-Design of Observation Tools and Practices for Informal Learning Environments.* Paper presented at the Connected Learning Summit, Irvine, CA.

Martin, J.P., Miller, M.K., and Simmons, D.R. (2014). Exploring the theoretical social capital "deficit" of first generation college students: Implications for engineering education. *International Journal of Engineering Education, 30*(4), 822–836.

Martin, J.P., Simmons, D.R., and Yu, S.L. (2013). The role of social capital in the experiences of Hispanic women engineering majors. *Journal of Engineering Education, 102*(2), 227–243.

Martin, L. (2015). The promise of the maker movement for education. *Journal of Pre-College Engineering Education Research (J-PEER), 5*(1), 4.

Martinez, S.L., and Stager, G. (2013). *Invent to Learn: Making, Tinkering, and Engineering in the Classroom.* Torrance, CA: Constructing Modern Knowledge Press.

Martinez-Garza, M. (2013). Digital games and the U.S. National Research Council's science proficiency goals. *Studies in Science Education, 49*(2), 170–208.

Marty, P.F., Alemanne, N.D., Mendenhall, A., Maurya, M., Southerland, S.A., Sampson, V., Douglas, I., Kazmer, M.M., Clark, A., and Schellinger, J. (2013). Scientific inquiry, digital literacy, and mobile computing in informal learning environments. *Learning, Media and Technology, 38*(4), 407–428.

Marx, D.M., and Roman, J.S. (2002). Female role models: Protecting women's math test performance. *Personality and Social Psychology Bulletin, 28*(9), 1183–1193.

Marx, D.M., Stapel, D.A., and Muller, D. (2005). We can do it: The interplay of construal orientation and social comparisons under threat. *Journal of Personality and Social Psychology, 88*(3), 432.

Master, A., Cheryan, S., and Meltzoff, A.N. (2016). Computing whether she belongs: Stereotypes undermine girls' interest and sense of belonging in computer science. *Journal of Educational Psychology, 108*(3), 424.

Master, A., Cheryan, S., Moscatelli, A., and Meltzoff, A.N. (2017). Programming experience promotes higher STEM motivation among first-grade girls. *Journal of Experimental Child Psychology, 160*, 92–106.

Mathewson, T. (2017, December 20). Internet access in schools and the end of net neutrality. *The Hechinger Report.* Available: https://hechingerreport.org/internet-access-in-schools-e-rate-trends-and-the-end-of-net-neutrality.

McComb, E.M., and Scott-Little, C. (2003). *A Review of Research on Participant Outcomes in After-School Programs: Implications for School Counselors.* ERIC Clearinghouse on Counseling and Student Services. Available: https://www.counseling.org/resources/library/ERIC%20Digests/2003-08.pdf.

McCombs, J., Whitaker, A., and Yoo, P. (2017). *The Value of Out-of-School Time Programs.* Santa Monica, CA: RAND Corporation. Available: https://www.rand.org/pubs/perspectives/PE267.html.

McGee, E.O. (2016). Devalued Black and Latino racial identities: A by-product of STEM college culture? *American Educational Research Journal, 53*(6), 1626–1662.

McGee, S., McGee-Tekula, R., Duck, J., Dettori, L., Rasmussen, A.M., Wheeler, E., and Greenberg, R.I. (2019). *Study of Equitable Access and Outcomes from Advanced Computer Science Coursework in an Urban Setting.* Paper presented at the American Education Research Association Annual Meeting, Toronto, ON.

McGee, S., McGee-Tekula, R., Duck, J., Dettori, L., Yanek, D., Rasmussen, A., Greenberg, R.I., and Reed, D.F. (2018). Does exploring computer science increase computer science enrollment? In *American Education Research Association Annual Meeting,* New York, April (Vol. 1, p. 2019).

Mehta, J., and Fine, S. (2019). *In Search of Deeper Learning: The Quest to Remake the American High School.* Cambridge, MA: Harvard University Press.

Mehus, S., Stevens, R., and Grigholm, L. (2010). *Interactional Arrangements for Learning about Science in Early Childhood: A Case Study Across Preschool and Home Contexts.* Paper presented at the 9th International Conference of the Learning Sciences, Chicago, IL.

Melchoir, A., Burack, C., Hoover, M., and Haque, Z. (2019). *FIRST® Longitudinal Study: Findings at 60 Month Follow-Up.* The Center for Youth and Communities, Heller School for Social Policy and Management, Brandeis University. Available: https://www.first-inspires.org/sites/default/files/uploads/resource_library/impact/first-longitudinal-study-60-months.pdf.

Mendelsohn, P., Green, T.R.G., and Brna, P. (1990). Programming languages in education: The search for an easy start. In J.-M. Hoc, T.R.G. Green, R. Samurçay, and D.J. Gilmore (Eds.), *Psychology of Programming* (pp. 175–200). London, UK: Academic Press.

Menekse, M. (2015). Computer science teacher professional development in the United States: A review of studies published between 2004 and 2014. *Computer Science Education, 25*(4), 325–350.

Merkouris, A., Chorianopoulos, K., and Kameas, A. (2017). Teaching programming in secondary education through embodied computing platforms: Robotics and wearables. *ACM Transactions on Computing Education (TOCE), 17*(2), 1–22.

Merolla, D.M., and Serpe, R.T. (2013). STEM enrichment programs and graduate school matriculation: The role of science identity salience. *Social Psychology of Education, 16*(4), 575–597.

Merolla, D.M., Serpe, R.T., Stryker, S., and Schultz, P.W. (2012). Structural precursors to identity processes: The role of proximate social structures. *Social Psychology Quarterly, 75*(2), 149–172.

Mesiti, L.A., Parkes, A., Paneto, S.C., and Cahill, C. (2019). Building capacity for computational thinking in youth through informal education. *Journal of Museum Education, 44*(1), 108–121.

Michalchik, V., Llorente, C., Lundh, P., and Remold, J. (2008). *A Place to Be Your Best: Youth Outcomes in the Computer Clubhouse.* SRI International. Available: https://theclubhousenetwork.org/wp-content/uploads/2018/12/A-Place-to-Be-Your-Best-FINAL-7-25.pdf.

Migus, L.H. (2014). *Broadening Access to STEM Learning through Out-of-School Learning Environments.* National Research Council Committee on Successful Out-of-School STEM Learning. Washington, DC: National Research Council. Available: http://citeseerx.ist.psu.edu/viewdoc/download?doi=10.1.1.674.7491&rep=rep1&type=pdf.

Miller, K., Sonnert, G., and Sadler, P. (2018). The influence of students' participation in STEM competitions on their interest in STEM careers. *International Journal of Science Education, Part B, 8*(2), 95–114.

Mitchell, M. (1993). Situational interest: Its multifaceted structure in the secondary school mathematics classroom. *Journal of Educational Psychology, 85*(3), 424.

Moallem, M., Hung, W., and Dabbagh, N. (Eds.). (2019). *The Wiley Handbook of Problem-Based Learning.* Boston, MA: Wiley-Blackwell.

Mogensen, F., and Schanck, K. (2010). The action competence approach and the "new" discourses of sustainable development, competence and quality criteria. *Environmental Education Research, 16*(1), 59–74.

Moll, L.C. (2015). Tapping into the "hidden" home and community resources of students. *Kappa Delta Pi Record, 51*(3), 114–117.

Moll, L.C., Amanti, C., Neff, D., and Gonzalez, N. (1992). Funds of knowledge for teaching: Using a qualitative approach to connect homes and classrooms. *Theory into Practice, 31*(2), 132–141.

Monterastelli, T., Bayles, T., and Ross, J. (2008). High school outreach program: Attracting young ladies with "engineering in health care." In *ASEE 2008 Annual Conference & Exposition.* Available: https://vtechworks.lib.vt.edu/bitstream/handle/10919/80378/RossHighSchoolOutreach2008.pdf?sequence=1&isAllowed=y.

Moore, T.J., Brophy, S.P., Tank, K.M., Lopez, R.D., Johnston, A.C., Hynes, M.M., and Gajdzik, E. (2020). Multiple representations in computational thinking tasks: A clinical study of second-grade students. *Journal of Science Education and Technology, 29*(1), 19–34.

Munro, D. (2015). Hosting hackathons: A tool in retaining students with beneficial side effects. *Journal of Computing Sciences in Colleges, 30*(5), 46–51.

Murai, Y., Kim, Y., Chang, S., Rosenheck, L., and Kirschmann, P. (2019). What maker assessment should look like: A closer look at the design process. In *Proceedings of the 2019 Connected Learning Summit* (pp. 225–226).

Murchison, L., Brohawn, K., Fanscali, C., Beesley, A.D., and Stafford, E. (2019). The unique challenges of afterschool research: A practical guide for evaluators and practitioners. *Afterschool Matters, 29*, 28–35.

Mystakidis, S., Lambropoulos, N., Fardoun, H.M., and Alghazzawi, D.M. (2014). Playful Blended Digital Storytelling in 3D Immersive Elearning Environments: A Cost Effective Early Literacy Motivation Method. In *Proceedings of the 2014 Workshop on Interaction Design in Educational Environments* (pp. 97–101).

Nager, A., and Atkinson, R.D. (2016). *The Case for Improving U.S. Computer Science Education.* Information Technology & Innovation Foundation. Available: http://www2.itif.org/2016-computer-science-education.pdf.

Nakajima, T., and Goode, J. (2019). Transformative learning for computer science teachers: Examining how educators learn e-textiles in professional development. *Teaching and Teacher Education, 85*, 145–189.

Naphan-Kingery, D.E., Miles, M., Brockman, A., McKane, R., Botchway, P., and McGee, E. (2019). Investigation of an equity ethic in engineering and computing doctoral students. *Journal of Engineering Education, 108*(3), 337–354.

Nasir, N.I.S., and Cook, J. (2009). Becoming a hurdler: How learning settings afford identities. *Anthropology & Education Quarterly, 40*(1), 41–61.

Nasir, N.I.S., Rosebery, A.S., Warren, B., and Lee, C.D. (2006). Learning as a cultural process: Achieving equity through diversity. In R.K. Sawyer (Ed.), *The Cambridge Handbook of the Learning Sciences* (pp. 626–646). Cambridge, UK: Cambridge University Press.

National Academies of Sciences, Engineering, and Medicine. (2018a). *Assessing and Responding to the Growth of Computer Science Undergraduate Enrollments.* Washington, DC: The National Academies Press.

——. (2018b). *How People Learn II: Learners, Contexts, and Cultures.* Washington, DC: The National Academies Press.

——. (2018c). *English Learners in STEM Subjects: Transforming Classrooms, Schools, and Lives.* Washington, DC: The National Academies Press.

——. (2019). *The Science of Effective Mentorship in STEMM.* Washington, DC: The National Academies Press.

——. (2020). *Promising Practices for Addressing the Underrepresentation of Women in Science, Engineering, and Medicine: Opening Doors.* Washington, DC: The National Academies Press.

National Center for Education Statistics. (2015). *Parent and Family Involvement in Education, from the National Household Education Surveys Program of 2012.* Washington, DC: Author.

National Conference of State Legislatures. (2019). *Expanding Learning Opportunities through Afterschool Programs.* Available: https://www.ncsl.org/research/education/expanding-learning-opportunities-through-afterschool-programs.aspx#research.

National Research Council. (1999). *How People Learn: Brain, Mind, Experience, and School.* Washington, DC: National Academy Press.

——. (2000). *How People Learn: Brain, Mind, Experience, and School* (Expanded ed.). Washington, DC: National Academy Press

——. (2001). *Knowing What Students Know: The Science and Design of Educational Assessment*. Washington, DC: National Academy Press.

——. (2009). *Learning Science in Informal Environments: People, Places, and Pursuits*. Washington, DC: The National Academies Press.

——. (2010a). *Surrounded by Science: Learning Science in Informal Environments*. Washington, DC: The National Academies Press.

——. (2010b). *Report of a Workshop on the Scope and Nature of Computational Thinking*. Washington, DC: The National Academies Press.

——. (2011a). *Report of a Workshop on the Pedagogical Aspects of Computational Thinking*. Washington, DC: The National Academies Press.

——. (2011b). *Learning Science Through Games and Simulations*. Washington, DC: The National Academies Press.

——. (2012). *Framework for K–12 Science Education*. Washington, DC: The National Academies Press.

——. (2014). *STEM Integration in K–12 Education: Status, Prospects, and an Agenda for Research*. Washington, DC: The National Academies Press.

——. (2015). *Identifying and Supporting Productive STEM Programs in Out-of-School Settings*. Washington, DC: The National Academies Press.

National Science Foundation (NSF). (2015). *World Premiere of "The Science Behind Pixar" Illustrates Power of Computational Thinking*. Available: https://www.nsf.gov/news/news_summ.jsp?cntn_id=135497.

——. (2017). *The National Science Foundation and Making*. Available: https://www.nsf.gov/news/news_summ.jsp?cntn_id=131770.

NGSS Lead States. (2012). *Next Generation Science Standards: For States, By States*. Washington, DC: The National Academies Press.

Ni, L. (2011). Building professional identity as computer science teachers: Supporting secondary computer science teachers through reflection and community building. In *Proceedings of the Seventh International Workshop on Computing Education Research* (pp. 143–144).

Nightingale, E.O., and Wolverton, L. (1993). Adolescent rolelessness in modern society. *Teachers College Record*, 94(3), 472–486.

Noam, G.G., Robertson, D.L., Papazian, A., and Guhn, M. (2014). *The Development of a Brief Measure for Assessing Science Interest and Engagement in Children and Youth: Structure, Reliability and Validity of the Common Instrument*. Cambridge, MA: Program in Education, Afterschool and Resiliency (PEAR), Harvard University.

Nugent, G.C., Barker, B.S., and Grandgenett, N. (2013). The impact of educational robotics on student STEM learning, attitudes, and workplace skills. In *Robotics: Concepts, Methodologies, Tools, and Applications* (pp. 1442–1459). Hershey, PA: IGI Global.

Nugent, G., Barker, B., Grandgenett, N., and Welch, G. (2016). Robotics camps, clubs, and competitions: Results from a US robotics project. *Robotics and Autonomous Systems*, 75, 686–691.

Nugent, G., Barker, B., Lester, H., Grandgenett, N., and Valentine, D. (2019). Wearable textiles to support student STEM learning and attitudes. *Journal of Science Education and Technology*, 28(5), 470–479.

Nussbaumer, L. (2018). *Human Factors in the Built Environment* (2nd ed.). New York, NY: Fairchild/Bloomsbury.

Nye, C.D., Su, R., Rounds, J., and Drasgow, F. (2012). Vocational interests and performance: A quantitative summary of over 60 years of research. *Perspectives on Psychological Science*, 7, 384–403.

Ok, M.W., Rao, K., Bryant, B.R., and McDougall, D. (2017). Universal design for learning in pre-K to grade 12 classrooms: A systematic review of research. *Exceptionality, 25*(2), 116–138.

O'Keeffe, P. (2013). A sense of belonging: Improving student retention. *College Student Journal, 47*(4), 605–613.

O'Neil, T. (2010). Fostering spaces of student ownership in middle school science. *Equity and Excellence in Education, 43*(1), 6–20.

Ouyang, Y., Hayden, K.L., and Remold, J. (2018). Introducing computational thinking through non-programming science activities. In *Proceedings of the 49th ACM Technical Symposium on Computer Science Educatio*n (pp. 308–313).

Papavlasopoulou, S., Giannakos, M.N., and Jaccheri, L. (2019). Exploring children's learning experience in constructionism-based coding activities through design-based research. *Computers in Human Behavior, 99*, 415–427.

Papert, S. (1980). *Mindstorms: Computers, Children, and Powerful Ideas.* New York, NY: Basic Books.

Paris, D. (2012). Culturally sustaining pedagogy: A needed change in stance, terminology, and practice. *Educational Researcher, 41*(3), 93–97.

Pasnik, S. (Ed.) (2019). *Getting Ready to Learn; Creating Effective, Educational Children's Media.* London, UK and New York, NY: Routledge.

Pe-Than, E., Herbsleb, J., Nolte, A., Gerber, E., Fiore-Gartland, B., Chapman, B., Moser, A., and Wilkins-Diehr, N. (2018). The 2nd workshop on hacking and making at time-bounded events: Current trends and next steps in research and event design. In *Extended Abstracts of the 2018 CHI Conference on Human Factors in Computing Systems* (pp. 1–8).

Penuel, W.R., Chang-Order, J., and Michalchik, V. (2018). Using research-practice partnerships to support interest-related learning in libraries. In V.R. Lee and A.L. Phillips (Eds.) *Reconceptualizing Libraries: Perspectives from the Information and Learning Sciences.* London, UK: Taylor & Francis.

Peppler, K.A. (2010). Media arts: Arts education for a digital age. *Teachers College Record, 112*(8), 2118–2153.

Peppler, K. (2013). STEAM-powered computing education: Using e-textiles to integrate the arts and STEM. *Computer, 9*, 38–43.

Peppler, K.A., and Warschauer, M. (2011). Uncovering literacies, disrupting stereotypes: Examining the (dis)abilities of a child learning to computer program and read. *International Journal of Learning and Media, 3*(3), 15–41.

Peppler, K., Halverson, E., and Kafai, Y.B. (Eds.). (2016). *Makeology: Makerspaces as Learning Environments* (Vol. 1). London, UK and New York, NY: Routledge.

Peppler, K., Keune, A., and Chang, S. (2018). *Open Portfolio Project, Phase 2: Research Brief Series.* Available: http:// makered.org/opp/publications.

Peppler, K., Sedas, R.M., and Dahn, M. (2020). Making at home: Interest-driven practices and supportive relationships in minoritized homes. *Education Sciences, 10*(5), 143.

Perkel, D. (2010). Copy and paste literacy? Literacy practices in the production of a MySpace profile. *Works in Applied Linguistics, 49*(2), 493–511.

Perkins Data Explorer. (2020). *IT Concentration Participation 2017–2018.* Available: https:// perkins.ed.gov/pims/DataExplorer/CTEConcentrator.

Petrich, M., Wilkinson, K., and Bevan, B. (2013). It looks like fun, but are they learning? In M. Honey and D.E. Kanter (Eds.), *Design, Make, Play* (pp. 68–88). London, UK and New York, NY: Routledge.

Phillips, A.L., Lee, V.R., and Recker, M. (2018). Small town librarians as experience engineers. In V.R. Lee and A.L. Phillips (Eds.), *Reconceptualizing Libraries: Perspectives from the Information and Learning Sciences* (pp. 158–169). London, UK and New York, NY: Routledge.

Pinkard, N., Martin, C.K., and Erete, S. (2020). Equitable approaches: Opportunities for computational thinking with emphasis on creative production and connections to community. *Interactive Learning Environments, 28*(3), 347–361.

Pinkard, N., Erete, S., Martin, C.K., and McKinney de Royston, M. (2017). Digital youth divas: Exploring narrative-driven curriculum to spark middle school girls' interest in computational activities. *Journal of the Learning Sciences, 26*(3), 477–516.

Pintrich, P.R. (2003). A motivational science perspective on the role of student motivation in learning and teaching contexts. *Journal of Educational Psychology, 95*(4), 667–686.

Plass, J., Homer, B.D., and Kinzer, C.K. (2014). *Playful Learning: An Integrated Design Framework*. Games for Learning Institute. Available: https://citeseerx.ist.psu.edu/viewdoc/download?doi=10.1.1.1081.645&rep=rep1&type=pdf.

Pöhner, N., and Hennecke, M. (2018). Learning problem solving through educational robotics competitions: First results of an exploratory case study. In *Proceedings of the 13th Workshop in Primary and Secondary Computing Education* (pp. 1–4).

Polman, J., and Miller, D. (2010). Changing stories: Trajectories of identification among African American youth in a science outreach apprenticeship. *American Educational Research Journal, 47*(4), 879–918.

Portelance, D.J., Strawhacker, A.L., and Bers, M.U. (2016). Constructing the ScratchJr programming language in the early childhood classroom. *International Journal of Technology and Design Education, 26*(4), 489–504.

Porter, E., Bopp, C., Gerber, E., and Voida, A. (2017). Reappropriating hackathons: The production work of the CHI4Good Day of Service. In *Proceedings of the 2017 CHI Conference on Human Factors in Computing Systems* (pp. 810–814).

Powers, A.L. (2004). An evaluation of four place-based education programs. *The Journal of Environmental Education, 35*(4), 17–32.

Preece, J., and Maloney-Krichmar, D. (2005). Online communities: Design, theory, and practice. *Journal of Computer-Mediated Communication, 10*(4), JCMC10410.

Qiu, K., Buechley, L., Baafi, E., and Dubow, W. (2013). A curriculum for teaching computer science through computational textiles. In *Proceedings of the 12th International Conference on Interaction Design and Children* (pp. 20–27).

Rafalow, M.H., and Tekinbas, K.S. (2014). *Welcome to Sackboy Planet: Connected Learning Among LittleBigPlanet 2 Players*. Connected Learning Lab. Available: https://dmlhub.net/publications/welcome-sackboy-planet-connected-learning-among-littlebigplanet-2-players/index.html.

Raffaelli, M., and Ontai, L.L. (2004). Gender socialization in Latino/a families: Results from two retrospective studies. *Sex Roles, 50*(5–6), 287–299.

Rahm, J. (2008). Urban youths' hybrid positioning in science practices at the margin: A look inside a school-museum-scientist partnership project and an after-school science program. *Cultural Studies of Science Education, 3*, 97–121.

Ralabate, P. (2016). *Your UDL Lesson Planner: The Step-by-Step Guide for Teaching all Learners*. Baltimore, MD: Brookes Publishing.

Rands, M., and Gansemer-Topf, A. (2017). The room itself is active: How classroom design impacts student engagement. *Journal of Learning Spaces, 6*(1), 26–33.

Raposa, E.B., Ben-Eliyahu, A., Olsho, L.E., and Rhodes, J. (2019). Birds of a feather: Is matching based on shared interests and characteristics associated with longer youth mentoring relationships? *Journal of Community Psychology, 47*(2), 385–397.

Rasmussen, B., and Håpnes, T. (1991). Excluding women from the technologies of the future?: A case study of the culture of computer science. *Futures, 23*(10), 1107–1119.

Real, B., and Rose, R.N. (2017). *Rural Libraries in the United States: Recent Strides, Future Possibilities, and Meeting Community Needs.* American Library Association. Available: http://www.ala.org/advocacy/sites/ala.org.advocacy/files/content/pdfs/Rural%20 paper%2007-31-2017.pdf.

Reed, D., Wilkerson, B., Yanek, D., Dettori, L., and Solin, J. (2015). How exploring computer science (ECS) came to Chicago. *ACM Inroads, 6*(3), 75–77.

Reilly, E.D., Rackley, K.R., and Awad, G.H. (2017). Perceptions of male and female STEM aptitude: The moderating effect of benevolent and hostile sexism. *Journal of Career Development, 44*(2), 159–173.

Renninger, K.A., and Hidi, S. (2011). Revisiting the conceptualization, measurement, and generation of interest. *Educational Psychologist, 46*(3), 168–184.

Repenning, A. (1991). Creating user interfaces with agentsheets. In *Proceedings of the 1991 IEEE Symposium on Applied Computing* (pp. 191–196).

Resnick, M. (2017). *Lifelong Kindergarten: Cultivating Creativity through Projects, Passion, Peers, and Play.* Cambridge, MA: MIT Press.

Resnick, M., and Rosenbaum, E. (2013). Designing for tinkerability. In M. Honey and D. Kanter (Eds.), *Design, Make, Play: Growing the Next Generation of STEM Innovators* (pp. 163–181). London, UK and New York, NY: Routledge.

Resnick, M., and Silverman, B. (2005). Some Reflections on Designing Construction Kits for Kids. In *Proceedings of the 2005 Conference on Interaction Design and Children* (pp. 117–122). Available: https://dl.acm.org/doi/proceedings/10.1145/1109540.

Resnick, M., Maloney, J., Monroy-Hernández, A., Rusk, N., Eastmond, E., Brennan, K., Millner, A., Rosenbaum, E., Silver, J., Silverman, B., and Kafai, Y. (2009). Scratch: Programming for all. *Communications of the ACM, 52*(11), 60–67.

Rich, K.M., Yadav, A., and Schwarz, C.V. (2019). Computational thinking, mathematics, and science: Elementary teachers' perspectives on integration. *Journal of Technology and Teacher Education, 27*(2), 165–205.

Rich, P.J., and Hu, H.H. (2019). Surveying the landscape: Statewide data on K-12 CS education implementation. In *2019 Research on Equity and Sustained Participation in Engineering, Computing, and Technology (RESPECT)* (pp. 1–8).

Rich, P.J., Jones, B.L., Belikov, O., Yoshikawa, E., and Perkins, M. (2017). Computing and engineering in elementary school: The effect of yearlong training on elementary teacher self-efficacy and beliefs about teaching computing and engineering. *International Journal of Computer Science Education in Schools, 1*(1), n1.

Rich, P.J., Browning, S.F., Perkins, M., Shoop, T., Yoshikawa, E., and Belikov, O.M. (2019). Coding in K-8: International trends in teaching elementary/primary computing. *TechTrends, 63*(3), 311–329.

Ringland, K.E., Boyd, L., Faucett, H., Cullen, A.L., and Hayes, G.R. (2017). Making in Minecraft: A means of self-expression for youth with autism. In *Proceedings of the 2017 Conference on Interaction Design and Children* (pp. 340–345).

Roberts, M., Prottsman, K., and Gray, J. (2018). Priming the pump: Reflections on training K–5 teachers in computer science. In *Proceedings of the 49th ACM Technical Symposium on Computer Science Education* (pp. 723–728).

Robinson, C.W., and Zajicek, J.M. (2005). Growing minds: The effects of a one-year school garden program on six constructs of life skills of elementary school children. *HortTechnology, 15*(3), 453–457.

Rodriguez, S.L., and Lehman, K. (2018). Developing the next generation of diverse computer scientists: The need for enhanced, intersectional computing identity theory. *Computer Science Education, 27*(3-4), 229–247.

Roorda, D.L., Koomen, J.M.Y., Spilt, J.L., and Oort, F.J. (2011). The influence of affective teacher-student relationships on students' school engagement and achievement: A meta-analytic approach. *Review of Educational Research, 81*(4), 493–529.

Rubio, J. (2017). Working together: Youth-adult partnerships to enhance youth voice. In L.W. Braun and S. Peterson, (Eds.), *Putting Teens First in Library Service: A Road Map* (pp. 69–95). Chicago, IL: YALSA.

Ruiz, R. (2019). Girl Scouts learn how to make a difference with new "Coding for Good" badges. *Mashable.* Available: https://mashable.com/article/girl-scouts-coding-for-good-badges.

Rushkoff, D. (2010). *Program Or Be Programmed: Ten Commands for a Digital Age.* New York, NY: Or Books.

Ruth, A., Hackman, J., Brewis, A., Spence, T., Luchmun, R., Velez, J., and Ganesh, T.G. (2019). Engineering projects in community service (EPICS) in high schools: Subtle but potentially important student gains detected from human-centered curriculum design. *Education Sciences, 9*(1), 35.

Ryan, R.M., and Deci, E.L. (2000). Self-determination theory and the facilitation of intrinsic motivation, social development, and well-being. *American Psychologist, 55*, 68–78.

Ryan, R.M., and Deci, E.L. (2017). *Self-Determination Theory: Basic Psychological Needs in Motivation, Development, and Wellness.* New York, NY: Guilford Publishing.

Ryoo, J.J., and Kekelis, L. (2018). Reframing "failure" in making: The value of play, social relationships, and ownership. *Journal of Youth Development, 13*(4), 49–67.

Ryoo, J.J., Goode, J., and Margolis, J. (2015). It takes a village: Supporting inquiry- and equity-oriented computer science pedagogy through a professional learning community. *Computer Science Education, 25*(4), 351–370.

Ryoo, J., Margolis, J., Tanksley, T., and Estrada, C. (2020) Take space, make space: How students use computer science to disrupt and resist marginalization in schools. *Computer Science Education, 30*(3), 337–361.

Ryoo, J.J., Bulalacao, N., Kekelis, L., McLeod, E., and Henriquez, B. (2015). *Tinkering with "Failure": Equity, Learning, and the Iterative Design Process.* Paper presented at the FabLearn 2015 Conference, Stanford, CA. Available: https://techbridgegirls.org/Tinkering+With+Failure_FabLearn_2015.compressed.pdf.

Ryoo, J.J., Margolis, J., Lee, C.H., Sandoval, C.D., and Goode, J. (2013). Democratizing computer science knowledge: Transforming the face of computer science through public high school education. *Learning, Media, and Technology, 38*(2), 161–181.

Ryoo, J.J., Chapman, G., Flapan, J., Goode, J., Margolis, J., Ong, C., Estrada, C., Skorodinsky, M., Tanksley, T., Burge, J.D., Yamaguchi, R., McAlear, F., Scott, A., Martin, A., Koshy, S., Bobb, K., and Diaz, L. (2019). Going beyond the platitudes of equity: Developing a shared vision for equity in computer science education. In *SIGCSE 2019* (pp. 657–658).

Sadker, M., and Sadker, D. (1994). *Failing at Fairness.* New York, NY: Charles Scribner.

Santo, R., Vogel, S., and Ching, D. (2019). *CS for What? Diverse Visions of Computer Science Education in Practice.* New York, NY: CSforALL.

Sax, L.J., Blaney, J.M., Lehman, K.J., Rodriguez, S.L., George, K.L., and Zavala, C. (2018). Sense of belonging in computing: The role of introductory courses for women and under-represented minority students. *Social Science, 7*(122).

Sax, L.J., Newhouse, K.N., Goode, J., Skorodinsky, M., Nakajima, T.M., and Sendowski, M. (2020). Does AP CS Principles broaden participation in computing? An analysis of APCSA and APCSP participants. In *Proceedings of the 51st ACM Technical Symposium on Computer Science Education* (pp. 542–548).

Seyranian, V., Madva, A., Duong, N., Abramzon, N., Tibbetts, Y., and Harackiewicz, J.M. (2018). The longitudinal effects of STEM identity and gender on flourishing and achievement in college physics. *International Journal of STEM Education, 5*(1), 40.

Schank, H. (2015). Science fairs aren't so fair. *The Atlantic.* March, 12.

Schanzer, E., Fisler, K., and Krishnamurthi, S. (2018). Assessing Bootstrap: Algebra Students on Scaffolded and Unscaffolded Word Problems. In *Proceedings of the 49th ACM Technical Symposium on Computer Science Education* (pp. 8–13).

Schanzer, E., Fisler, K., Krishnamurthi, S., and Felleisen, M. (2015). Transferring Skills at Solving Word Problems from Computing to Algebra Through Bootstrap. In *Proceedings of the 46th ACM Technical symposium on computer science education* (pp. 616–621).

Scherer, R., Siddiq, F., and Sánchez Viveros, B. (2019). The cognitive benefits of learning computer programming: A meta-analysis of transfer effects. *Journal of Educational Psychology, 111*(5), 764.

Schmidt, F.L. (2014). A general theoretical integrative model of individual differences in interests, abilities, personality traits, and academic and occupational achievement: A commentary on four recent articles. *Perspectives on Psychological Science, 9*(2), 211–218.

Schneider, M. (2002). *Do School Facilities Affect Academic Outcomes?* National Clearinghouse for Educational Facilities. Available: https://files.eric.ed.gov/fulltext/ED470979.pdf.

Schulte, C., and Knobelsdorf, M. (2007). Attitudes towards computer science-computing experiences as a starting point and barrier to computer science. In *Proceedings of the Third International Workshop on Computing Education Research* (pp. 27–38).

Schusler, T.M., and Krasny, M.E. (2010). Environmental action as context for youth development. *The Journal of Environmental Education, 41*(4), 208–223.

Schusler, T.M., Krasny, M.E., Peters, S.J., and Decker, D.J. (2009). Developing citizens and communities through youth environmental action. *Environmental Education Research, 15*(1), 111–127.

Scott, A., Martin, A., McAlear, F., and Koshy, S. (2017). Broadening participation in computing: Examining experiences of girls of color. In *Proceedings of the 2017 ACM Conference on Innovation and Technology in Computer Science Education* (pp. 252–256).

Scott, A., Koshy, S., Rao, M., Hinton, L., Flapan, J., Martin, A., and McAlear, F. (2019). *Computer Science in California's Schools: An Analysis of Access, Enrollment, and Equity.* Kapor Center. Available: https://www.kaporcenter.org/wp-content/uploads/2019/06/Computer-Science-in-California-Schools.pdf.

Scott, K.A., and Garcia, P. (2016). Techno-social change agents: Fostering activist dispositions among girls of color. *Meridians, 15*(1), 65–85.

Scott, K.A., and White, M.A. (2013). COMPUGIRLS'standpoint: Culturally responsive computing and its effect on girls of color. *Urban Education, 48*(5), 657–681.

Scott, K., and Zhang, X. (2014). Designing a culturally responsive computing curriculum for girls. *International Journal of Gender, Science and Technology, 6*(2), 264–276.

Scott, K.A., Aist, G., and Hood, D.W. (2009). CompuGirls: Designing a culturally relevant technology program. *Educational Technology, 49*(6), 34–39.

Scott, K.A., Sheridan, K.M., and Clark, K. (2015). Culturally responsive computing: A theory revisited. *Learning, Media and Technology, 40*(4), 412–436.

Scott-Little, C., Hamann, M.S., and Jurs, S.G. (2002). Evaluations of after-school programs: A meta-evaluation of methodologies and narrative synthesis of findings. *American Journal of Evaluation, 23*(4), 387–419.

Sefton-Green, J., Watkins, S.C., and Kirshner, B. (2019). *Young People's Transitions into Creative Work: Navigating Challenges and Opportunities.* London, UK and New York, NY: Routledge.

Sengupta, P., Kinnebrew, J.S., Basu, S., Biswas, G., and Clark, D. (2013). Integrating computational thinking with K–12 science education using agent-based computation: A theoretical framework. *Education and Information Technology, 81*, 351–380.

Settles, I.H. (2006). Use of an intersectional framework to understand Black women's racial and gender identities. *Sex Roles, 54*(9–10), 589–601.

Sfard, A., and Prusak, A. (2005). Telling identities: In search of an analytic tool for investigating learning as a culturally shaped activity. *Educational Researcher, 34*(4), 14–22.

Sharma, R., and Ali, S. (2018). Embedding concepts of sustainability in secondary school mathematics through games based learning. In *European Conference on Games Based Learning* (pp. 583–589).

Shapiro, J.R., and Williams, A.M. (2012). The role of stereotype threats in undermining girls' and women's performance and interest in STEM fields. *Sex Roles, 66*(3–4), 175–183.

Shein, E. (2014). Should *everybody* learn to code? *Communications of the ACM, 57*(2), 16–18.

Sheridan, K., Halverson, E.R., Litts, B., Brahms, L., Jacobs-Priebe, L., and Owens, T. (2014). Learning in the making: A comparative case study of three makerspaces. *Harvard Educational Review, 84*(4), 505–531.

Shrestha, N., Barik, T., and Parnin, C. (2018). It's like python but: Towards supporting transfer of programming language knowledge. In *2018 IEEE Symposium on Visual Languages and Human-Centric Computing (VL/HCC)* (pp. 177–185).

Siebert-Evenstone, A., and Shaffer, D.W. (2019). Location, location, location: The effects of place in place-based simulations. *A Wide Lens: Combining Embodied, Enactive, Extended, and Embedded Learning in Collaborative Settings, 13th International Conference on Computer Supported Collaborative Learning (CSCL)* (Vol. 1, pp. 152–159).

Simpson, A., and Bouhafa, Y. (2020). Youths' and adults' identity in STEM: A systematic literature review. *Journal for STEM Education Research*, 1–28.

Simpson, A., Bannister, N., and Matthews, G. (2017). Cracking her codes: Understanding shared technology resources as positioning artifacts for power and status in CSCL environments. *International Journal of Computer-Supported Collaborative Learning, 12*(3), 221–249.

Sirinides, P., Fink, R., and DuBois, T. (2016). A study of early learning services in museums and libraries. *Early Children Education Journal, 45*, 563–573. Available: https://williampennfoundation.org/sites/default/files/reports/A%20Study%20of%20Early%20Learning%20Services%20in%20Museums%20and%20Libraries.pdf.

Smith, G.A. (2002). Place-based education: Learning to be where we are. *Phi Delta Kappan, 83*(8), 584–594.

Sobel, D. (2004). *Place-Based Education: Connecting Classrooms and Communities.* Great Barrington, MA: Orion Society.

Sobel, K. (2019). *Immersive Media and Child Development: Synthesis of a Cross-Sectoral Meeting on Virtual, Augmented, and Mixed Reality and Young Children.* The Joan Ganz Cooney Center at Sesame Workshop. Available: http://joanganzcooneycenter.org/wp-content/uploads/2019/05/jgcc_immersive_media_and_child_development.pdf.

Squire, K. (2006). From content to context: Videogames as designed experience. *Educational Researcher, 35*(8), 19–29.

Stanton, J., Goldsmith, L., Adrion, W.R., Dunton, S., Hendrickson, K.A., Peterfreund, A., Yongpradit, P., Zarch, R., and Zinth, J.D. (2017). *State of the States Landscape Report: State-Level Policies Supporting Equitable K–12 Computer Science Education.* Available: https://www.ecs.org/wp-content/uploads/MassCAN-Full-Report-v10.pdf.

Stapleton, S.C., Royster, M., Bharti, N., Birch, S., Bossart, J., Butts, S., Tobin Cataldo, T., Russell Gonzalez, S., Minson, V., Putnam, S.R., and Yip, C. (2019). Girls tech camp. *Issues in Science and Technology Librarianship*, (92).

Statti, A., and Villegas, S. (2020). The use of mobile learning in grades K–12: A literature review of current trends and practices. *Peabody Journal of Education, 95*(2), 139–147.

Steele, C.M., and Aronson, J. (1995). Stereotype threat and the intellectual test performance of African Americans. *Journal of Personality and Social Psychology, 69*(5), 797.

Steinke, J. (2017). Adolescent girls' STEM identity formation and media images of STEM professionals: Considering the influence of contextual cues. *Frontiers in Psychology, 8*, 716.

Sternberg, R.J., and Lubart, T.I. (1991). Creating creative minds. *Phi Delta Kappan, 72*(8), 608–614.

Stets, J.E., Brenner, P.S., Burke, P.J., and Serpe, R.T. (2017). The science identity and entering a science occupation. *Social Science Research, 64,* 1–14.

Stout, J.G., and Wright, H.M. (2016). Lesbian, gay, bisexual, transgender, and queer students' sense of belonging in computing: An intersectional approach. *Computing in Science & Engineering, 18*(3), 24–30.

Stornaiulo, A., and Nichols T. (2018). Making publics: Mobilizing audiences in high school makerspaces. *Teachers College Record, 120*(8).

Strayhorn, T.L. (2012). *College Students' Sense of Belonging: A Key to Educational Success for All Students.* New York, NY: Routledge.

Strobel, J., Wang, J., Weber, N.R., and Dyehouse, M. (2013). The role of authenticity in design-based learning environments: The case of engineering education. *Computers & Education, 64,* 143–152.

Strong-Wilson, T., and Ellis, J. (2007). Children and place: Reggio Emilia's environment as third teacher. *Theory into Practice, 46*(1), 40–47.

Subramaniam, K. (2016). Teachers' organization of participation structures for teaching science with computer technology. *Journal of Science Education and Technology, 25*(4), 527–540.

Subramaniam, M., Scaff, L., Kawas, S., Hoffman, K.M., and Davis, K. (2018). Using technology to support equity and inclusion in youth library programming: Current practices and future opportunities. *Library Quarterly, 88*(4), 1–17.

Svihla, V., and Reeve, R. (2016). *Design as Scholarship: Case Studies from the Learning Sciences.* London, UK and New York, NY: Routledge.

Swan, D.W. (2014). *The Effect of Informal Learning Environments during Kindergarten on Academic Achievement during Elementary School.* Paper presented at the annual meeting of the American Education Research Association, Philadelphia, PA.

Tajfel, H., and Turner, J.C. (1986). The social identity theory of intergroup behaviour. In W.G. Austin and S. Worchel (Eds.), *Psychology of Intergroup Relations* (pp. 7–24). Chicago, IL: Nelson.

Takeuchi, L.M., and Vaala, S. (2014). *Level Up Learning: A National Survey on Teaching with Digital Games.* The Joan Ganz Cooney Center of Sesame Workshop. Available: https://www.joanganzcooneycenter.org/wp-content/uploads/2014/10/jgcc_leveluplearning_final.pdf.

Tan, E., Calabrese Barton, A., Kang, H., and O'Neill, T. (2013). Desiring a career in STEM-related fields: How middle school girls articulate and negotiate identities-in-practice in science. *Journal of Research in Science Teaching, 50*(10), 1143–1179.

Taylor, N.G., Moore, J., Visser, M., and Drouillard, C. (2018). Incorporating computational thinking into library graduate course goals and objectives. *School Library Research, 21.* Available: https://files.eric.ed.gov/fulltext/EJ1202969.pdf.

Teague, J. (2002). Women in computing: What brings them to it, what keeps them in it? *ACM SIGCSE Bulletin, 34*(2), 147–58.

Tedre, M., and Denning, P.J. (2016). The long quest for computational thinking. In *Proceedings of the 16th Koli Calling International Conference on Computing Education Research* (pp. 120–129).

Thomas, J.O., Joseph, N., Williams, A., and Burge, J. (2018). Speaking truth to power: Exploring the intersectional experiences of Black women in computing. In *2018 Research on Equity and Sustained Participation in Engineering, Computing, and Technology (RESPECT)* (pp. 1–8).

Todd, C. (2015). COMMENTARY: GamerGate and resistance to the diversification of gaming culture. *Women's Studies Journal, 29*(1), 64–67.

Torres, C., and Hager, P. (2007). De-emphasizing competition in organized youth sport: Misdirected reforms and misled children. *Journal of the Philosophy of Sport, 34*, 194–210.

Townsend, B. (1996). Room at the top for women. *American Demographics, 18*, 28–37.

Traill, S., Traphagen, K., and Devaney, E. (2015). *Assessing the Impacts of STEM Learning Ecosystems: Logic Model Template & Recommendations for Next Steps.* STEM Ecosystems. Available: http://stemecosystems.org/ wp-content/uploads/2015/11/Assessing_ Impact_ Logic_Model_Template_STEM_Ecosystems_Final.pdf.

Trainer, E.H., and Herbsleb, J.D. (2014). Beyond code: Prioritizing issues, sharing knowledge, and establishing identity at hackathons for science. In *CSCW Workshop on Sharing, Re-use, and Circulation of Resources in Scientific Cooperative Work.*

Tran, L.U. (2006). Teaching science in museums: The pedagogy and goals of museum educators. *Science Education, 91*(2), 278–297.

Tran, L.U., and King, H. (2007). The professionalization of museum educators: The case in science museums. *Museum Management and Curatorship, 22*(2), 131–149.

Tran, Y. (2018). Computational thinking equity in elementary classrooms: What third-grade students know and can do. *Journal of Educational Computing Research, 57*(1), 3–31.

Traphagen, K., and Traill, S. (2014). *How Cross-Sector Collaborations Are Advancing STEM Learning.* Palo Alto, CA: Noyce Foundation.

Tripp, L. (2011). Digital youth, libraries, and new media literacy. *The Reference Librarian, 52*(4), 329–341.

Van Laar, C., Meeussen, L., Veldman, J., Sterk, N., Van Grootel, S., and Jacobs, C. (2019). Coping with stigma in the workplace: Understanding the role of threat regulation, supportive factors, and potential hidden costs. *Frontiers in Psychology, 10*, 1879.

Van Merriënboer, J.J., and Sweller, J. (2005). Cognitive load theory and complex learning: Recent developments and future directions. *Educational Psychology Review, 17*(2), 147–177.

Vance, F., Nielsen, K., Garza, V., Keicher, A., and Handy, D. (2016). *Design for Success: Developing a STEM Ecosystem.* University of San Diego. Available: https://stemecosystems.org/ wp-content/uploads/2017/01/USD-Critical-Factors-Final_121916.pdf.

Vee, A. (2013). Understanding computer programming as a literacy. *Literacy in Composition Studies, 1*(2), 42–64.

Veety, E., Sur, J.S., Elliott, H.K., and Lamberth, III, J.E. (2018). Teaching engineering design through wearable device design competition (Evaluation). *Journal of Pre-College Engineering Education Research, 8*(2), 1.

Vickery, J. (2014). Youths teaching youths: Learning to code as an example of interest-driven learning. *Journal of Adolescent and Adult Literacy, 57*(5), 361–365.

Vincent-Ruz, P., and Schunn, C.D. (2018). The nature of science identity and its role as the driver of student choices. *International Journal of STEM Education, 5*(1), 48.

Vogel, S., Santo, R., and Ching, D. (2017). Visions of computer science education: Unpacking arguments for and projected impacts of CS4All initiatives. In *Proceedings of the 2017 ACM SIGCSE Technical Symposium on Computer Science Education* (pp. 609–614).

Vogel, S., Hoadley, C., Ascenzi-Moreno, L., and Menken, K. (2019). The role of translanguaging in computational literacies: Documenting middle school bilinguals' practices in computer science integrated units. In *Proceedings of the 50th ACM Technical Symposium on Computer Science Education* (pp. 1164–1170).

Volk, T.L., and Cheak, M.J. (2003). The effects of an environmental education program on students, parents, and community. *The Journal of Environmental Education, 34*(4), 12–25.

Vossoughi, S., and Bevan, B. (2014). *Making and Tinkering: A Review of the Literature.* National Research Council Committee on Out of School Time STEM. Washington, DC: The National Academies Press.

Vossoughi, S., and Vakil, S. (2018). Towards what end? A critical analysis of militarism, equity and STEM education. In A. Ali and T. Buenavista (Eds.), *At War!: Challenging Racism, Materialism, and Militarism in Education* (pp. 117–140). New York, NY: Fordham University Press.

Vossoughi, S., Hooper, P.K., and Escudé, M. (2016). Making through the lens of culture and power: Toward transformative visions for educational equity. *Harvard Educational Review, 86*(2), 206–232.

Wai, J., Lubinski, D., Benbow, C.P., and Steiger, J.H. (2010). Accomplishment in science, technology, engineering, and mathematics (STEM) and its relation to STEM educational dose. *Journal of Educational Psychology, 102*(4), 860–871.

Walton, G.M., and Cohen, G.L. (2007). A question of belonging: Race, social fit, and achievement. *Journal of Personality and Social Psychology, 92*(1), 82.

Wang, M.-T., and Degol, J. (2013). Motivational pathways to STEM career choices: Using expectancy-value perspective to understand individual and gender differences in STEM fields. *Developmental Research, 33*(4).

Wang, M.T., and Eccles, J.S. (2013). School context, achievement motivation, and academic engagement: A longitudinal study of school engagement using a multidimensional perspective. *Learning and Instruction, 28*, 12–23.

Wanzer, D.L., McKlin, T., Freeman, J., Magerko, B., and Lee, T. (2020). Promoting intentions to persist in computing: An examination of six years of the EarSketch program. *Computer Science Education*, 1–26.

Wardrip, P.S., and Brahms, L. (2016). Taking making to school. *Makeology: Makerspaces as Learning Environments, 1*, 97–10.

Wardrip, P.S., Brahms, L., Reich, C., and Carrigan, T. (2016). Supporting learning in museum makerspaces: A national framework. *Museum*, Sept/Oct., 18–24.

Watson, S. (Ed.). (2007). *Museums and Their Communities*. London, UK and New York, NY: Routledge.

Weinberg, A.E., Basile, C.G., and Albright, L. (2011). The effect of an experiential learning program on middle school students' motivation toward mathematics and science. *RMLE Online, 35*(3), 1–12.

Weintrop, D., and Wilensky, U. (2015). Using commutative assessments to compare conceptual understanding in blocks-based and text-based programs. In *ICER '15: Proceedings of the Eleventh Annual International Conference on International Computing Education Research* (pp. 101–110).

Weintrop, D., Beheshti, E., Horn, M., Orton, K., Jona, K., Trouille, L., and Wilensky, U. (2016). Defining computational thinking for mathematics and science classrooms. *Journal of Science Education and Technology, 25*(1), 127–147.

Weitze, C.L. (2017). Reflective, creative and computational thinking strategies used when students learn through making games. In *Proceedings of the 11th European Conference on Game-Based Learning* (pp. 744–753).

Wenger, E. (1998). Communities of practice: Learning as a social system. *Systems Thinker, 9*(5), 2–3.

Weston, T.J., Dubow, W.M., and Kaminsky, A. (2019). Predicting women's persistence in computer science-and technology-related majors from high school to college. *ACM Transactions on Computing Education (TOCE), 20*(1), 1–16.

Whitehouse, A. (2019). *Pilot Testers Wanted for New Computer Science and Engineering Units!* Engineering Is Elementary, Museum of Science, Boston, MA. Available: https://blog.eie.org/pilot-testers-wanted-for-new-computer-science-units.

Wilson, G., and Randall, M. (2010). Implementing and evaluating a "Next Generation Learning Space": A pilot study. In *Curriculum, Technology & Transformation for an Unknown Future. Proceedings Ascilite Sydney 2010* (pp. 1096–1100).

Wing, J.M. (2006). Computational thinking. *Communications of the ACM, 49*(3), 33–35.

Witherspoon, E.B., Schunn, C.D., Higashi, R.M., and Baehr, E.C. (2016). Gender, interest, and prior experience shape opportunities to learn programming in robotics competitions. *International Journal of STEM Education, 3*(1), 1–12.

Wong, B. (2016). "I'm good, but not that good": Digitally-skilled young people's identity in computing. *Computer Science Education, 26*(4), 299–317.

Woszczynski, A.B., and Green, A. (2017). Learning outcomes for Cyber Defense competitions. *Journal of Information Systems Education, 28*(1), 21–42.

Yadav, A., and Berges, M. (2019). Computer science pedagogical content knowledge: characterizing teacher performance. *ACM Transactions on Computing Education, 19*(3), Article 29.

Yadav, A., Stephenson, C., and Hong, H. (2014). Computational thinking for teacher education. *Communications of the ACM, 60*(4), 55–62.

Yadav, A., Gretter, S., Hambrusch, S., and Sands, P. (2016). Expanding computer science education in schools: Understanding teacher experiences and challenges. *Computer Science Education, 26*(4), 235–254.

Yang, Z., Becerik-Gerber, B., and Mino, L. (2013). A study on student perceptions of higher education classrooms: Impact of classroom attributes on student satisfaction and performance. *Building and Environment, 70*, 171–188.

Yin, Y., Hadad, R., Tang, X., and Lin, Q. (2019). Improving and assessing computational thinking in maker activities: The integration with physics and engineering learning. *Journal of Science Education and Technology, 29*(2), 189–214.

Yip, J.C., Lee, K.J., and Lee, J.H. (2019). Design partnerships for participatory librarianship: A conceptual model for understanding librarians co-designing with digital youth. *Journal of the Association for Information Science and Technology, 71*(10).

Young Adult Library Services Association. (2017). *Teen Services Competencies for Library Staff.* Available: http://www.ala.org/yalsa/guidelines/yacompetencies.

Zander, C., Boustedt, J., McCartney, R., Moström, J.E., Sanders, K., and Thomas, L. (2009). Student transformations: Are they computer scientists yet? In *Proceedings of the Fifth International Workshop on Computing Education Research Workshop* (pp. 129–140).

Zhou, C., Bell, P., Bang, M., Kuver, R. Twito, A. and Braun, A. (2019). Building expansive family STEAM programming through participatory design research. In V. Lee and A. Phillips, (Eds.), *Reconceptualizing Libraries: Opportunities from the Learning and Information Sciences* (pp. 72–93). London, UK and New York, NY: Routledge.

Zickuhr, K., Rainie, L., and Purcell, K. (2013). *Library Services in the Digital Age.* Pew Internet & American Life Project. Available: https://files.eric.ed.gov/fulltext/ED539071.pdf.

Zimmer, C. (2016). Science fairs are as flawed as my solar-powered hot dog cooker. *STAT.* April 13. Available: https://www.statnews.com/2016/04/13/science-fairs-white-house.

Appendix A

Search Strategy and Data Coding

The committee sought to assemble a set of studies that represented the extent of available evidence. The review focused on literature and programs centered around three categories of outcomes: (1) affective (such as interest, identity/belonging, motivation, and self-efficacy); (2) cognitive (such as knowledge and skills); and (3) behavioral (such as engagement, persistence, and retention). A search was conducted through Scopus requesting studies from the past two decades (2000–2020) and limited to English. Table A-1 shows the syntax used to identify studies. The search parameters were set to be broad and inclusive, which yielded a large number of studies (n = 2,974).

The list was culled down by removing studies that did not meet committee-determined standards for quality and relevance. Specifically, studies were classified based on the following attributes: goal, intervention type, study type, findings reported, outcome category, STEM field, methods, setting, authentic, and the age/grade range. To determine the type of study, the committee used the common guidelines for education research and development (Earle et al., 2013). Box A-1 briefly documents the guide and summarizes the different study types. From this analysis, 309 studies were identified as potentially relevant and requiring additional review.

The committee then reviewed the abstracts for each of the 309 studies. Table A-2 illustrates the systematic culling down of studies that were reviewed at each stage, whereas Table A-3 highlights the ones described in the chapter on outcomes. In Table A-2, studies with measurable impact estimates are those studies that can be characterized as Impact and Effectiveness Research based on Box A-1.

TABLE A-1 Search Syntax for Locating Studies

Criteria and Syntax
Computing focus
(STEM
STEM OR science OR technology OR engineering OR mathematic* OR computing OR "computer science" OR "computer program*")
AND Personalized learning focus
("hands-on" OR "design based" OR "maker ed" OR "maker space" OR "place based" OR authentic OR "technology education" OR "project based" OR "problem based" OR "activity design" OR "maker movement*" OR "problem solving" OR "game design")
AND Setting
("in school" OR "out of school" OR formal OR informal OR librar* OR museum* OR "community setting*" OR YMCA OR "boy scout*" OR "girl scout*" OR club* OR "summer camp")
AND Target youth
("K–12" OR "elementary school*" OR "middle school*" OR "high school*" OR child* OR youth* OR adolescent* OR teenager* OR "young student*")
(student* AND NOT {college* OR undergraduate* OR graduate* OR university})
AND Focal outcomes
(engagement OR {time on task} OR "future course*" OR "future class*" OR "future club*" OR persistence OR "choice major" OR "curriculum choice*" OR "class choice" OR "career choice")
(interest OR awareness OR attitude*)
(knowledge OR skill* OR disposition* OR network*)
AND Recency
PUBYEAR AFT 2000
Citations returned = 2,974

*Focal outcomes were aligned with commonly stated program goals.

Search Syntax Strategies and Yield								
1	2	3	4	5	6	7	8	9
	X			X			X	
X		X	X		X	X		X
X	X	X	X	X	X	X	X	X
X	X	X	X	X	X	X	X	X
X			X			X		
		X			X			X
X	X	X						
			X	X	X			
						X	X	X
X	X	X	X	X	X	X	X	X
172	74	154	382	179	331	655	225	802

BOX A-1
Types of Research and Their Purposes

__Foundational Research:__ Studies of this type seek to test, develop, or refine theories of teaching or learning and may develop innovations in methodologies and/or technologies that will influence and inform research and development in different contexts.

__Exploratory/Early-stage Research:__ Studies of this type investigate approaches to education problems to establish the basis for design and development of new interventions or strategies, and/or to provide evidence for whether an established intervention or strategy is ready to be tested in an efficacy study. Studies in this genre should establish initial connections to outcomes of interest (usually correlational rather than causal) and support the development of a well-explicated theory of action that can inform the development, modification, or evaluation of an intervention or strategy.

__Design and Development Research:__ Studies of this type draw on existing theory and evidence to design and iteratively develop interventions or strategies, including testing individual components to provide feedback in the development process. Typically, this research involves four components:

1. Development of a solution based on a well-specified theory of action appropriate to a well-defined end user.
2. Creation of measures to assess the implementation of the solution(s).
3. Collection of data on the feasibility of implementing the solution(s) in typical delivery settings by intended users.
4. Conducting a pilot study to examine the promise of generating the intended outcomes.

__Impact and Effectiveness Research:__ Studies of this type assess how well a program, policy, or practice works. They use comparisons of individuals who do and do not experience the intervention to judge the impacts. In some cases, impact evaluations are designed to determine effectiveness under ideal conditions (Efficacy Research). Impact evaluations also may test the effectiveness of a strategy or intervention under circumstances that would typically prevail in the target context (Effectiveness Research) and, in other cases, may be to test the scalability of the intervention across a broad spectrum of populations and settings (Scale-up Research) or the replicability of the studies in similar or different contexts (Replication Research).

SOURCE: Adapted from Earle et al. (2013, pp. 1–53).

TABLE A-2   Search Summary

Outcome Domain	Abstracts Retrieved & Reviewed	Studies Retrieved & Reviewed	Studies Referenced in the Text	Studies with Credible Impact Estimate
Affective	107	76	24	3
Cognitive	149	102	37	1
Behavioral	53	40	16	3
Total	309	218	77	7

TABLE A-3 Evaluation Studies Identified Through the Literature Search

Author (Date)	Study Type	Intervention/ Practice
Affective Outcomes		
Barker et al. (2018)	Exploratory	Wearable technologies
Bugallo and Kelly (2014)	Exploratory	Participatory STEM activities
Bugallo et al. (2015)	Exploratory	Participatory STEM activities
Choudhury et al. (2010)	Exploratory	Participatory STEM activities
Denault et al. (2008)	Exploratory	Participatory CS activities
Doerschuk et al. (2013)	Exploratory	Participatory CS activities
Evans and Schares (2017)	Exploratory	Makerspaces/activities
Gardner-McCune et al. (2013)	Exploratory	Participatory CS activities
Harriger et al. (2012)	Exploratory	Participatory CS activities
Jagiela et al. (2018)	Exploratory	Participatory STEAM activities
Krayem et al. (2019)	Exploratory	Participatory STEM activities
Ladeji-Osias et al. (2018)	Exploratory	Participatory STEM activities
Monterastelli et al. (2008)	Exploratory	Participatory STEM activities
Nugent et al. (2016)	Exploratory	Participatory STEM activities
Nugent et al. (2019)	Exploratory	Wearable technologies
Stapleton et al. (2019)	Exploratory	Participatory STEM activities
Ahn et al. (2014)	Design & Development	Participatory STEM activities
Erete et al. (2016)	Design & Development	Participatory STEM activities
Jin et al. (2018)	Design & Development	Participatory CS activities
Lau et al. (2009)	Design & Development	Wearable technologies
Pinkard et al. (2017)	Design & Development	Participatory STEM activities
Scott and White (2013)	Design & Development	Participatory CS activities
Klopfer et al. (2004)	Impact & Effectiveness	Participatory STEM activities
Loksa et al. (2016)	Impact & Effectiveness	Participatory CS activities

Setting	Grade/ Age Group	Outcomes for Impact Estimates
After-school, on site	Elementary; Middle school	Self-efficacy
Summer program/camp	High school	Identity; Self-efficacy
Summer program/camp	High school	Interest; Motivation; Self-efficacy
Summer program/camp	High school	Identity
Summer program/camp	High school	Interest
Summer program/camp	High school	Interest
University	K–12	Interest
University	High school	Interest
Summer program/camp	High school	Interest
University	High school; Middle school	Interest; Self-efficacy
University	High school	Interest
Summer & Saturday Program	Middle school	Engagement; Interest
University	High school	Interest
Camps, Clubs & Competitions	Middle school	Self-efficacy
Classroom—traditional & after-school	Elementary school (K–5)	Self-efficacy; Programming design & knowledge
University; Summer camp	Middle school	Self-efficacy
After-school, on site	Middle school	Identity
Community—other	Middle school	Identity
Summer program/camp	High school	Knowledge & Skills; Motivation
Summer program/camp	Middle school	Knowledge & Skills; Motivation; Interest
Multiple OST	Elementary school (K–5)	Identity
Multiple OST	High school	Motivation
Classroom—traditional	Middle school; High school	Motivation
Summer camp	High school	Self-efficacy

continued

TABLE A-3 Continued

Author (Date)	Study Type	Intervention/ Practice
Cognitive Outcomes		
Bicer et al. (2017)	Exploratory	Makerspaces & activities
Brooks and Sjöberg (2019)	Exploratory	Games
Bugallo et al. (2015)	Exploratory	Participatory STEM activities
Dasgupta et al. (2019)	Exploratory	Makerspaces & activities
de Paula et al. (2018)	Exploratory	Participatory STEM activities
Denault et al. (2008)	Exploratory	Participatory STEM activities
Folk et al. (2015)	Exploratory	Unplugged STEM activities
Freina et al. (2019)	Exploratory	Games
Gardeli and Vosinakis (2019)	Exploratory	Mobile apps
Nugent et al. (2013)	Exploratory	Participatory STEM activities
Nugent et al. (2016)	Exploratory	Participatory STEM activities
Nugent et al. (2019)	Exploratory	Wearable technologies
Ouyang et al. (2018)	Exploratory	Participatory CS activities
Sharma and Ali (2018)	Exploratory	Participatory STEM activities
Weitze (2017)	Exploratory	Making games/sims
Jenson et al. (2018)	Design & Development	Course
Yin et al. (2019)	Design & Development	Makerspaces/activities
Garneli et al. (2015)	Impact—Efficacy	Games

Setting	Grade/ Age Group	Outcomes for Impact Estimates
Summer program	High school	Perception of skills & creativity
Research Lab setting	Elementary school (K–5)	Interactions with technology, design, decision making
Summer program	High school	Engineering knowledge
Classroom—traditional	Middle school	Technology & science knowledge; Experimental strategies & graph interpretation
After School Program—at a school	Middle school	Computational & game development skills
Summer program/camp	High school	Computer programming
Classroom—traditional	K–12 (across grade bands)	CT concepts & terms; Recognition of CT
Classroom—traditional	Elementary school (K–5)	Programming & documentation skills
Classroom—traditional	Elementary school (K–5)	Problem-solving, algorithmic concepts & game design
After school, on-site	Middle school	Computer programming, engineering & design, GPS & science, math, robotics & workplace skills
Camps, clubs & competitions	Middle school	Computer programming, engineering & design, GPS & science, math, robotics & workplace skills
Classroom—traditional	Elementary school (K–5)	Knowledge of circuity & programming; engineering design
Classroom—traditional	Elementary school (K–5)	CT concepts
Classroom—traditional	High school	Cartesian coordinate system; Applied geometry
Classroom—traditional	High school	Disciplinary content; Game design & making
Classroom—traditional	Middle school	Computer programming; Academic achievement
Summer academy	Middle & High school	Physics & engineering, CT definition & CT skills
ns	Middle school	Problem-solving, programming & use of CS constructs

continued

TABLE A-3 Continued

Author (Date)	Study Type	Intervention/ Practice
Behavioral Outcomes		
Amo et al. (2019)—study 2	Exploratory	Hands-on cyber security workshops
Freudenthal et al. (2011)	Exploratory	Media-propelled CT
Gardeli and Vosinakis (2019)	Exploratory	Game: Mobile augmented reality
Klein (2013)	Exploratory	Casual mobile game
Simpson et al. (2017)	Exploratory	Computer-supported collaborative learning
Vickery (2014)	Exploratory	Web design workshop
Folk et al. (2015)	Exploratory	Deliberate instruction in CT & algorithm design (unplugged)
Weston et al. (2019)	Exploratory	AP and computing courses
Charlton and Poslad (2016)	Exploratory (Descriptive)	Maker events: Shareable wearables
Mystakidis et al. (2014)	Development	Immersive multi-media learning experience
Amo et al. (2019)—study 1	Impact & Effectiveness (RCT)	Cyber-networking workshop
Klopfer et al. (2004)	Impact & Effectiveness (RCT)	Palm versus wearable supported participatory simulations
Wanzer et al. (2020)	Impact & Effectiveness	Web-based introductory computing experience

NOTE: ns means not specified. For each outcome category, the articles are organized by study type and then alphabetized.

Setting	Grade/ Age Group	Outcomes for Impact Estimates
Summer camp	13–17-year-olds	Cyber security engagement & self-efficacy
High school math & college calculus class	High school students First year college students	Enrollment in CT courses, engagement in problem-solving, math course enrollment& college grades
Primary school classrooms	Age 9–10	Enjoyment & collaboration
Play Club	10–15-year-olds	Level of emersion & reflection
Summer camp	Rising high school freshmen	Positions of power
Public library	8–16-year-olds	Sustained enjoyment
K–12 STEM classes	Middle & High school instructors & students.	Recognition & definition of algorithms; engagement in CT
High school	High school students	Persistence in computing post high school & technology majors
Community setting	Age 14–15	Engagement in design and development & product application
Library	Grades 2–6	Interest in books & positive mentality toward reading
Museum	Middle school (low-income)	General problem solving, science engagement, cyber & digital awareness
Science classes	Study 1: 14–16-year-olds Study 2: 11–13-year-olds	Engagement in collaborative problem-solving, motivation to participate in problem-solving & self-reported learning
Workshops; summer camps, traditional classes	Middle school; High school	Intent to persist in computing

Appendix B

Committee and Staff Biographies

BARBARA M. MEANS (*Chair*) is executive director of Learning Sciences Research at Digital Promise. Previously the founder and director of the Center for Technology in Learning at SRI International, she is an educational psychologist whose research focuses on ways technology can support students' learning of advanced skills and the revitalization of classrooms and schools. Her 2014 book, *Learning Online: What Research Tells Us About Whether, When, and How*, provides a critical appraisal of the research base for practices in online learning from kindergarten through higher education and adult learning. Means has been an author or editor for eight books on topics in education, learning technology, and education reform. She was a member of the National Academies of Sciences, Engineering, and Medicine committee that produced the report *How People Learn II: Learners, Contexts, and Cultures*. She earned her bachelor's degree in psychology from Stanford University and her Ph.D. in educational psychology from the University of California, Berkeley.

KAREN BRENNAN is an associate professor at the Harvard Graduate School of Education, where she directs the Creative Computing Lab. Her research is primarily concerned with the ways in which learning environments can be designed to cultivate young people's creativity and agency as learners and designers. Brennan's research and teaching activities focus on constructionist approaches to designing learning environments— encouraging learning through designing, personalizing, connecting, and reflecting to maximize learner agency. She led the design and development of ScratchEd, an online environment for educators who are interested in supporting computational literacy. Brennan also received funding from the National Science Foundation (NSF) for a project that documented the concepts, practices, and perspectives children cultivate through computational design activities with the Scratch programming language. She has a B.Sc. in computer science and mathematics, a B.Ed. in computer science and mathematics, and a M.A. in curriculum studies from the University of British Columbia. Brennan completed her Ph.D. in media arts and sciences at the MIT Media Lab, where she was a member of the team that developed the Scratch programming environment.

KERRY BRENNER is a senior program officer for the Board on Science Education at the National Academies of Sciences, Engineering, and Medicine. She is the lead staff person for the Roundtable on Systemic Change in Undergraduate STEM Education and for the Symposium on Imagining the Future of Undergraduate STEM Education. She was the study director for projects that produced the reports *Undergraduate Research Experiences for STEM Students: Successes, Challenges, and Opportunities* and *Science and Engineering for Grades 6–12: Investigation and Design at the Center*. She led the planning of workshops on Recognizing and Evaluating Teaching of Science in Higher Education and one on Service Learning in Undergraduate Geosciences Education as well as helping to organize workshops on Increasing Student Success in Developmental Mathematics and a Convocation on Integrating Discovery-Based Research into the Undergraduate Curriculum. She earned her bachelor's degree from Wesleyan University and her Ph.D. in molecular biology from Princeton University.

STEPHANIE CHANG currently works as the director of Impact at Maker Ed, having spent 5 years previously leading and designing Maker Ed's program offerings for educators and institutions around the country. Her current maker-centered work focuses on research and evaluation efforts related to educator practices and learning outcomes of youth, while also encompassing organizational development, sustainability, and storytelling. Chang's work has been situated in experiential education, whether defined as STEM, STEAM, hands-on, project-based, or maker-centered. Overall, she is deeply interested in bridging formal and informal learning; working to best leverage the affordances of technology for learning; and designing inclusive, equitable, and authentic environments for learning and teaching. Prior to Maker Ed, Chang supported makerspaces and programs with 15 California high schools, worked in educational research, led science and technology summer programs, and taught environmental and marine science. She holds a B.S. in biology from MIT and a master's degree from the Learning, Design, and Technology program at Stanford University's Graduate School of Education.

SHAUNDRA B. DAILY is an associate professor of practice in electrical and computer engineering and computer science at Duke University. She is also co-founder and creative director of DEEP Designs, LLC. Prior to joining Duke, she was an associate professor at the University of Florida in the Department of Computer & Information Science & Engineering. She also served as an associate professor and interim co-chair in the School of Computing at Clemson University. Daily's research and teaching interests include promoting alternative pathways to engage with computing in order to diversify the computing landscape and developing and integrating applications of affective computing into a variety of contexts. She received NSF funding to develop new methods to utilize a virtual environment and movement as an embodied pedagogical approach to support computational thinking. Daily earned a B.S. and M.S. in electrical engineering from the Florida Agricultural and Mechanical University-Florida State University College of Engineering, and a S.M. and Ph.D. in media art and sciences at the MIT Media Lab.

CHERI FANCSALI is deputy director of the Research Alliance for New York City Schools, where she provides leadership for strategic planning and organizational development. She advances the Research Alliances' mission by collaborating with the New York City Department of Education, other local stakeholders, and education researchers across the country. She also directs the development, design, and execution of a variety of studies, including the external evaluation of NYC's Computer Science for All initiative and the National Science Foundation-funded Maker Partnership, a project to develop teacher training and curricular supports to integrate computer science into science instruction. Fancsali has extensive research and evaluation experience with a focus on school- and community-based educational programs, teacher professional development and capacity building, school reform initiatives, STEM education, aftershool programs, and socio-emotional learning. Previously, Fancsali was an early childhood and special education teacher in New York City. She holds a B.S. in special education from the University of Wisconsin, an M.S. in education policy from Teachers College, Columbia University, and a Ph.D. in sociology and education from Columbia University.

JUAN E. GILBERT is the Andrew Banks Family Preeminence Endowed Professor and Chair of the Computer and Information Science and Engineering Department at the University of Florida where he leads the Human Experience Research Lab. Gilbert has research projects in advanced learning technologies, usability and accessibility, Brain-Computer Interfaces (BCI), AI/machine learning, and ethnocomputing (culturally relevant computing). He is an Association for Computing Machinery (ACM) fellow, a fellow of the American Association of the Advancement of Science, and a member of the National Academy of Inventors. Honors and awards include a mural painting in New York City by City Year New York, the Presidential Award for Excellence in Science, Mathematics, and Engineering Mentoring from President Barack Obama, the American Association for the Advancement of Science (AAAS) 2014 Mentor Award, and the 2018 Computer Research Association's A. Nico Habermann Award. He is a Senior Member of the IEEE. He earned a B.S. in systems analysis from Miami University (Ohio) and a Ph.D. in computer science from the University of Cincinnati.

JOANNA GOODE is the Sommerville Knight Professor in the College of Education at the University of Oregon. Her research examines issues of access and equity for underrepresented students of color and females in computer science education. For the past several years, she has studied the institutional and psychological reasons preventing many underrepresented young people from entering the computer science pipeline in high school. As a former urban high school mathematics and computer science teacher, Goode's research considers the relationship between teacher development and opportunities to learn for students. She also serves as the director of a program aimed at preparing and supporting the efforts of LAUSD computer science educators in diversifying the high school computing pipeline. Goode earned her Ph.D. in the education division of urban schooling at the University of California, Los Angeles.

MARK GUZDIAL is a professor in computer science and engineering and engineering education research at the University of Michigan. He studies how people come to understand computing and how to make that more effective. Guzdial was one of the founders of the International Computing Education Research conference. He also was one of the leads on the NSF alliance *"Expanding Computing Education Pathways,"* which helped U.S. states improve and broaden their computing education. He invented and has written several books on the "Media Computation" contextualized approach to computing education. With Barbara Ericson, his wife and colleague, he received the 2010 Association for Computing Machinery Karl V. Karlstrom Outstanding Educator award. Guzdial is an ACM Distinguished Educator and a fellow of the ACM. His most recent book is *Learner-Centered Design of Computing Education: Research on Computing for Everyone*. He received the 2019 ACM SIGCSE Outstanding Contributions to Education award. He received his Ph.D. in education and computer science (a joint degree) at the University of Michigan.

MIZUKO ITO is a cultural anthropologist of technology use, examining children and youth's changing relationships to media and communications. Her work centers on how to tap student interests and digital media to fuel learning that is engaging, relevant, and socially connected. She is director of the Connected Learning Lab, professor in residence and John D. and Catherine T. MacArthur Foundation Chair in Digital Media and Learning at the University of California, Irvine, with appointments in the Department of Anthropology, the Department of Informatics, and the School of Education. She is also co-founder of Connected Camps, a non-profit that provides online creative learning in Minecraft for kids in all walks of life. She co-edited *Personal, Portable, Pedestrian: Mobile Phones in Japanese Life* and *Fandom Unbound: Otaku Culture in a Connected World*, on mobile technologies and fandom in Japan. Her research on youth digital media engagement in the United States appears in several co-authored books. She is the recipient of the Jan Hawkins Award for Early Career Contributions to Humanistic Research and Scholarship in Learning Technologies from the American Educational Research Association. Ito earned an M.A. in anthropology and Ph.D. degrees in education and anthropology from Stanford University.

LEAH H. JAMIESON is Ransburg Distinguished Professor of Electrical and Computer Engineering at Purdue University, John A. Edwardson Dean Emerita of the College of Engineering, and holds a courtesy appointment in Purdue's School of Engineering Education. She is a member of the National Academy of Engineering and the American Academy of Arts and Sciences and a fellow of the American Society for Engineering Education and IEEE. She is co-founder and past director of the Engineering Projects in Community Service (EPICS) program. Awards include the NSF Director's Award for Distinguished Teaching Scholars, the NAE Bernard M. Gordon Prize for Innovation in Engineering and Technology Education, and the IEEE James H. Mulligan, Jr. Education Medal. Jamieson has served as president and CEO of IEEE, board chair of the Anita Borg Institute, and co-chair of the Computing Research Association's Committee on the Status of Women in Computing Research. She received a B.S. in mathematics from MIT and an M.A., M.S.E., and Ph.D. in electrical engineering and computer science from Princeton University. She has been awarded honorary doctorates by Drexel University and the New Jersey Institute of Technology.

ERIC KLOPFER is professor and director of the Scheller Teacher Education Program and The Education Arcade at MIT. He is also a co-faculty director for MIT's J-WEL World Education Lab. Klopfer's research focuses on the development and use of computer games and simulations for building understanding of science, technology, engineering, and mathematics. The games that he works on are designed to build understanding of scientific practices and concepts as well as critical knowledge, using both mobile and web-delivered game platforms. He is the co-author of the books,

Adventures in Modeling, The More We Know, and *Resonant Games,* and author of *Augmented Learning.* His lab has produced software (including the massively multiplayer online game The Radix Endeavor) and platforms (including StarLogo Nova and Taleblazer) used by millions of people, as well as online courses that have reached hundreds of thousands. He is also the co-founder and past president of the non-profit Learning Games Network. Klopfer earned a B.S. in biology from Cornell University and a Ph.D. in zoology from the University of Wisconsin–Madison.

IRENE LEE is a research scientist at the Scheller Teacher Education Program and The Education Arcade. She is the founder and program director of Project GUTS: Growing Up Thinking Scientifically and Teachers with GUTS. The programs she develops enable participants to create computer models and use them to gain a scientific understanding of the world around them. Lee's research focuses on students' and teachers' understanding of complex adaptive systems and their development of computational thinking skills. She served as the chair of the Computer Science Teachers Association (CSTA) Computational Thinking Task Force and as a lead writer of the K–12 Computer Science Frameworks and the 2011 CSTA K–12 Computer Science Standards. Lee is serving as an advisor to the AI4K12 initiative and is guest editor of the *Journal of Science Education and Technology*'s Special Issue on Computational Thinking from a Disciplinary Perspective. She is a past president of the Supercomputing Challenge and the Swarm Development Group, and previously was the director of the Learning Lab at Santa Fe Institute. Lee has a B.A. in pure mathematics from the University of Chicago and a M.Ed. from the Harvard Graduate School of Education.

VICTOR R. LEE is associate professor at Stanford University and was an associated professor of Instructional Technology and Learning Sciences at Utah State University. His research explores learning through wearables and self-tracking technologies, maker education in out-of-school settings, and unplugged and screen-free computer science education at the elementary school level. Prior research involved studying the use and design of science curriculum materials and conceptual change. Lee is past recipient of a National Academy of Education and Spencer Foundation Post-doctoral fellowship, NSF's CAREER award, and the Jan Hawkins Early Career Award from the American Educational Research Association. He has published two academic volumes, *Learning Technologies and the Body: Integration and Implementation in Formal and Informal Learning Environments* and *Reconceptualizing Libraries: Perspectives from the Information and Learning Sciences* (with Abigail Phillips). He serves on several major journal editorial boards. He holds a Ph.D. in learning sciences from Northwestern University.

REBECCA MAYNARD is professor emeritus of education and social policy at the University of Pennsylvania. A leading expert in the design and conduct of randomized controlled trials in the areas of education and social policy, she has advanced the application of research synthesis methods in education and social policy. She co-developed Power*UP* to support efficient sample designs for causal inference studies, and designed and directed the University's Predoctoral Training Program in Interdisciplinary Methods for Field-based Education Research. She also served as Commissioner of the National Center for Education Evaluation and Regional Assistance at the Institute of Education Sciences (IES). She is a fellow of the American Education Research Association, and an elected member of the Society for Research Synthesis Methodology. Awards include the Peter H. Rossi Award for Contributions to the Theory and Practice of Program Evaluation and the Society for Research on Adolescence Social Policy Best Book Award for *Kids Having Kids*. She also is past president of both the Association for Public Policy Analysis and Management and the Society for Research on Educational Effectiveness. Prior to joining the University of Pennsylvania faculty in 1993, she was senior vice president at Mathematica Policy Research, Inc.

DANIEL A. RABUZZI is founder and lead consultant at Indigo Pheasant, LLC. Prior to this, he served as the executive director of Mouse, senior director of Operations & Strategy at Year Up NY, and National Program Director at The Network for Teaching Entrepreneurship. He has been an evaluator for the Echoing Green fellowship and for Carnegie Corporation grants, a member of the advisory team for the Brooklyn Navy Yard's Science Technology Engineering Arts & Math Center, and a member of the advisory team for the Urban Assembly Maker Academy in New York City, among other advisory roles. He is the 2005 silver award winner from the Society of National Association Publications for his cover story in the American Society of Association Executives journal. Rabuzzi earned a B.A. at Harvard University, an M.A. at The Fletcher School at Tufts, and an M.A. and Ph.D. in history from Johns Hopkins University.

HEIDI SCHWEINGRUBER is the director of the Board on Science Education at the National Academies of Sciences, Engineering, and Medicine. She has served as study director or co-study director for a wide range of studies, including those on revising national standards for K–12 science education, learning and teaching science in grades K–8, and mathematics learning in early childhood. She also co-authored two award-winning books for practitioners that translate findings of the National Academies' reports for a broader audience, on using research in K–8 science classrooms and on information science education. Prior to joining the National Academies, she worked as a senior research associate at the Institute of Education Sciences in the U.S. Department of Education. She also previously served on the faculty of Rice University and as the director of research for the Rice University School Mathematics Project, an outreach program in K–12 mathematics education. She has a Ph.D. in psychology (developmental) and anthropology and a certificate in culture and cognition, both from the University of Michigan.

AMY STEPHENS (*Study Director*) is a senior program officer for the Board on Science Education of the National Academies of Sciences, Engineering, and Medicine. She is also an adjunct professor for the Southern New Hampshire University Psychology Department, teaching graduate-level on-line courses in cognitive psychology and statistics. She has an extensive background in behavioral and functional neuroimaging techniques and has examined a variety of different populations spanning childhood through adulthood. She was the study director for the workshop on Graduate Training in the Social and Behavioral Sciences and *English Learners in STEM Subjects: Transforming Classrooms, Schools, and Lives* and *Changing Expectations for the K–12 Workforce: Policies, Preservice Education, Professional Development, and the Workplace*. She is also currently the study director for the study on Enhancing Science and Engineering in Prekindergarten through Fifth Grades. She holds a Ph.D. in cognitive neuroscience from The Johns Hopkins University and was a postdoctoral research fellow at the Center for Talented Youth and the university's School of Education.

MEGA SUBRAMANIAM is an associate professor and the co-director of the Youth Experience (YX) Lab at the College of Information Studies (known as the iSchool) at the University of Maryland. Subramaniam's research focuses on enhancing the role of libraries in fostering the mastery of emerging digital literacies that are essential for STEM learning among underserved young people. Subramaniam is currently the lead PI for the IMLS-funded Graduate Certificate of Professional Studies in Youth Experience (YX), and co-lead for two other funded projects, ConnectedLib and Safe Data Safe Families, all intended to bring together research and practice to enhance the pedagogical skills of in-service and preservice youth librarians. She also currently serves as the fellow and chair of the Task Force for the Libraries Ready to Code initiative, spearheaded by the American Library Association. She is a recipient of the *Library Journal's* Movers and Shakers award. She currently serves as a board member for Young Adults Library Services Association (YALSA) and as a co-editor of the *School Library Research Journal*. Subramaniam received her M.S. in instructional systems technology from Indiana University, Bloomington, and her Ph.D. in information studies from Florida State University.